A GRAND ADVENTURE

THE HERITAGE OF GRAND RAPIDS, MICHIGAN

Larry B. Massie

DEDICATION

IN MEMORY OF

my dear Scottish grandparents, William and Elspeth Massie, in whose Hall Street home I spent the first two years of my life.

First Edition • • ISBN: 1-886483-50-7 • LIBRARY OF CONGRESS CARD CATALOG NUMBER: 00-111238 • AUTHOR: Larry B. Massie • PROJECT EDITOR: John Woodward • COORDINATING EDITORS: Betsy Lelja, Sara Rufner • PROJECT SALES COORDINATOR: Robin Martino • PRODUCTION STAFF: Jeff Caton, Dave Hermstead, Jay Kennedy, Vincent Kornegay, Marianne Mackey, Charlie Silvia • PROFILE WRITERS: Jennifer Cramer, Kim Delmar Cory, Sharon Hanks, Kelly Hill, Thea Rozetta Lapham, Katerie Prior, Kate Wilder • HUMAN RESOURCES MANAGER: Ellen Ruby • ADMINISTRATION: Juan Diaz, Debbie Hunter, Azalea Maes, Majka Penner, Scott Reid, Cory Sottek • PUBLISHER: C.E. Parks • EDITOR-IN-CHIEF: Lori M. Parks VICE PRESIDENT OF SALES: Jill DeLeary • VP/CORPORATE DEVELOPMENT: Bart Barica • CFO: Randall Peterson • PRODUCTION MANAGER: Deborah Sherwood • MANAGING EDITOR: Betsy Baxter Blondin • ART DIRECTOR: Gina Mancini • ASSISTANT ART DIRECTOR: Susie Passons

Published By

HERITAGE

Heritage Media Corp. • Heritage Building

1954 Kellogg Avenue • Carlsbad, California • 92008

www.heritagemedia.com

Printed by Heritage Media Corp. in the United States of America

Published in cooperation with the Grand Rapids Historical Society, www.grhistory.org

Unless otherwise noted, all photographs courtesy of Larry B. Massie

3
DEDICATION

TABLE OF CONTENTS

PART ONE

PART TWO

PREFACE

Superfluous — more than enough — redundant. Those were the words that came to mind when I was first approached about writing yet another history of Grand Rapids. Setting aside the honor I felt in being asked and my long thirst to write a book about the city where I was born, how could I in 40,000 words and 200 images contribute anything to the rich and vast body of Grand Rapids histories previously published?

I thought about the region's rich historiographic heritage. Beginning with the pioneering efforts of Jackson Dillenback and Prof. Franklin Everett in the 1870s, each generation recorded memories, facts and varying interpretations of the city's past. The year 1881 witnessed publication of a thick Kent County history and a series of biographical "mug books" would follow. Albert Baxter's monumental *History of the City of Grand Rapids* appeared in 1891. The early decades of the 20th century brought Dwight Goss' and Ernest B. Fisher's two-volume histories. The Roaring 20s produced Charles Belknap's fascinating volume of reminiscences, George E. Fitch's historic photograph collection and William Etten's history compiled to commemorate the centennial of Louis Campau's arrival. Z.Z. Lydens edited an encyclopedic review of the city's past in 1967. In more recent years a variety of lavishly illustrated volumes by Lynn Mapes, Richard Harms and others have appeared. And, of course, City Historian Gordon Olson's excellent works have set the standard for scholarly yet popular accounts. In addition, over the decades numerous monographs on the furniture industry, periodical articles, promotional pamphlets and ephemeral sources have chronicled many other aspects of Grand Rapids' past.

Yet as I pondered, I detected some interesting episodes and fascinating characters that had "slipped through the cracks" of standard historical accounts. And because the writing of history is at best a subjective process with each writer, however subconsciously, interpreting the record through his own knowledge, experiences and perspectives, I concluded that perhaps there was room for one more book about an amazing city's evolution.

So within the matrix of a general history of the city up to the start of World War II, I have attempted to re-examine some widely accepted interpretations, delineate some under-explored aspects such as the literary heritage of the area, and season the account with a cast of little-known personalities including medical quacks, con men, pugilists, ladies of the night and other colorful characters. I have also tried, whenever possible, to include pictorial sources that have not been previously widely used.

I want to thank my wife, friend and partner, Priscilla, for her understanding and support as I faced the travail of the blank page. Among the others who have kindly helped me in this endeavor, including the dean of Michigan bibliopolists Ralph Casperson, Calvin College Archivist Richard Harms and the staff of the Grand Rapids Public Library's Local History Room, I want to single out my longtime friend Gordon Olson. His support, generous assistance with research problems and especially his reading of the manuscript have made this book a far better product. I, however, take full responsibility for any errors or misinterpretations that remain.

I hope you enjoy reading this as much as I have enjoyed exploring and writing about this vibrant city's heritage.

Larry B. Massie

Allegan Forest, Michigan

FOREWORD

From Gerald R. Ford's political journey from Grand Rapids to the White House to the outrageous fraud schemes of the Bidwell brothers, Grand Rapids has produced its share of outstanding leaders and intriguing characters. Some are well known to local residents, and in the case of Ford, to the nation as a whole. Others, like the Bidwells, are mysterious figures in the shadows at the edges of history.

My longtime friend and colleague, Larry Massie, believes that whether they are remembered for their business acumen, their political savvy, their community contributions or their criminal cunning, our leaders, entrepreneurs and cultural scions, together with a few scoundrels and scamps, deserve their day in the sun. They are part of the same system that produced our community. Larry contends — and I concur — that if we are to comprehend the men and women who make the headlines today, we must know better the saints and sinners in our past.

In *A Grand Adventure,* Larry has carefully selected people who left their mark on Grand Rapids and has used their lives to tell the larger story of the growth of a city. He tells the Grand Rapids story from its beginnings as an Ottawa Indian village, to its years as the home of Baptist and Catholic Indian missions and fur trading, to its half-century as the nation's furniture capital and its 20th-century prominence as Michigan's second city. Regardless of your interests, you will find something to hold your attention. His tale, spun with a relaxed, comfortable narrative, is accompanied by more than 200 photographs and is guaranteed to make many new fans of Grand Rapids history.

Larry Massie is no stranger to Michigan history. He has written many other books, ranging from popular histories of several West Michigan communities to an extremely popular historic cookbook, *Walnut Pickles and Watermelon Cake,* with his wife, Priscilla. The Grand Rapids Historical Society and Heritage Media Corp. are fortunate that this son of Grand Rapids has decided to write a history of the city where he spent his formative years.

I recommend that you take this book to your favorite chair and get comfortable. You are about to embark on a pleasant time-journey through Grand Rapids history. It will be an enjoyable trip. You have an excellent guide.

Gordon L. Olson

Grand Rapids City Historian

PROLOGUE

THE SULLEN SLOP OF A LONELY SEA

Only the sullen slop of a lonely sea disturbs the tomb-like silence. No trees sway in the breeze, no furry creatures scurry and no bird wings its way over the future site of Grand Rapids. But beneath the brackish waves scuttle primeval creatures; crinoids, brachiopods and huge horseshoe crabs.

Thousands of millennia flow unrecorded but by the broad strokes of geology. Life forms later to become extinct battle for survival, consume one another and die in turn, leaving the stony imprint of their existence. The 500-foot seas dry up and come again, and each succeeding ebb and flow leaves deposits of salt, limestone, gypsum, shale and clay.

Eons more pass, until one day the wind quickens from the north and mile-high glaciers begin their inexorable advance. Their great weights metamorphose the rock into new minerals. They gouge and shape, scour and scoop, then slowly retreat and advance five times. And when the ice has had its final way with the land, there lay valleys and hollows, ridges and hillocks of drift dragged from the far north.

The melting waters of the ice fields etch river beds and fill lakes. The rich alluvial soil awakens with plant life. First come the spruce and later white, red and jack pine. Then follow aspen and birch, sugar maple and hemlock, and finally great oak, beech, walnut, sycamore, wild cherry and hickory trees interspersed with vines, grasses and shrubs. Huge herbivores, mammoths and mastodons roam the terrain, masters of all save the wily Paleo hunters who leave only distinctive fluted spear points to mark their culture.

Centuries pass and the mastodons go, replaced by elk, deer, caribou and moose. Immense flights of ducks, vees of geese and the ghostly whirr of swans signal the seasons. Nature's bounty yields tender fern shoots, mushrooms, blackberries, huckleberries and cranberries, walnuts and hickory nuts, edible roots, maple sap and wild rice. The crystal-clear waters teem with great prehistoric-looking sturgeon, bass, muskellunge, pike, trout, suckers and perch. Washtub-sized snapping turtles wallow from the swamp to lay egg broods in the

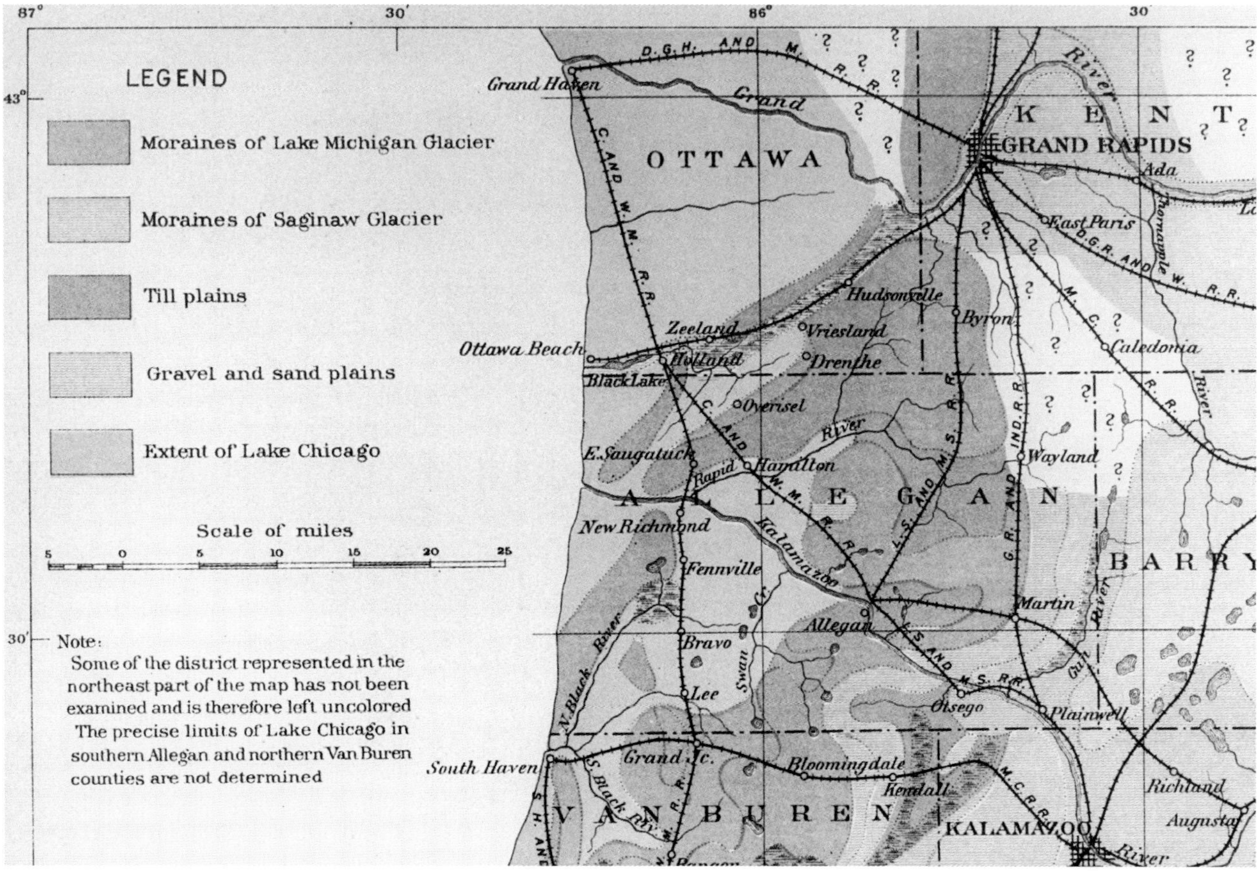

(Opposite page)
The bones of mastodons that were hunted by paleolithic Indians have been discovered in Kent County.

This geological map published in 1898 portrays some prominent glacial related features of southwestern Michigan. Note how close to Grand Rapids prehistoric Lake Chicago once lapped.

sun-warmed sandy uplands. Blue racers, blacksnakes, puff adders and ugly-tempered little massasuagas slither in search of prey.

Fur-bearing mammals abound — chattering squirrels, fat woodchucks, rabbits, raccoon, skunk, ermine, mink, fishers, otters, badgers and wolverines. The chilling scream of wildcats, the roar of cougars, the plaintive howl of wolves, the piping of coyotes and the haunting hoot of great horned owls enliven the night. Legions of wild turkeys gobble and strut and great flights of passenger pigeons darken the skies. Beaver further alter the landscape with tooth and dam.

Lured by the peninsula's natural riches, successive aboriginal cultures people the Grand River Valley. Notched projectile points document the Early Archaic Indian presence some 9,000 years ago. By 5,000 B.C. Indians of the Late Archaic culture leave behind distinctive "turkey tail" spear heads, banner stones and mysterious bird stones. Members of the Early Woodland culture construct conical earthen burial mounds and mold broad-mouthed pottery containers beginning 2,500 years ago. Four to five hundred years later they have been supplanted by the Hopewell Indians, mound builders who bring to the area elaborate ceremonial motifs, finely wrought grave offerings, puzzling garden beds and the first agricultural traditions. By 800 A.D. the Late Woodland period begins, and it is an era of dramatic cultural diversity that contributes effigy mounds, stone pipes and distinctive pottery to the Grand River Valley's prehistory.

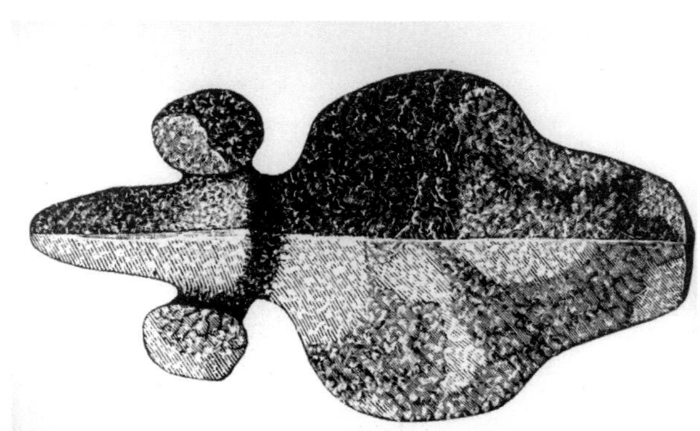

This "popeye" birdstone excavated from a mound on the west side of the river in the 19th century may be 3,000-5,000 years old.

1 THE REAL McCOY

With the arrival in the 17th century of the first Europeans, charting the past is no longer the exclusive domain of aboriginal oral tradition and archaeological speculation. French explorers in quest of a passage to the fabled riches of the Orient, Jesuit priests thirsting to save Indian souls and hardy coureurs de bois and voyageurs in pursuit of an empire of fur bring recorded history to the upper Great Lakes.

Those first Europeans to describe the peninsulas found most of what would become Michigan, a "no man's land" devoid of population. The Lower Peninsula had long been the ancestral homeland of the Mascoutens and other Algonquian-speaking tribes generically known as the "fire nations." But these peoples and their allies,

the Ottawa, Chippewa and Huron to the north, had fled before the murderous onslaught of the Iroquois Federation.

By the end of the 17th century, the survivors of the Iroquois holocaust and the European-introduced diseases that decimated entire villages returned to the peninsulas — the Potawatomi making their home south of the Kalamazoo River into Indiana and the Ottawa the Grand River Valley and the western half of the Lower Peninsula north to the Straits of Mackinac. The Lake Huron shore, the eastern Lower Peninsula and most of the Upper Peninsula remained the domain of the Chippewa or Ojibwa.

Hardy French-Canadian voyageurs explored the Great Lakes in the 17th century.

Thomas McKenney's narrative of his 1826 tour of the Great Lakes contains this lithograph of Algonquin women and children.

Known as the "people of the three fires" and the "three brothers," the Ottawa, Chippewa and Potawatomi spoke dialects of the Algonquian linguistic stock. They shared similar religious beliefs, oral traditions, life styles, decorative arts and general appearance. The tribal members sometimes intermarried and frequently went on the warpath together to battle their common enemies, the Iroquois to the east and the Sioux and Fox to the west.

The Ottawa or "Odowa," an Algonquian term meaning trader, gained fame as intertribal barterers, dealing in cornmeal, sunflower oil, furs, woven mats, tobacco, medicinal plants and other products garnered from the natural bounty of a pristine Michigan. They practiced a semi-sedentary existence, dividing into smaller groups to hunt, fish and trap throughout the lean days of winter, which ended with maple sugar time in the spring. In the heat of the summer, the Ottawa of the Grand River Valley relinquished their villages to the hordes of blood-sucking insects and paddled birchbark canoes along the shore of Lake Michigan to the Leelanau Peninsula, a region later vacationers would continue to covet for its cool breezes. In autumn the bands migrated back to their respective villages to harvest the corn, beans, squash and other crops sown in the spring.

The Ottawa invariably established their villages on the banks of streams, their watery highways. Preferred locations included the mouths of rivers, the confluence of two or more streams and at rapids where fishing was the

The Ottawa were skilled fishermen.

best. Ancient settlements on the Grand River occurred at the present sites of Grand Haven, both sides of the river at Grand Rapids, Ada, Lowell and Ionia.

Ottawa families dwelt most of the year in conical wigwams — simply constructed frameworks of poles, lashed together and sided with sheets of birchbark or woven mats for better ventilation. A small opening at the top allowed some campfire smoke to escape but wigwams were notoriously smoky. Benches fashioned from brush and covered with skins, fur robes and mats served as beds. Larger accommodations, sometimes in the form of domed long houses, sheltered several families during the cold months.

The Ottawa observed a distinct division of duties between men and women. Braves hunted, fished, trapped, practiced archery and made war. They watched in solemn approval as women struggled under loads of firewood, lugged buckets of water, took down the wigwam and moved it when necessary, made maple syrup, tanned hides and crafted moccasins and artifacts of sweetgrass and birchbark.

Despite the seeming inequality of domestic duties, the Ottawa enjoyed a close-knit family life. Early chroniclers observed numerous expressions of deep affection between husband and wife. The entire band doted on papooses, and older children, given the run of the camp, rarely suffered corporal punishment. Men furnished leadership in most matters of tribal concern but within the wigwam the woman stood in absolute command.

The arrival of the first Europeans in the 17th century would spell the beginning of the end for the vibrant native cultures that had evolved in harmony with the land. Jean Nicolet and other explorers carried to New

McKenney's 1827 publication pictured this Michigan Indian lodge.

(Far left) The fur of the beaver inspired the British/French century-long battle for control of the North American continent.

To the Ottawa women fell laborious tasks such as gathering firewood.

Unscrupulous traders bartered "firewater" for furs.

France news of a treasure trove of furs. Beaver pelts, in an era when felt hats fashioned from the furs of those mammals were the height of fashion, proved especially desirable. Soon squads of intrepid coureurs de bois, unlicensed traders, explored much of the peninsulas in quest of furs. The 18th century witnessed a winner-take-all rivalry for the lucrative Great Lakes' fur trade that pitted European armies in bloody conflict as the British Hudson's Bay Company succeeded the French at the close of the French and Indian wars. Following the War of 1812, John Jacob Astor's American Fur Company replaced the British traders.

During this fight for empire Sault Ste. Marie and Mackinac Island emerged as hubs of the Great Lakes fur trade, where legions of Indian trappers and white traders held their annual rendezvous. Not content to await Indian delivery to those depots, intense competition drove the most ambitious entrepreneurs to establish a network of small trading posts throughout the Michigan wilderness. The shrewdest of the lot transported their trade goods directly to Indian settlements to get a jump on rivals.

French-Canadian voyageurs, the workhorses of the Great Lakes fur trade, paddled birchbark canoes up and down Michigan's many streams, pausing once every hour for a few puffs of their clay pipes. They carried cargos of steel knives and hatchets, woolen blankets, copper kettles, guns, ammunition, pocket mirrors and gaudy baubles. The Indians eagerly swapped their peltry for these trade goods and they increasingly came to depend on them. Unfortunately, most traders' canoes also conveyed numerous casks of liquor.

Voyageurs hefted one or more 90-pound packs during portages around rapids.

Laws against trafficking in ardent spirits proved unenforceable on the frontier. In 1832 alone, nearly 9,000 gallons of whiskey flowed to Mackinac Island for distribution throughout the peninsulas. Traders routinely diluted their alcoholic commodity and then added pepper and chewing tobacco for an extra kick. The aptly named firewater, for which culturally, psychologically and, probably, physiologically the Indian held little defense, became a recognized evil of the fur trade. Many a tribesman bartered his entire winter's catch for draughts of "white man's milk" and earned an early grave as a dividend.

Lost to history are many of the names of the generations of French Canadian and "metis" or mixed blood traders who carried canoe loads of prime Grand River furs to Mackinac Island each June. However, it is known that Charles de Langlade was appointed commandant of the Grand River trading operations following the 1755 battle in which he led Michigan and Wisconsin tribesmen to rout Gen. Edward Braddock's army in Pennsylvania. Sometime in the 1790s, an independent French trader named Joseph Laframboise established another trading network. He married the beautiful metis woman Magdalene Marcot in 1796 and together they operated prosperous posts at Muskegon Lake, Crockery Creek in northern Ottawa County and near the future site of Ada at the confluence of the Grand and Thornapple rivers.

En route from Mackinac Island to the Grand River one fall day in 1806, they camped near the mouth of the Muskegon River to trade and parley with local tribesmen. As was the deplorable necessity of his occupation,

This modern painting of Madame Laframboise hangs in Mackinac Island's Harbour View Inn, once her home.

This reconstruction of Laframboise's trading post was built for the 1876 Centennial Celebration in Grand Rapids.

Laframboise ladled samples of fiery liquor to establish rapport. But when one ugly-tempered Ottawa brave, White Ox, demanded more, the Frenchman turned him down. Soon after, as Laframboise knelt in evening prayer in his tent, White Ox exacted his revenge. A musket shot rang out and the trader pitched forward dead.

Stifling her grief, Magdalene transported her husband's body to her native village at the mouth of the Grand River and pushed on to the trading post at Ada. Determined to continue the business, Magdalene returned the following June to Mackinac Island, her bateau heavily laden with gleaming bales of pelts and her husband's disinterred body for reburial in the family plot. On the island she sold the furs at a handsome profit, restocked her trade goods and three months later retraced her arduous voyage to the Grand River. Year after year she plied the seasonal cycle of the fur trade, building upon her husband's reputation for fairness and amassing \$5,000 to \$10,000 in profits annually in an era when her voyagers drew less than \$1 per day for their dawn to dusk labors.

Following the War of 1812, John Jacob Astor's American Fur Company achieved a near monopoly in the American fur trade. Nevertheless Magdalene adroitly fended off his attempts to swallow up her operations through cunning, compromise and diplomacy. But in 1821, heartbroken at the sudden death of her beloved daughter, Josette, and her infant grandson, Benjamin, Magdalene retired from the fur trade, selling her flourishing post on the Grand River to Rix Robinson of the American Fur Company.

Rix Robinson carved out a remarkable career as a Grand River fur trader.

Robinson had been born in Massachusetts in 1789. Eleven years later he and his family migrated to the western New York frontier. The outbreak of the War of 1812 found Robinson in Detroit where he became a sutler for the U.S. Army. Following the war, he made his way to Mackinac Island, where Robert Stuart, the resident American Fur Company agent, hired him as an Indian trader. After gaining valuable experience trading in the Illinois country for several seasons, Robinson purchased Laframboise's operation and also established trading posts at the mouth of the Grand and Kalamazoo rivers. Following the death of his first Ottawa wife he married Se-Be-Quay (River Woman), the granddaughter of a Grand River chief. Robinson continued his remarkable career until he retired to his large land holdings near Ada in 1837. Gurdon Hubbard, another colorful character whom the Indians dubbed "Swift Walker" because of his ability to stride as many as 75 miles in a day, was a contemporary of Robinson's who also traded briefly in the Grand River country.

Garrulous old Louis Campau convinced pioneer Grand Rapidians that he alone founded the community.

By the time of the dominance of the American Fur Company, the days of the Indian in the Grand River Valley were already numbered. In one sense, the tribesmen had sealed their own fate by consistently backing the losing side in the warfare that periodically bloodied the frontier. Michigan warriors took up the tomahawk against the British and their allies, the hated Iroquois, to back the French during the intermittent French and Indian wars. Following the defeat of the French and their loss of New France in 1763, the Michigan-based tribes switched loyalty to the British, conducting repeated frontier forays against the Americans in the Revolutionary War. Again during the War of 1812 many a bloody American scalp swung from an Ottawa belt.

When the war ended in 1815, the Ottawa were a defeated nation. And while the French and British had been content to trade with the tribes and leave them in possession of their domain, the ever westward-pushing Americans campaigned to extinguish Indian title to land via treaties negotiated from a position of power. Treaty makers such as Michigan Territorial Governor Lewis Cass who had fought the tribesmen in the War of 1812, and Henry Rowe Schoolcraft, despite his marriage into a half-Chippewa family, were not above such tactics as stupefying the signers with whiskey, outright bribery and the recognition of lesser chiefs in favor of more legitimate leaders not inclined to sign.

This steel engraving of Michigan Territorial Governor Lewis Cass appeared in a biography promoting his 1852 presidential campaign.

Beginning with the 1795 Treaty of Greenville, the Michigan tribes found themselves divested of increasingly larger blocks of their ancestral land. A treaty negotiated by Gen. William Hull at Detroit in 1807 ceded most of the southeastern Lower Peninsula to the United States. The Indians lost the eastern part of the Grand River Valley as well as a six million-acre wedge to the northeast via the 1819 Treaty of Saginaw.

Cass had utilized the services of Louis Campau to summon the Chippewa chiefs and prepare the site of the Saginaw Treaty. Born in Detroit in 1791, Campau had learned the art of Indian trading from his uncle, Joseph Campau, a prominent Detroiter who became the territory's first millionaire through trading and land speculation. The younger Campau, who had been trading in the Saginaw country since 1815, had advanced the local Chippewa goods for which he expected to pocket half of the $3,000 in silver coins owed the Indians as one of the treaty provisions. But Jacob Smith, a Flint-area trader, outfoxed Campau by convincing two chiefs to demand payment directly to them and he ultimately collected the entire sum. The enraged Campau punched Smith in the face and secured further revenge by adding 10 barrels of his own whiskey to the five barrels allotted by Cass for the celebration that evening. The resulting drunken pandemonium nearly resulted in an Indian massacre of the Cass party. Campau had gotten his satisfaction and, what is more, learned a valuable lesson about being in the right spot at the right time when Indian payments were made.

Two years later Cass negotiated the Treaty of Chicago in which the Ottawa and Potawatomi surrendered title to all Michigan land south of the Grand River. That 1821 treaty established several reservations and awarded tracts of land to a number of metis children of traders. Madame Laframboise's son, Joseph, received a square mile of land, curiously, not on the Grand but the St. Joseph River. Other provisions awarded the Ottawa $1,000 annually, forever, and $1,500 annually was to be appropriated for the following 10 years for the support of a blacksmith, a teacher, an agricultural agent and the purchase of cattle and farming utensils in an effort to aculturate the Indians to the white man's ways. The Ottawa's blacksmith, teacher and agricultural agent were to reside on a one-square-mile tract to be designated somewhere on the north bank of the Grand River. Eight Ottawa, two Chippewa and 55 Potawatomi "chiefs"

This 19th-century print depicts 1836 treaty negotiations.

(Both photos this page) Isaac and Christiana McCoy endured extreme hardships during their Baptist missionary activities at Niles and Grand Rapids.

signed the 1821 treaty. Cass then distributed seven barrels of liquor for the ensuing celebration. The Indians got roaring drunk and during the melee seven were stabbed to death.

That is where Isaac McCoy, a man destined to be of vital importance in the development of Grand Rapids, enters the story. Born near Uniontown, Fayette County, Pennsylvania, in 1784, McCoy immigrated to Kentucky with his father six years later. At the age of 17 he cast his lot with the Baptist faith and joined the Buck Creek Church. Two years later he married Christiana Polk whose mother and several sisters, ironically, had been captured and carried back to Michigan during the Revolutionary War by a raiding party of Ottawas. In 1804 the newlyweds moved to southern Indiana where McCoy began preaching in the pioneer settlements. In 1810 he was ordained a Baptist minister.

Appointed a missionary to the Indians of Indiana and Illinois seven years later, he launched his life's work. After laboring briefly in western Indiana, he decided to establish a mission at Fort Wayne. Financial support that was promised from the Baptist Church failed to materialize and by the winter of 1821 the McCoys and their mission, which included 48 Miami Indian pupils, were in dire need.

In desperation McCoy made a hazardous horseback trek in the dead of winter to Detroit seeking support from Cass who, in addition to his duties as Michigan's territorial governor, also served as ex officio superintendent of Indian affairs for most of the original Northwest Territory. Cass listened to McCoy's story of suffering with sympathy and allotted him some $450 worth of clothing and rations for the Miami scholars.

More importantly, the missionary established rapport with Cass. On July 16, 1822, he appointed McCoy teacher to the Potawatomi as decreed by the provisions of the Treaty of 1821. He would receive an annual stipend of $400 which McCoy applied to his missionary endeavors. He would also be responsible for overseeing the operations to be established on the St. Joseph River and among the Ottawa on the Grand River. At the same time, John Sears received appointment as teacher to the Ottawa.

On October 8, 1822, McCoy led a contingent of 21 Miami pupils from Fort Wayne to the new mission site about one mile west of what would become the city of Niles. After building six log structures, he returned to Fort Wayne for the remaining 32 members of the mission and his family. In the meantime, typhoid fever had struck. McCoy's 9-year-old daughter died during his absence and on November 3 Sears' brother, Benjamin, who had joined the missionary endeavor, succumbed to the disease. Disheartened at the sickness and privation he envisioned to be his prolonged lot, the first teacher assigned to the Ottawa retreated back east, never having even visited his Grand River post.

McCoy spent the winter and spring of 1823 improving his establishment on the St. Joseph River, which he named Carey Mission in honor of the Reverend William Carey, a celebrated Baptist missionary to India. On May 26, 1823, he left Carey in company with a French guide named Paget on an exploratory tour to the Grand River to begin the process of setting up an operation similar to that on the St. Joseph River.

The five-day trek through the wilderness proved arduous, more so because Paget got them lost, but finally on May 30 an Indian carried them in his canoe across the Grand River to the village of Kewikishkun (Long Nose) at the mouth of the Flat River. The chief being absent, McCoy borrowed a canoe and spent a day vainly searching up and down the river for the mission site that had been described to him. Cass had previously appointed Charles C. Trowbridge, Indian

The green corn ceremony marked an important cycle of the Ottawa calendar.

agent, interpreter and later mayor of Detroit, as the commissioner to locate the sites of the St. Joseph and Grand rivers missions. Trowbridge initially selected a location some 30 to 40 miles farther up the river from the rapids.

Returning to Long Nose's village, McCoy found that the Indians had gotten hold of some whiskey. McCoy pleaded with them not to get drunk until he could address them about establishing the mission. They responded that no business could be transacted without the presence of Long Nose and "When they were among the whites on business they had to await their will; and as I was now among them I must do the same, and wait until they were ready to hear me."

McCoy soon learned the real reason for the delay. The main body of the tribe, it seems, denied the legality of the sale of their ancestral land at the Treaty of Chicago. They blamed Long Nose for signing the treaty and he, fearing retaliation, dared not appear in counsel on any matter that stemmed from the treaty provisions. Furthermore, to accept McCoy's mission with a school, blacksmith and agricultural agent would weaken the case they intended to appeal.

Given the situation and because his family at the Carey Mission desperately needed food, McCoy decided to return home without further negotiations. He reached the Carey Mission on June 5, having stopped to beg food at several Indian villages including the home of Gosa, an Ottawa subchief who lived on the Kalamazoo River. With funds from the Baptist church not forthcoming, McCoy depended on his government salary and federal money appropriated by treaty provisions as the only sources of revenue for the Potawatomi mission, which had grown to 60 students.

In order to increase that government subsidy, McCoy needed to get the Ottawa mission in operation. Because of the opposition McCoy had detected during his visit to Long Nose's village, he decided to set up a temporary blacksmith shop on the southern edge of Ottawa territory, the Kalamazoo River, and hopefully its success would convince the Indians to allow a more permanent mission on the Grand River.

McCoy departed on foot September 30, 1823, and three days later arrived at Ottawa Chief White Sparrow's village on the Kalamazoo River. He was elated when the Indians accepted his overtures to establish a blacksmith shop at the site. But with the onset of winter McCoy shelved plans for the Ottawa blacksmith shop. In December, 1823, he left the Carey Mission in the hands of his wife and launched what would become a more than five-month trip to Washington, D.C. to lobby numerous officials for increased support of his endeavors. On his return in early June, 1824, he stopped off at Detroit for a visit with Cass and at that time obtained the appointment of William Polke, formerly of Indiana, as teacher to the Ottawa, a position that had remained vacant since Sears had resigned nearly two years before.

On June 29, Polke loaded an ox-cart with tools and supplies and in company with a newly hired blacksmith and two Potawatomi youths, set out for the station on the Kalamazoo. The teacher returned 10 days later having left

Roads in territorial Michigan were little more than wheel tracks through the wilderness.

Ottawa Chief Kanapima or Augustin Hamelin Jr. from Northern Michigan adopted the white man's apparel to participate in the 1836 Treaty of Washington.

the blacksmith and the Indian boys to continue plying their trade. It did not take long for McCoy's anticipated results to be felt. On July 15, 1824, a delegation of Ottawa visited the Carey Mission and asked that the blacksmith shop be relocated to a more accessible site on the Grand River.

Then in mid-November Gosa arrived at the Carey Mission to deliver an urgent message from Naoqua Keshuch, Noonday, chief of a village at the rapids of the Grand River, earnestly requesting McCoy to visit his people. Accordingly, McCoy, in company with a Potawatomi interpreter, blacksmith William Sawyer and a French laborer left with Gosa on November 24. Three days later they reached Gun Lake and found Noonday and his family encamped on the shore. Noonday urged McCoy to establish a mission at his village on the Grand River, declaring that he and others desired to embrace civilized life and for the guidance of the missionary.

As McCoy recorded, the chief delivered a moving speech.

"I am an Indian," said Noonday, "nevertheless I think of God, and of religion, and had we a preacher among us perhaps I could become good." But when McCoy explained what he could do for the Ottawa, as he had for the Potawatomi, Noonday became apprehensive. Other white men had broken their promises — would McCoy put his in writing? When the missionary wrote and signed his proposals, Noonday arose and said "In token of friendship I take hold of your hand. I take fast hold of it. God sees us take hold of each other's hands and will be witness against him that shall deceive."

Guided by Noonday, the party continued north toward the Grand Rapids on November 29. That night McCoy suffered a violent attack of dysentery and despite Noonday's herbal remedies he remained miserable for the remainder of the tour. Reaching the Grand River two days later, Noonday conveyed the missionary across to his village in a tiny canoe he had secreted along the shore. On December 1, 1824, McCoy, though scarcely able to walk, with the chief's assistance selected and marked out the site for the mission on the west bank of the river (currently the approximate site of the Gerald R. Ford Museum). As was the Baptist custom, he dubbed it the Thomas Mission in honor of Dr. John Thomas, one of Carey's fellow preachers in India.

And thus McCoy, through the urgings of Noonday, made the unilateral decision to change the site of the Baptist mission to the Ottawa from that designated by Trowbridge some 30 miles upstream, to the Indian village at the rapids of the Grand River. Although he soon requested Cass to confirm the new location (and ultimately Secretary of War John C. Calhoun approved it), McCoy's decision would prove of paramount significance in the subsequent development of the city that would evolve into Grand Rapids.

On December 17th, William Sawyer, the blacksmith at the Carey Mission, left with two additional laborers to get the primitive metal working facility, Grand Rapids' original manufacturing site, functional. Throughout the winter the blacksmith shop continued to operate with Sawyer and Polke bouncing back and forth between it and the Carey Mission. On March 10, 1825, Sawyer, Polke and two additional laborers journeyed in a dugout canoe from Carey to Lake Michigan and up the Grand River to the rapids. There they encountered a vast encampment of the Ottawa, an annual spring gathering at the prime fishing grounds. Some mischief maker had distributed whiskey to the Indians. A drunken brave's attempt to shoot Polke was thwarted only by the fortuitous intercession of Gosa.

In May Polke again visited the Grand River site and found the Ottawa, now sober, in a more receptive mood. He reported the construction of log buildings and fields being plowed and fenced. Then suddenly in June he resigned, expressing doubts as to his fitness to endure the harsh life of an Indian missionary. The following month Johnston Lykins was appointed to succeed Polke as government teacher to the Ottawa — the third such appointment in as many years with still no school established.

Clearly, if the Thomas Mission was to become a reality McCoy could not delegate the responsibility — he would have to spend considerable time and energy doing it himself. Furthermore, drunkenness and anti-Baptist feelings flared both at Carey and the Thomas missions. In August the three men stationed as blacksmiths at Thomas barely escaped being murdered during one bacchanalian revel by barricading themselves in a cabin. McCoy came to realize that "the devil and whiskey sellers appeared to pull down faster then we could build up." He began devoting more and more of his zeal toward promoting his long cherished dream — removal of the Michigan Indians to the west out of reach of the whiskey peddlers. Although he sincerely believed he was doing the right thing, he became the architect of the federal policy that resulted in the tragic Indian Removal Act and subsequent "trail of tears."

Despite his conviction in Indian removal, McCoy intended to establish the long-awaited Ottawa school in the interim. On November 28, 1826, his wife Christiana, three of their young children, including a sick infant, and several others began what became a miserable eight-day-long wagon trek through the snow-covered wilderness to the rapids. At one point the wagon tipped over on the side of a hill, pinning Christiana and the children beneath and the baby barely escaped suffocation.

Upon reaching the rapids the McCoys moved into one of the log cabins. On Christmas day 1826 the newly

Indian Commissioner Thomas McKenney included a depiction of an Indian school in his 1848 memoirs.

Baptist Missionary Leonard Slater arrived at the Thomas Mission in 1827.

Henry Rowe Schoolcraft's monumental six-volume history of the Indians contains this illustration of a medicine man administering to a patient.

constructed log schoolhouse opened with five Indian pupils. By April, 1827, the scholars numbered 15.

In the meantime McCoy had contracted a severe cold in early January. Four weeks later he was still so weak that he could only preach feebly while sitting in a chair. Nevertheless, the school, taught sometimes by Lykins, a young printer named Jotham Meeker who had joined the mission, and by McCoy himself, continued to function. By May 1827, 21 students were in attendance, the buildings had been improved and 10 acres planted in corn, potatoes and other vegetables. That month the Rev. Leonard Slater and his wife arrived at the Thomas Mission to relieve McCoy. Feeling "much like going from home" McCoy left for Carey on May 22, having become "much attached" to the Ottawa.

Born in Worcester, Massachusetts, in 1802, Slater had studied for the ministry and joined the Baptist Church at the age of 16. In 1826 he and his wife traveled 200 miles on horseback from Detroit to Niles to assist McCoy in his missionary endeavors. At the Thomas Mission, Slater began learning the Ottawa language, a skill that would prove invaluable during his subsequent long career. He was assisted during the summer of 1827 by Meeker, whom McCoy appointed superintendent of the mission. During a visit in August McCoy noted many improvements. The Ottawa seemed quite content with their new white instructors, and enlarged fields at Noonday's village and that of Chief Blackskin farther upstream had been fenced and planted.

But beneath the apparent calm trouble brewed. A severe intestinal illness broke out among the staff and the Indians. Meeker, who attempted to act as a doctor, killed one young Indian suffering from diarrhea by administering an emetic to him. In early 1828, a blacksmith named Secord, who McCoy had hired to work at the Mission, proved to be a drunkard. Worse yet, he got Gosa, sober for three years, to start drinking again. During an inspection tour in March, 1828 McCoy found matters at Thomas, "to be retrograding." The school had shrunk to 12 pupils and Blackskin and many other Ottawa appeared unfriendly.

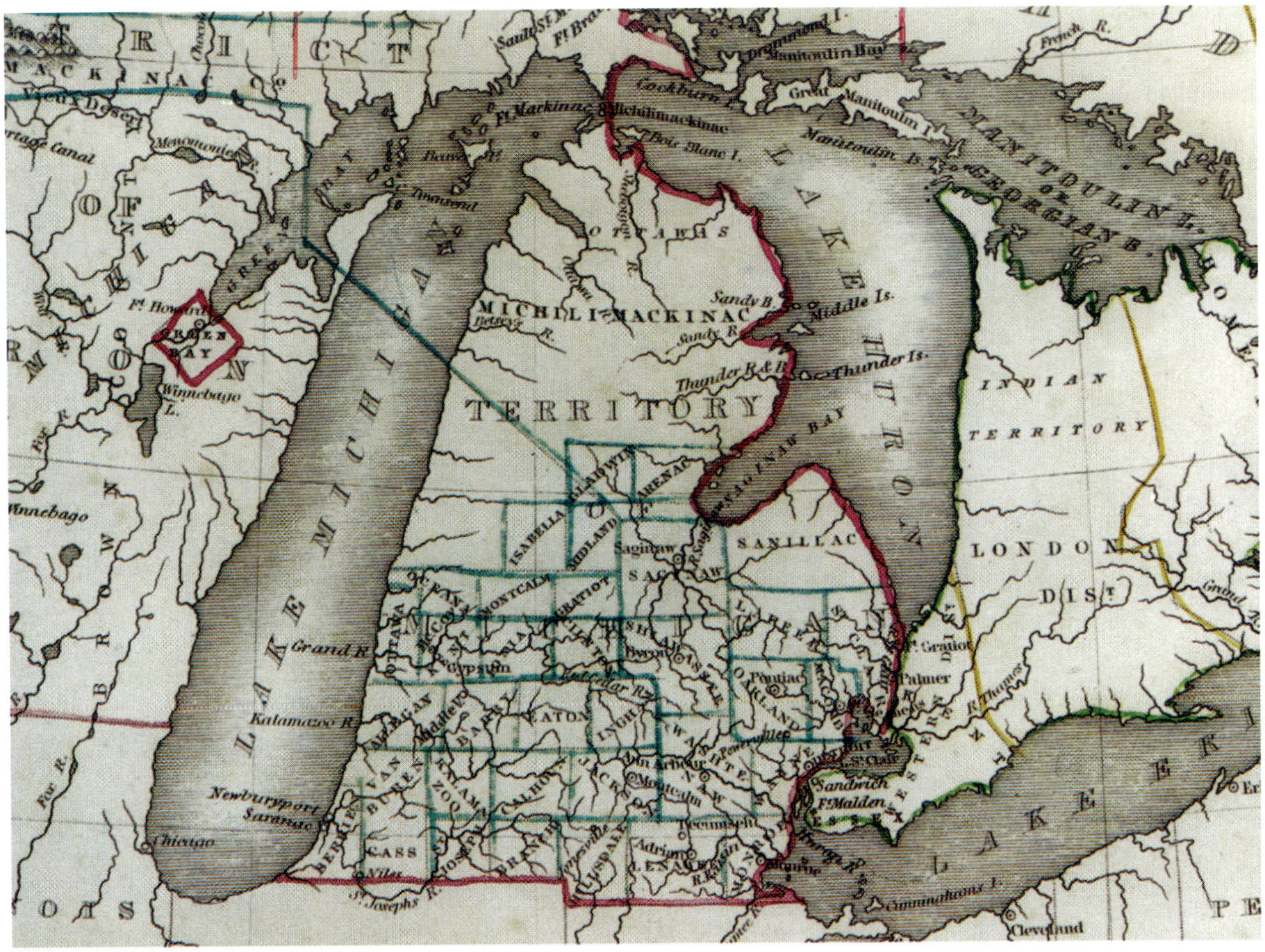

This 1834 map of the Lower Peninsula is one of several that identify Grand Rapids simply as McCoy.

During the summer of 1828 McCoy took Noonday, Gosa, an Ottawa chief named Wesauogaua and a number of Potawatomi on a tour to the prairies of Kansas in an effort to convince them to move their people to the west. Not until July 1829 did he return to Thomas to find "the condition of the station such as to occasion grief." Meeker had gone to Ohio on personal business leaving Slater in charge. The school was closed, the fields lay uncultivated and "the whole establishment appeared in a state of dilapidation." Slater, it seems, devoted nearly all his energies to preaching, feeling the Indian's spiritual salvation more important than the temporal needs of education and food. Slater differed philosophically from McCoy on another matter as well. He had no intention of supporting McCoy's campaign for removal to Kansas.

Disgusted at these developments, McCoy left the Thomas Mission for the last time. In 1830 he closed down the Carey Mission and led a band of refugee Indians to Kansas where he established the Shawano Mission. There, Meeker established the first press in Kansas, ultimately printing dozens of pamphlets in Indian hieroglyphics and English.

McCoy continued his labors in Indian Territory, which became the states of Kansas and Oklahoma, until he accepted a position as general agent of the Indian Mission Association at Louisville, Kentucky, in 1842. He died four years later, uttering these last words, "Tell the brethren, never to let the Indian Mission fail."

The importance of McCoy's selection and establishment of the original settlement at the rapids of the Grand River is reflected in contemporary cartographic evidence. At least three different maps of Michigan published in the early 1830s identify the site not as Thomas Mission, Slater's Mission or Campau's Trading Post but as McCoy's Mission or simply McCoy — Grand Rapids' original appellation.

2 WITH A BIBLE IN ONE HAND & WHISKEY IN THE OTHER

Despite McCoy's role, history has chosen to honor as Grand Rapids' founding father the French fur trader last encountered ladling out barrels of whiskey to the Indians at Saginaw — Louis Campau. Sometime in 1825 Campau had resolved to shift his trading operations from Saginaw to the Grand River Valley in rivalry with Robinson's American Fur Company endeavors. In the fall of 1826 Campau packed his trade goods in on ponies and with four employees launched a two-pronged attack on the Grand River fur trade. He left two subordinates in charge of a small trading post he had established at the mouth of the Flat River and pushed on in November to his primary objective, the big villages at the rapids.

Beyond the size of the Indian settlement, of even more significance was the presence of McCoy's mission, the site of the annual distribution of treaty payments to the Ottawa. Campau, or Wagoosh, "the Fox," as the Indians named him, knew well from experience in the Saginaw Valley the importance of being on site in order to grab off the gold.

Campau set up his first trading post on the west side of the river near the mission structures and apparently enjoyed a successful season. The following year he brought in his family and a greater supply of goods and erected three hewn-log structures on the other side of the river near where the entrance to the Civic Auditorium is now. For the following five or six years little change came to the incipient Grand Rapids. Annually the Ottawa gathered, then dispersed to ply their nomadic lifestyle. The foxy Frenchman continued to build his reputation as a cunning trader on the east side of the river, and across the stream dour Slater beat the Bible in an all but futile effort to Christianize the Ottawa.

Meanwhile, the Grand River, the Ottawa's O-wash-to-nong, or "far away water" dashed and churned over the rapids — Ba-wa-ting — "where the water falls down." The rapids of the Grand River were the Ottawa Ba-wa-tang. The Chippewa Ba-wa-ting lay at the Sault Rapids and the Potawatomi Ba-wa-ting or Pa-wa-ting (b and p are interchangeable in Algonquin) was the future site of Niles on the St. Joseph River.

What was the Ottawa Ba-wa-ting like at this time? In 1926, when the city celebrated the centennial of Campau's arrival, local historian William J. Etten penned a detailed word picture of the city's appearance a century before. He described a river much wider than at present with two channels separated by four islands below the rapids. The river dropped 18 feet as it raced over a mile-long, boulder-studded rapids. A narrow border of lowland comprised the east bank of the river. Behind it lay hills, vales and swamps including a high mass of hard clay (later leveled) the settlers called Prospect Hill. Shallows between two of the islands allowed a fording place and north of the rapids a deer and bear "run" crossed the stream.

The decade after McCoy's pioneering efforts at the rapids had witnessed tremendous growth for Michigan Territory. Due in part to U.S. Surveyor General Edward Tiffin's erroneous report in 1817, which maligned

The Rev. John Booth sketched the McCoy settlement in 1831. Across the river from Campau's trading post is the Baptist mission. Chief Noonday's camp is in the foreground.

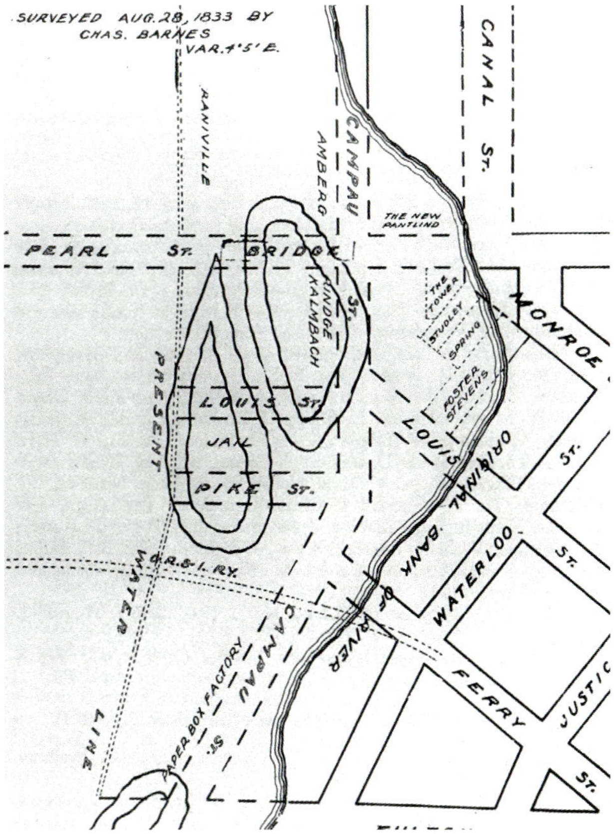

This map shows the original lay of the land superimposed on the streets as they were in 1926.

Michigan as a vast swamp filled with malarial mosquitoes, the territory had been largely bypassed by westward migration. But when government surveyors laid out the first road across the Lower Peninsula, the Chicago Military Road, roughly the present route of U.S. 12, and the Erie Canal opened in 1825 to link the Hudson River with Detroit, news of the lush land found by early arrivals circulated back east and launched a mass migration to "Michigania." Homesteaders quickly staked out the fertile prairies and oak openings in the southern tier of counties and then pushed the frontier northward.

Hordes of New Englanders and the sons and daughters of those who had pioneered western New York generations before rushed for the Michigan bonanza. They included genuine settlers anxious to start a new life in the territory as well as numerous speculators who had no intention of settling. They planned to acquire large tracts of prime farmland or stands of giant white pine at the standard $1.25 per acre government price and when the best acreage had been taken up, resell to late comers at a tidy profit. Other investors sought sites with good water power potential for industrial development to plat out towns and sell lots for hundreds of times their cost.

Among the cagiest of the speculators were surveyors who earmarked for their own profit the best lands they encountered during their government work. That is where one Lucius Lyon entered the story. Born near Shelburne Falls, Vermont, in 1800, the eldest of eight siblings, Lyon received a common school education and studied engineering and surveying in nearby Burlington. He cast his lot with Michigan in 1822. Arriving in Detroit penniless, he found employment as a school teacher. Befriended by Cass, Schoolcraft and Judge Solomon Sibley, Lyon received appointment as deputy surveyor in 1823. Three years later he first visited the Grand River country when he surveyed the meanders of the stream. He met Robinson at his trading post near Ada and purchased various supplies from him.

In 1831 Lyon was busy surveying on the Kalamazoo River when he received an urgent request from Campau that he relocate his crew to the rapids of the Grand and survey the locale ahead of schedule. Slater, it seems,

Wilderness surveyors established section lines that made purchase of government land at $1.25 an acre possible.

Lucius Lyon used the information he gathered as a surveyor to invest in numerous town sites.

had threatened to buy the land on which Campau's trading post lay and force him to move because he continued to sell whiskey to the Indians. After decades of debate Congress had passed a Preemption Act in 1830 that allowed those who had "squatted" on and made improvements to government land before it was placed on the market to apply for pre-emptive rights to purchase up to 160 acres. But the act was to continue in force for only one year and during that year the land in question had to be legally surveyed. Time was running out for Campau.

Lyon, who would ultimately use his surveying knowledge to invest in land in Chicago, Ypsilanti, Pontiac, Ann Arbor, Battle Creek, Kalamazoo, Schoolcraft, Hastings, Niles, Lyons (named after him) and dozens of other locations, evidently perceived Campau's plea as an opportunity to invest in another potentially lucrative town site. Accordingly, he shifted his entire crew to the Grand River and in 1831 he and John Mullett surveyed the land that would become the city of Grand Rapids. While there, A.S. Cotton, a member of the survey crew, overheard Campau tell Lyon "that he was not anxious to purchase all the land that his pre-emption claim would cover, but was desirous to secure about an acre on which his house stood so he might trade with the Indians without risk of being driven away by Mr. Slater." Furthermore, as Cotton testified by affidavit in 1835 when questions arose about the propriety of Lyon's dealings, Campau "also seemed to fear that the Americans, or Whites, by coming on and settling the country, would destroy his Indian trade, and he seemed to calculate on leaving the country whenever that should take place. He told Mr. Lyon he might have the whole of his claim, excepting the land where his house stood (for his trouble and expense in surveying it and procuring preemption) by paying the government price for all but the acre aforesaid, or a spot large enough for a garden."

After Lyon had completed his survey, at Campau's request he dispatched Aaron Adams, one of his chainmen, to the surveyor general's office in Cincinnati with the field notes in order to bring back the plat of the township before the Preemption Act expired. What is more, Lyon advanced Campau the funds needed to pay for the land.

Campau journeyed to the newly opened land office in White Pigeon and on September 20, 1831, he purchased in his and his wife Sophie's name 72 acres encompassing what would evolve into downtown Grand Rapids bounded by Michigan and Fulton streets, Division Avenue and the river. He paid the standard rate for government land — $1.25 an acre or $90. Having secured the site "the fox" seems to have had a change of heart concerning his retaining but an acre. The following summer he deeded only the northern half of the tract to Lyon and thus began a long-standing quarrel between the two.

Campau proceeded to plat out a town he called Grand Rapids and in contradiction to his earlier concerns about settlers spoiling his Indian trade, actually began soliciting immigrants. The first to heed his overtures, the Joel Guild family, lured from New York promoter Samuel Dexter's Ionia colony, arrived on June 23, 1833. Guild purchased a lot from Campau and erected the first frame house in the incipient village some 200 feet from the trading post on the present site of McKay Tower.

Lyon and associates, officially known as the Proprietors of Kent, including Trowbridge, the commissioner who had designated the mission site on the Grand River to be

This 1833 sketch of Grand Rapids depicts Joel Guild's house in the center.

HE VILLAGE IN 1836—SHOWING EAST BANK OF THE RIVER AND THE ISLANDS OPPOSITE THE NOW CENTRAL PART OF THE CITY—FROM THE ORIGINAL PLAT.

The origins of Grand Rapids' confusing downtown street pattern can be seen in this 1836 plat.

located elsewhere than Grand Rapids, and Eurotas P. Hastings, for whom the Barry County seat was named, purchased an additional 135 acres. They effectively boxed Campau's tract in by 1834. One nagging little problem, however, stood in the way of Lyon's platting his parcel to the north of Campau's — at the time of the transfer Sophie Campau had failed to sign off on her interest in the land. Lyon filed a suit against her and her husband, whom he had come to refer to by then as "a jealous, selfish and troublesome Frenchman." Ultimately he settled out of court by deeding Sophie two valuable lots. On February 8, 1836, Lyon filed a plat of his land as the Village of Kent.

Lyon's plat featured streets laid out in a conventional north-south grid. But Campau had already established a more haphazard street arrangement oriented to the old Indian trail (Monroe Street) which led to his trading post. The adjoining plats whose streets crossed diagonally or not at all fueled the stubborn town founders' feud and despite some later adjustments left a legacy of downtown confusion.

Bishop Frederic Baraga, "apostle to the Chippewa," posed shortly before his death in 1868.

The civic discord that clouded Grand Rapids' nativity mirrored a spiritual rift that erupted with the arrival of Father Frederic Baraga on June 15, 1833. Born 36 years before in the Austrian Duchy of Carniola (later part of Yugoslavia), Baraga received an excellent university education before renouncing his wealthy estate to become a priest in 1823. Seven years later he joined the Leopoldine Society that promoted missionary activity among the American Indians and sailed for New York City. Early summer of 1831 found him establishing a mission among the Ottawa of L'Arbre Croche, the present site of Harbor Springs. Baraga enjoyed such success in northern Michigan that he sought new fields of conquest.

Word had reached him of the major Ottawa villages on the Grand River, where reportedly there dwelt 900 Indians, who, he wrote his superior, were "practically all genuine heathens." Campau, also Catholic, greeted him warmly during his initial visit to Grand Rapids. But the hand of friendship was not offered by Slater, who like most contemporary Protestant missionaries regarded Catholic priests as hated competitors for Indian souls. Particularly galling was the Ottawas' preference for the mysteries of Catholic dogma over the austere tenets of Calvinism. During his three-week sojourn at the rapids, Baraga gained 86 converts, simply by baptizing them without the religious indoctrination stressed by the Baptists, which encouraged him to establish a permanent mission there.

Following a tour to his northern mission, he returned to Grand Rapids in September 1833 to found the Mission of St. Mary. By April 1834 Baraga had erected a hewn-log chapel on the west side of the river between Watson and Butterworth streets, east of Lexington Avenue. Before the year ended he also established an Indian school nearby. He faced

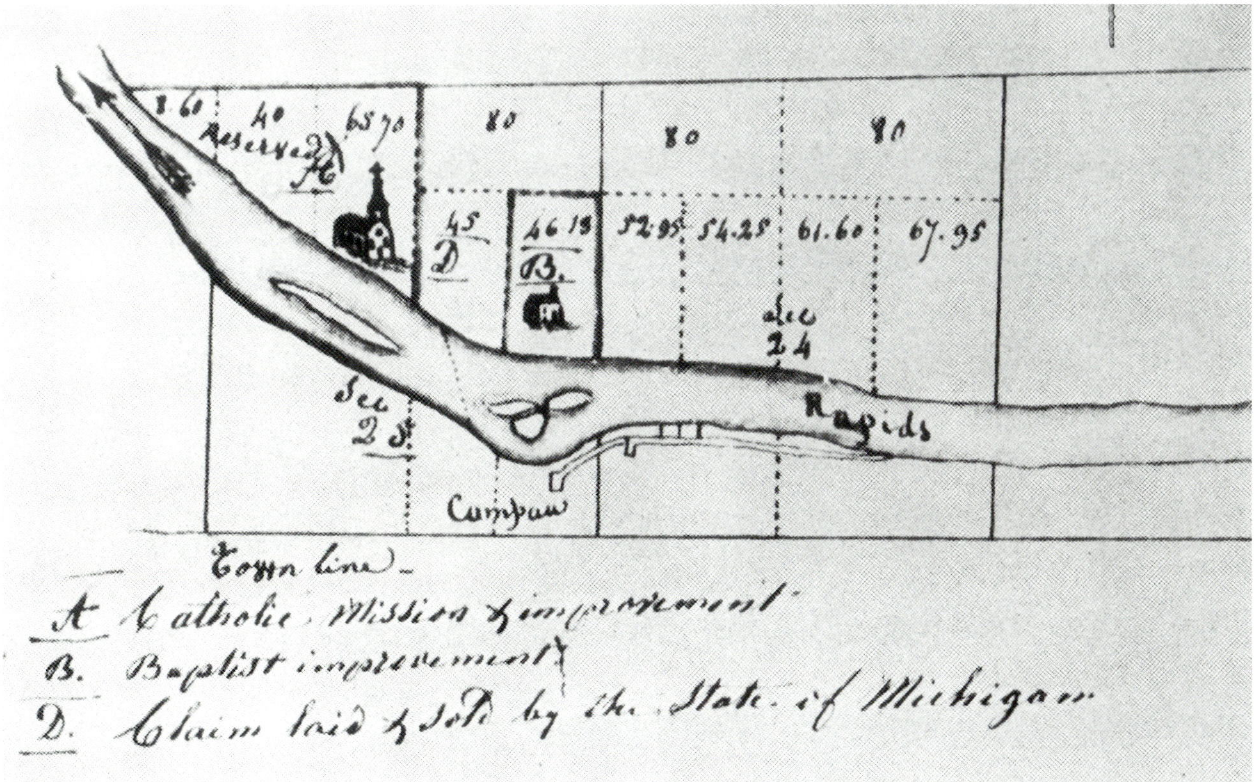

This 1840 surveyor's sketch identified the Catholic and Baptist mission sites.

continuing opposition from Slater, who had been appointed the community's first postmaster, as well as Campau who wanted him to build the church on his side of the river. The French trader wanted to be a good Catholic but when Baraga interfered with his lucrative profession of swapping firewater for furs, it was another matter. One night his antagonists instigated a drunken mob of Indians into attacking him. For hours they besieged his cabin, howling in anger as he knelt on the floor in prayer until an acting U.S. marshall dispersed them. Not long after that harrowing experience Baraga evidently decided to compromise with Campau. The Catholic Indian mission and school remained on the west side of the river, but the priest allowed the partially finished church to be moved over the ice to Campau's village.

The only known photograph of Father Andreas Viszosky was taken as he lay in state in 1853.

In February 1835 Baraga relinquished his Grand Rapids mission to Father Andreas Viszosky, a Hungarian priest who would continue to serve the Grand Rapids parish until his death in 1853. Baraga returned to his beloved north country to establish a mission among the Indians at LaPointe, Wisconsin. Over the next three decades he devoted his life to the spiritual welfare of the Chippewa who dwelt along the southern shore of Lake Superior. In 1843 he moved his headquarters to L'Anse, at the foot of Keweenaw Bay, and 10 years later he was consecrated the first bishop of the newly created Diocese of the Upper Peninsula. Prior to his death in 1868 the "Apostle to the Chippewa" published nine religious volumes in their language.

During the summer of 1836 a tornado struck the little community couched at the rapids of the Grand "leveling many of the buildings and carrying the furnishings some distance." The local Ottawa undoubtedly viewed this as symbolic of the disaster that had been visited

Michigan Indian Agent Henry Rowe Schoolcraft thought he knew what was best for the Ottawa despite their objections.

upon them as a result of the Washington Treaty that year which, with the exception of a few reservations, effectively stripped the Ottawa of all remaining land in the Lower Peninsula. In exchange all the Ottawa living between the Grand and Cheboygan rivers would divide for 20 years an annual payment of $18,000 and a few other minor dispensations. That paltry sum would be doled out annually at Grand Rapids.

Slater, as outlined by McCoy in his 1840 *History of Baptist Indian Missions*, played a rather dubious role in the treaty negotiations conducted by Schoolcraft. The Grand River Ottawa had met in council twice near the Thomas Mission and both times resolved not to sell their tribal land. When they learned, however, that a small contingent of Ottawa at L'Arbre Croche would probably sign away all the land without the approval of the Grand River Indians, they decided to send a delegation to Washington to prevent it. That delegation was deliberately composed of men who were not chiefs and had no power to sign a treaty. Slater accompanied the delegation and presented to Schoolcraft a document signed by all but one of the Grand River chiefs "remonstrating against the ceding of any portion of their country."

But what the Indians actually wanted would prove of little concern during the treaty negotiations. Schoolcraft and others with vested interests including fur traders Robinson and Lyon, who had been elected senator in 1836 but could not take his seat until Michigan officially entered the union in 1837, had their own ideas of what was best for the Ottawa and, incidently, themselves. As Schoolcraft wrote in reference to the Grand River Ottawa, "they require the proper course to be pointed out and can readily be induced to conform to it." Slater, evidently, was also of a similar mind and, as he confessed to McCoy, may also have been influenced by the several thousand dollars in bribes offered by traders who had much to gain via annuity payments. In any event, the 1836 Treaty of Washington was indeed signed by the delegation of non-chiefs sent by the Grand River Ottawa expressly to prevent it. Slater, Robinson and Lyon also signed the document. One of the provisions of the treaty awarded Robinson more than $20,000 because he had an Indian wife.

Another treaty article placed $6,400 under Slater's control. With a portion of that sum he purchased an 80-acre tract between Indian Lake and Long Lake in Barry County's Praireville Township. He led some 300 Grand River Ottawa including Noonday there and re-established his mission and Indian school. Slater's Barry County mission prospered for a decade or so, but following the death of the stalwart Noonday in 1845 and the inroads of land-hungry settlers, his Indian flock melted away. In 1852 Slater moved to Kalamazoo where prior to his death in 1866 he devoted his evangelistic efforts to the black citizens of that community.

Following the 1836 Treaty some Ottawa lingered in the Grand Rapids area, dispossessed and unwanted except during each year's annuity payment days, when, as Franklin Everett noted, "it was amusing to observe the great number of 'friends' that would gather around the Indian after he had received his money from the paymasters." Other Ottawa families moved north out of harm's way until the tide of immigration reached them. Some shifted to northern Allegan County and the future site of Holland where the Reverend George Nelson Smith established the Old Wing Mission in 1839. But after the arrival of Albertus Van Raalte's Dutch colonists in 1846, the Indians found life among them intolerable and moved with Smith to the Leelanau Peninsula. In 1854 most of the remaining Grand River Ottawa walked up the gangplank of a steamer at Grandville and journeyed north to land reserved for them in Oceana County. Charles E. Belknap, who came to Grand Rapids as a boy that year, offered a fitting tribute to the city's native people: "Until the white man came with a Bible in one hand but a jug of whiskey in the other, the Indian was a pretty good fellow."

The Rev. John Frost, a Crow Indian, visited the Rev. Leonard Slater's grave in Kalamazoo's Riverside Cemetery in the 1930s.

3 THE ROCHESTER OF THE WEST

With most of the Indians gone and the west side of the river open for settlement, Grand Rapids, or Kent as the post office was called until 1844, entered a period of bustling development. Nine-year-old Marion Hinsdale who moved with her family to Grand Rapids in 1836 recalled her first summer there: "The arrival of so many strangers; the rapid changes; the hurry of people to get some place to live before cool weather, the peculiar ways in which people did live; the feverish excitement of speculation; so many events crowded into the space of a few months, make those months seem now, like so many years."

In 1834, while Kent County was attached to Kalamazoo County for governmental purposes, Grand Rapids citizens had

gathered in Guild's house to establish Kent Township (renamed Grand Rapids Township in 1842) and elected the first township officials, including Robinson as supervisor and Slater as justice of the peace. With the arrival of scores of new settlers, on March 24, 1836, Kent County created its own government and legal system. A shipment of spoiled flour sold in the settlement the year before gave rise to the first Kent County Circuit Court litigation, the 1836 case of Savoy R. Beals vs. Lewis Morean.

In addition to numerous speculators the mid-1830s witnessed the arrival of increasing numbers of citizens who would lay the foundations for a community. The first

(Far right) William Haldane opened one of Grand Rapids' first furniture shops in the house he constructed in 1835.

A half century after pioneering in primitive log cabins some prosperous Kent County residents continued to preserve their original homes.

physician, Dr. Stephen A. Wilson, hung out his shingle in 1835. The following year an English immigrant named John Pannell pioneered in an another aspect of community life when he constructed a diminutive brewery over a creek that flowed at the base of Prospect Hill (the current site of the Old Kent Bank parking lot). That same year a 29-year-old son of Scottish immigrants, William Haldane, drove his horse and buggy from Ohio to Grand Rapids and constructed a small dwelling at the corner of Pearl and Ottawa streets. In a back room he opened one of the village's first cabinet shops, a pioneering venture in the industry that would ultimately bring Grand Rapids international fame.

Even some of the speculators opted to cast their lots with the little settlement. One destined to make his mark, John Ball, rode into town in October 1836. Born in 1795 near Hebron, New Hampshire, then the western New England frontier, Ball developed the same adventurous spirit that had characterized his pioneer ancestors. The youngest of 10 children, he remembered little of his youth other than the constant labors required to eke an existence out of stony New England farm fields. Yearning for more education than could be acquired in the two month "winter school" available to him, he convinced his father to let him leave the farm. He worked his way through a private school taught by a minister, nearby Salisbury Academy and Dartmouth College.

Following graduation he taught school and studied law but then succumbed to wanderlust. During a sailing voyage, his vessel was wrecked off the coast of Georgia and he narrowly escaped a watery grave. Other adventures on the trip included an overland journey to Oregon in 1832, a visit to California and Hawaii and a cruise aboard a whaling vessel. In 1836 Ball caught the Michigan land fever then raging in the east. Three New York investors backed him in a venture to purchase land on the territorial frontier in return for 25 percent of the profits.

During Ball's first trip to Michigan in August, 1836, he invested unwisely in some nearly worthless Monroe County swampland. But the New York investors remained confident and, equipped with more gold pieces, Ball returned to Detroit on October 1. He made his way through the wilderness to the newly opened land office in Ionia, where he acquired maps outlining the available government land in the Grand River Valley.

Honest John Ball cast his lot with the pioneer village in 1837.

After his initial foray to Grand Rapids where he found 50-foot-wide lots selling for $2,500, he soon determined his best chance for investment lay in the wilderness of Ottawa and Allegan counties. From his subsequent land looking adventures he gained a thorough knowledge of prime tracts of timber land which eventually netted him a modest fortune. In the spring of 1837, Ball took up permanent residence in Grand Rapids, first boarding at the Eagle Hotel where he supplemented his income as a lawyer and a banker. That fall he won election as the state representative for Ottawa, Kent, Ionia and Clinton counties. Later, Ball purchased a large Greek Revival house on East Fulton Street where he resided until his death in 1884. His will granted the original 40-acre tract of the park named in his honor to the city he loved and helped build.

The year that Ball began his long residence in Grand Rapids, 1837, also witnessed the birth of the first newspaper. How the original Washington hand press got to Grand Rapids is a story of pioneer determination and pluck. In the fall of 1836, Lyon's Kent company purchased the press, type and other printing equipment of the Niagara Falls *Journal* and had it shipped west on the steamer *Don Quixote*. Under command of Captain William Kanouse, the vessel left Detroit on October 10, 1836, for Grand Rapids. A gale struck nine days later and the ship took refuge off Thunder Bay Island. The anchor line broke and the *Don Quixote* ran aground and filled with water. The crew managed to save the press and store it in a hastily erected log cabin. Repeated efforts to save the ship failed and finally the press and type were transferred to a sailing vessel that reached Grand Haven on December 31. At that point veteran printer George W. Pattison purchased the outfit and hired some locals to convey it up the river on dog sleds. A few miles below the rapids the sled carrying the press broke through the ice and plunged to the bottom of the river. After being fished out of the water it finally arrived in Grand Rapids.

On April 18, 1837, Pattison triumphantly issued the first copy of the Grand River *Times* at the original office

(Far left)
The Greek Revival facade of the Eagle Hotel, the city's first hostelry, greeted patrons from 1834 to 1883.

John Ball lived in this Greek Revival home on East Fulton Street until his death in 1884.

Louis Campau erected this Greek Revival mansion on the corner of Fulton Street and Gay Avenue in 1838.

on Canal Street. The lead article, titled "The Rochester of Michigan," captures the ebullience of the era: "Though young in its improvements, the site of this village has long been known, and esteemed for its natural advantages... Who would have believed, to have visited this place two years since, when it was only inhabited by a few families, most of whom were of French origin... that this place would now contain its twelve hundred inhabitants? The rapidity of its settlement is beyond the most visionary anticipation; but its location, its advantages, and its clime, were sufficient to satisfy the observing mind, that nothing but the frown of Providence could blast its prospects!

"....A canal is nearly completed around the rapids at this place, sufficiently large to admit boats to pass up and down, with but little detention. Several steamboats are now preparing to commence regular trips... The citizens are of the most intelligent enterprising and industrious character. Their buildings are large, tasty, and handsomely furnished — the clatter of mallet and chisel — the clink of hammer — the many newly raised and recently covered frames — and the few skeleton boats upon the wharves of the river, speak loudly for the enterprise of the place! Mechanics of all kind find abundance of employ, and reap a rich reward for their labor. Village property advances in value, and the prospect of wealth is alike flattering to all! What the result of such advantages and prospects will be, time alone must determine."

In 1837 this Washington hand press arrived in the village via dog sled after many vicissitudes.

Alas, those rosy predictions soon faced bleak reality. Before 1837 had ended, a severe depression gripped the eastern states, precipitated, in part, by President Andrew Jackson's Specie Circular of 1836, which required government land be purchased in gold, not the nearly worthless wildcat currency being churned out by scores of underfunded institutions including Campau's People's Bank and the Proprietors of Kent's Grand River Bank. Initially, Michigan remained insulated from the worst effects of the depression, largely because of the new state's boundless optimism. But by 1839 the rush of new settlers into Michigan dwindled and commodity prices on the frontier came crashing down. Businesses went bankrupt, banks closed forever, and much of the prime land grabbed by speculators reverted to the public domain via unpaid taxes.

Grand Rapids, which had been incorporated in 1838, fell on hard times, or as Jackson D. Dillenback noted in his 1870 *History and Directory of Kent County,* the village was for several years "a blue place." Campau became one of the first casualties of the depression. Overextended in building and banking ventures based on the inflated value of his Grand Rapids land holdings, when the bubble burst and land prices plummeted, he was forced to surrender his downtown lots to bankruptcy assignees in 1839. Four years later all his debts had been paid and the assignees deeded back to Campau what little was left of his downtown property. He never fully recovered from that debacle, although he continued to live in style in the mansion he had erected in 1838 on the southwest corner of Fulton Street and Gay Avenue and wisely deeded to his mother prior to the bankruptcy. Tradition has it that he papered the cupola of the big Greek Revival home with unsigned bills of his People's Bank and other valueless wildcat notes.

In 1863 with four mortgages on the mansion, he sold it. He and Sophie moved into a modest home at Ellsworth Avenue and Elm Street.

As the decades wore on, time tempered the reputation of the garrulous old trader as a cunning if not altogether scrupulous entrepreneur to that of a eccentric fatherly city founder. Local newspapers regularly quoted the imaginative recollections of "the old settler." After his move to Ellsworth Avenue, "his resources failing he lived on the bounty of his friends, who were unwilling that he should feel poverty." Grief-stricken when Sophie died in 1869, Campau lingered on in sickness until his death on April 13, 1871. The man worth an estimated $100,000 in the halcyon days of the mid-1830s left an estate valued at $2,500.

Louis Campau and wife Sophie posed for the camera shortly before her death in 1869.

Campau's old nemesis Lyon fared little better. When the depression hit, he lost most of his widespread real estate holdings to creditors and back taxes. He sought to recoup his fortune through a salt-making operation. Salt, in great demand as the primary preserving agent, was a recognized medium of exchange on the frontier. Lyon had long known about some salt springs on the banks of the Grand River. Following a visit to a salt-making enterprise on the Kanawah River, West Virginia, he determined to attempt a similar operation in Grand Rapids. He planned to drill a well, pump up the brine, evaporate it and market the remaining residue. Using a machine powered by water from the nearby canal that he had partially dredged around the rapids, Lyon commenced boring on the west bank of the canal in January 1840. Over the succeeding decade he would sink more than $20,000 into the experiment. By 1843 some salt was produced and successfully marketed locally but ultimately the operation proved a dismal failure in part because of the inability to keep fresh water from diluting the brine. Although he carved out a notable career as one of Michigan's original senators, a regent of the University of Michigan and U.S. Congressman in 1843-45, Lyon's many land speculations ultimately resulted in naught. He died in Detroit in 1851, nearly penniless.

Franklin Everett interviewed Grand River Valley pioneers to compile a monumental history of the region.

The depression also claimed numerous other Grand Rapids stalwarts as well as the newspaper, which gave up the ghost in 1840. Franklin Everett, who arrived in Grand Rapids during the bleak days of 1846 and would compile an excellent history of the Grand River Valley in 1878 based largely on his own observations and interviews with other pioneers, cast much of the blame for those losses on over optimism. He wrote: "Improvements — and some of them great ones — had been made, but in almost every case they had ruined those who had invested their capital. The fact was, at the start there was too much enterprise — a throwing away of capital in works that should have awaited their demand. In attempting to do business where there was not the business to do, the capital was sunk. Abram S. Wadsworth had bankrupted himself in developing water power; and Daniel Ball the same, by running good steamboats, when only the cheapest craft would pay. Lucius Lyon had sunk a fortune in developing various interests too soon. And the natural consequences of the whole was a general abandonment of enterprises begun and the beginning of no new ones. Discouraged, some of the leading spirits had withdrawn; and capital seeking investment, was not to be found."

The hard times bottomed in 1846. It was almost impossible to acquire money in Grand Rapids because nobody had any to spend. Barter and trade became the economic standby. Few went hungry because their labor could be traded for victuals, but getting ahead in the world appeared next to impossible. Lumber sent down the river to Grand Haven and hence to Chicago markets might bring less than the cost of cutting and transportation. Firewood was the local medium of exchange and an entire cord hauled six miles or so brought only $1. Wheat sold for 50 cents a bushel, corn 25 cents, venison two

(Far right) Campau's "Old Yellow Warehouse" stood on the riverbank from 1834 to 1889.

Teamsters laboriously graded Ottawa Street in 1865.

pounds for a penny and beef or pork less than three cents a pound.

Civic improvements went by the wayside. Everett remembered Canal Street as ""the muddiest hole in all creation." Frank Little, a clerk in Jefferson Morrison's store at the foot of Monroe Avenue in 1844, wrote: "In the late fall and early spring, Monroe Street from Division to Canal, became literally a river of mud — this mud from six to eight inches deep, the whole width of the street and thick, like hasty pudding."

Yet some progress continued to be made. A directory issued in 1845 enumerated 15 stores, two saw mills, three flour mills, two furnace and machine shops, two pail factories, two tanneries, a woolen factory, a sash factory, the salt works, a plaster mill, two hatters, several blacksmiths, three hotels, two printing offices, four churches and one incorporated academy. Three physicians bled patients with lancets and leeches and doled out a poisonous mercury compound called calomel as a panacea. That year also witnessed completion of the first wagon bridge across the river at Bridge Street, supplanting a primitive pedestrian bridge erected two years before.

The following year, when choice downtown lots went begging for $400 and other city lots brought less than $10, the village authorities invested $325 in the first fire engine, a small hand pumper called a "tub." To cheer themselves up a group of citizens organized a brass band in 1846 and others enjoyed lectures and amateur theatrics in the recently constructed Irving Hall. Before the decade ended, Grand Rapids hosted professional acting troupes that arrived via Grand Haven.

Another early amusement, a performance by a traveling magician staged in the "Yellow Warehouse" built on the river bank by Campau in 1834, nearly ended in disaster for the crowd that attended. Albert Baxter recalled what happened in his 1891 history of the city: "In one part of [the magician's] performance he lifted Warren Mills' hat from his head, and nearly a peck of potatoes rolled over that gentleman's shoulders to the floor. Then amid the cheering and stamping of feet came a crackling of timbers and the floor began to settle. This caused a stampede for exit, and those in the audience tumbled over each other in their haste to get downstairs. Fortunately the sills settled but two or three inches and were on solid blocking. No one was seriously hurt."

While some buoyed their spirits through entertainment others engaged

Albert Baxter included in his 1891 history a depiction of the city's first fire engine, known as the "Tub."

Dutch immigrants poured into southwestern Michigan beginning in 1846.

in altruistic endeavors. A group of local ladies founded the Union Benevolent Association in 1846 to raise and distribute funds for indigent families. That organization would plant the seeds for the city's first health care center, which would evolve into Blodgett Hospital.

By 1847 the village had recovered enough from the depression to begin some rudimentary attempts at civic betterment. To improve the slough called Canal Street south of Michigan, workmen shoveled a thin layer of sand and gravel over the mud and dressed the top with pulverized limestone from the river bed. That same year the State Legislature cast a plumb in Grand Rapids' direction by appropriating 25,000 acres of land to fund expansion of the mile-long canal Lyon had dug between 1835 and 1842. The plan called for enlargement and improvement of the race, completion of a dam at its head and construction of a series of locks at its foot that would allow steamboats to navigate the river from Grand Haven to Lyons.

In the meantime the Reverend Albertus Van Raalte had led a ragtag band of peasant followers from a motherland they considered too liberal to found a Zion in the wilderness near the mouth of Ottawa Gounty's Black River. Van Raalte selected that isolated site in part to keep his countrymen away from the temptations of the flesh to be found in urban centers like Kalamazoo and Grand Rapids. But as the vanguards of 1846 swelled to a torrent of thousands of Dutch immigrants arriving in western Michigan annually, many found their way to Grand Rapids to work and live.

As work continued on the canal, in August 1849, Charles H. Taylor, editor of the Grand Rapids *Enquirer* commented: "Any one may now see the 'Dutch Buggies' in full operation, at the foot of Canal Street. The dirt is taken from the lock excavation, near the bank of the river, is used to raise a lot belonging to Mr. Davis, upon Canal Street, and the files of Dutchmen engaged in transporting the 'raw material' are well worth watching. These men are mostly hired 'for land', and a few months labor will make each of them the proprietor in fee of a forty-acre lot, which in their notion is a domain, equaling in size some of the petty Dukedoms or Principalities into which their native country is cut up. They are not only

The Alabastine Company's factory was a busy place in 1891.

an industrious but very steady set of laborers. No rows mark their hours or days of rest, to which peculiarity their general temperance undoubtedly contributes."

Despite the efforts of the Dutch laborers the lock system was never completed. But having tasted Grand Rapids opportunities the Dutch continued to be drawn there. By the spring of 1851 some 400 Hollanders called Grand Rapids home. In 1860 that number had swelled to 2,000 and by the turn of the 19th century more than one-quarter of Grand Rapids' 87,565 residents claimed Dutch heritage, a ratio that continues to this day.

Even as the Dutch laborers shoveled and sweated in 1849, a British immigrant named Richard Butterworth was busy excavating a geologic resource that would bring wealth and fame for Grand Rapids. The presence of gypsum in the Grand Rapids area had been known as early as 1827 when an Ottawa gave Slater a chunk of the mineral found near the mouth of aptly named Plaster Creek. Seven years later, James Clark settled in Grand Rapids to ply his trade as a plasterer. While finishing a house constructed for Campau he collected some gypsum, hammered it into small pieces, ground it in an old Indian corn mill and calcined the powder into plaster by burning it in a cauldron. He used it to apply some artistic stucco ornaments to the gables of the structure.

However, the primary use for gypsum at the time was as land plaster, a fertilizer applied to farmlands. In 1838 State Geologist Douglass Houghton noted in his annual report the presence of a considerable bed of gypsum in Grand Rapids. Houghton thought the Grand Rapids lode "cannot fail to prove a subject of much value to the agricultural interests of the state." Two years later in another report he lamented that the rich Grand Rapids deposits had "been entirely neglected."

In 1841 Daniel Ball and Warren Granger took the hint and began quarrying gypsum and grinding it into land plaster in a small water-powered mill. They shipped their initial output down the river and via schooner to Detroit. When they advertised locally, within a week 40 tons of plaster had been carted away in horse-drawn farm wagons. In 1843 Ball sold his interest in the enterprise to Henry R. Williams, Grand Rapids' first mayor, who aggressively promoted the product to area farmers. Soon, demand surpassed output, the price rose and by 1849 with the mill running day and night "teams coming 100 miles were forced to return without a load."

That is when Butterworth entered the plaster sweepstakes. He had settled on a farm two miles southwest of Grand Rapids in 1843. While plowing a field he dislodged a big boulder of gypsum and located major deposits in a nearby hillside. In 1849 he built a water-powered mill and began producing land plaster. His success, as well as that of producers on the east side of the river, brought long lines of wagons to Grand Rapids to convey an annual output that reached 2,000 tons a year by the early 1850s. Butterworth sold out in 1856 for $35,000, a fortune in those days, which he parlayed into a Grand Rapids machine shop that specialized in gypsum machinery. Butterworth's original gypsum site was renamed the Eagle Mill, part of the Grand Rapids Plaster Company's

Miners posed before the entrance to the Grand Rapids Plaster Company's quarry in 1876.

(Far left)
The sidewheel steamer *L. Jenison* plied the river above the rapids beginning in 1867 until it burned in 1875. *Calvin College Archives*

This stagecoach that ran between Grand Rapids and Kalamazoo lurched along the plank road in the 1850s and 1860s.

extensive holdings. By 1869, the various operations in Grand Rapids shipped 12,000 tons of plaster yearly.

By the 1880s, experiments revealed land plaster's value as fertilizer to be much overrated and various phosphorous compounds supplanted its use. But mining of the mineral for other purposes expanded. Producers developed techniques to efficiently calcine mass quantities of gypsum into a fine powder ideal for plaster of Paris, stucco, wall plaster and a glossy paint-like material called alabastine patented by Melvin B. Church in 1875. Eight years later Church and partners relocated their mammoth mill from Grandville to Grand Rapids.

By the 1890s Grand Rapids miners sank shafts 90 feet deep to reach vast deposits of gypsum as much as 50 feet thick. The city retained title as "America's leading supplier of gypsum products" into the 1960s.

The early development of the gypsum industry helped promote a vital need — improved transportation facilities. Since 1837 with the launching of the first steamboat on the river, the *Governor Mason,* which incidently was powered by the engine from the ill-fated *Don Quixote,* the Grand River and the Great Lakes served as the primary transportation route. The *Owashtanong* was also launched in 1837 and the following year the *Patronage* and the *John Almy* began running on the Grand. Ultimately more than 20 steamers plied the Grand Rapids to Grand Haven stretch. But for the city to achieve economic success once it had shaken off the effects of the depression, it need better access to markets.

The Michigan Central Railroad had snaked its way westward from Detroit to reach Kalamazoo in 1846, thereby spurring a boom in that community's economy. Grand Rapids promoters clamored for a railroad also until they realized that it was simply too expensive a proposition given the city's economic problems. So they turned to a cheaper alternative — a plank road linking Grand Rapids with the nearest rail line in Kalamazoo.

The Kalamazoo and Grand Rapids Plank Road Company began soliciting subscriptions in the summer of 1849. That fall the principal contractor, Titus Doan, begun acquiring planks, the route was surveyed and right of way secured. Two years later the company had raised $37,000 and under the direction of Charles Shepard and William Withey of Grand Rapids and Israel Kellogg and former Michigan Governor Epaphroditus Ransom of Kalamazoo, construction began.

Normally constructed of eight- to 16-foot-long, three-inch-thick pine or oak boards laid across wooden stringers, plank roads, when properly maintained, offered a smooth and easy ride. By the summer of 1855 the entire 48-mile length of the Grand Rapids and Kalamazoo Plank Road, covering a course due south on Division Avenue along the route of old U.S. 131 had been completed. Travelers paid tolls ranging from one cent per mile for a horse and rider to two cents per mile for a wagon drawn by two horses at toll booths located at 12 mile intervals. That is, unless they veered off at "shunpikes," as the short stretches of road that bypassed the toll gates were called. A spur of the plank road ran to Allegan. At the intersection of the two roads, a community originally called the Junction sprang up. Later, citizens changed its name to Plainwell.

The plank road soon became "a principal and very serviceable avenue of communication, for business, for passengers and for freighting" between Grand Rapids and the outside world. Dillenback recalled counting as many as 170 wagons daily on the road en route to the plaster mills. Many of those freight wagons undoubtedly bore the name Harrison on their sides.

William Harrison moved his wagon factory from Kalamazoo to Grand Rapids in 1856.

Spurred by the opening of the plank road, William Harrison had relocated his wagon factory from Kalamazoo to Grand Rapids in 1856. He built a big stone structure along the riverbank near the intersection of Front and Third streets and a long wagon train conveyed his machinery and materials from Kalamazoo over the plank road. Harrison's carpenters, metal workers, spokeshavers, painters and other skilled artisans hand-crafted quality wagons. In the early days Harrison often had to accept lumber, produce or whatever else farmers had in payment for wagons. But his enterprise flourished and became an important Grand Rapids industry, eventually producing an annual output second only to the famed Studebaker Company of South Bend, Indiana.

Not only did wagons made by Harrison carry away the vast output of the gypsum mines, they also transported to Grand Rapids loads of corn, pork, produce and other provisions which local merchants sold in immense quantities to the lumber camps located along tributaries of the Grand River and to the north.

The river remained the primary means of transporting lumber to market. As early as 1838 James M. Nelson had sent lumber rafts from Grand Rapids to the mills in Grand Haven. But until the 1850s the lumbering business grew modestly. By 1855 with increasing demand from burgeoning Chicago and the western prairies, lumber shipments from the mouth of the Grand River reached 45 million feet annually, most of which floated down from the rapids in rafts or single logs.

The city's own sawmills date from 1832 when a small up-and-down type mill was constructed at government expense on Indian Mill Creek for the Thomas Mission. Over the following two decades Grand Rapids proprietors established several other water power mills but the up-and-down saws were slow and wasteful. In 1853, Powers, Ball and Company erected the first steam-powered mill equipped with a circular saw and by the next year four million feet of lumber were being cut annually. Bigger and more sophisticated mills followed and by the 1870s Grand Rapids industrialists were converting extensive tracts of white pine growing along the Rouge, Flat, Maple and other tributaries into billions of feet of lumber.

Even after the arrival of the railroads the preferred method of delivering lumber to the mouth of the Grand River remained rafts. Skilled raft makers assembled them to withstand the rigors of shooting the chute in the dam

(Far right) The output of this typical 19th-century Michigan sawmill helped build Chicago, twice.

At boom yards millions of board feet of logs were sorted out by brand marks hammered onto their ends.

at Grand Rapids. Belknap described how rafts were constructed: "First came long, heavy stuff for a foundation, then shorter lumber for cross piling. By a system of overlapping or shingling, the lumber was woven into many layers. In times of good water the rafts were two feet thick. Heavy pieces at the top were pinned at the ends and to the bottom sills with tough hardwood split from river bank trees. All the tools needed were an ax and an auger. When the raft was finished there was often added a deck load of shingles and lath."

Often as long as 200 feet, rafts could be no wider than 16 feet to squeeze through the chute in the dam. They were usually manned by a crew of five raftsmen, French-Canadians skilled at steering the ungainly craft with a long heavy sweep at the rear out of the way of steamboats, around sand bars and through the dangerous rush below the chute.

In 1850 the state legislature approved Grand Rapids' new charter that made it a city with wards. Four years later the state census taker arrived, and he recorded some interesting statistics. The city's population stood at 4,278, composed of nearly equal numbers of men and women and 33 "colored persons." Within the city limits grazed 284 horses, 266 beef cattle, 316 milk cows and 24 sheep, as well as 362 hogs, most of whom ran at large rooting in the garbage dumped in gutters. A mere 147 employees worked in manufacturing trades. The previous year they had produced items worth a total of $147,600. A lone beer maker, German immigrant Christoph Kusterer, had brewed 700 barrels of his "family drink" for local consumption in 1853. Merchants comprised the city's main economic base, having imported goods valued at more than $750,000 that year.

Despite its growth, Grand Rapids remained in many respects little changed from its founding. The four islands were still the campgrounds of occasional Ottawa. Indian youths sometimes attended classes with the white students. Belknap related an interesting story about one of the Indian students. Principal James Ballard had been attempting to teach him elocution by repeated drilling with many gestures and exaggerated rolling of the R's the phrase "the ragged rascal ran." The Indian boy who spoke a pidgin mixture of Ottawa, French and English was finally allowed to attempt the exercise in his own words. Whereupon, imitating Ballard's gestures he gravely uttered, "The damn thief run like hell." And that was the end of the lesson for that day. Soon after, some parents complained of the mingling of races in the classroom and the Indian students were sent elsewhere.

Along the river grew giant sycamores and huge water elms festooned with wild grape vines. As late as 1858, three black bears were shot within the city limits. Belknap noted that each spring the inhabitants feasted on immense quantities of suckers working their way through the rapids to spawn. They were "fried with salt pork, boiled with cream and butter, stuffed with dressing, the platter garnished with watercress and always a few barrels salted for winter consumption." Spring also brought runs of spawning sturgeon weighing 150 pounds and more. Caught in nets spread below the dam or speared by canoeists, the monster fish were so plentiful they brought only 25 cents apiece. Citizens boiled the fish to remove the oil and used it in making soap, for burning in torches and lanterns, and for greasing their boots.

In 1861 Mary Cuming sketched the islands in the Grand River which later disappeared into the city's downtown.

Grand Rapidians harvested another coveted source of food in the form of immense flocks of passenger pigeons that flew so low over the city that boys batted them down with poles. In the spring pioneers made a beeline for the salt meadows along the west bank of the river, a

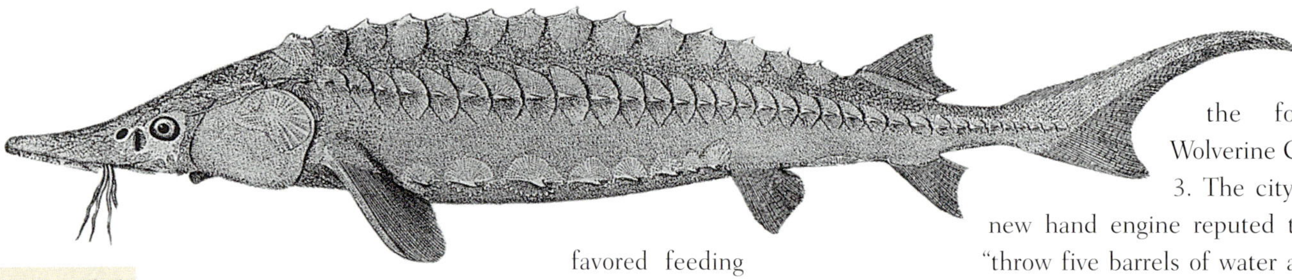

Lake sturgeon worked their way up the rapids to spawn. They reached a length of 12 feet or more.

favored feeding place of the pigeons, to net, trap or shoot the avian windfall by the thousands. What they did not consume fresh were pickled in apple cider and sealed in stone crocks. Despite each year's slaughter there seemed no limit to the bird's fecundity. But by the century's end few were seen and the last one on earth died in a Cincinnati zoo in 1914.

While hunting and fishing offered sport for many, other athletically inclined young men joined volunteer fire companies. Three companies had been attempted with little success as early as 1844. But in the fall of 1849, 29 citizens banded together to form Alert Fire Company, No. 1, with Charles H. Taylor as its captain. Protection Fire Company, No. 2, was organized before the year ended. In 1850 another dozen recruits launched Hook and Ladder, No. 1, and the west side got its first unit with the formation of Wolverine Company, No. 3. The city purchased a new hand engine reputed to be able to "throw five barrels of water a minute over the highest building on Monroe Street" to bolster the original "tub" engine. Soon parades, foot races and pumping demonstrations became a colorful part of village festivities as the rival companies competed.

Despite the fire companies, the decade of the 1850s witnessed numerous conflagrations. Early in the morning of December 16, 1851, Charles W. Taylor's big tannery at Coldbrook burned to the ground at an uninsured loss of $10,000. The fire engine house on Prospect Hill also burned that same morning. The next day Taylor received the following letter: "Damn you, you have got it at last. I told you I would have revenge. Yours truly, in trouble." Testimony during the ensuing circuit court case over the arson revealed details of the plot stemming from a feud between Taylor and local grocer George Mills: "Mills then said he would give any man who would burn

The Kent Street fire laddies posed with their pumper in 1865.

Prominent 19th-century banker Harvey J. Hollister (in right foreground) stood with his staff in the lobby of the old National Bank in 1889.

Taylor's Tannery $150. I enquired how he would set fire to it. He said that was easy for a man if he was not afraid. He said take a box like a cigar box and fill it with shavings and cotton dipped in turpentine. I said what good will that do? He said that there was a door that stood open about four or five feet from the ground. He said in there was a pile of bark. He said put two sticks in the door and put a board edgewise on the sticks in the door, then the light would show but little below. Then take a stick and shove the box across the floor into the bark. I said that was a good idea.

"I asked Mills how soon he wanted it done. Mills said he did not care, the sooner the better. Mills then said better let it be until it comes freezing nights. We shall have to see to the engine on Prospect Hill for the damn thing will piss out more fire than ten man can kindle. I asked how he would work it? He said one man would cut holes in the hose and pour water into it and let it freeze up shut. Then Mills asked me if I would join him. I said I thought I would..."

The court record does not confirm the outcome of the case but it is known that Mills left Grand Rapids for the far west soon after. Nevertheless, Taylor's Tannery burned a second time in 1856. Other major conflagrations of the era include a fast-spreading fire that destroyed 25 businesses on Monroe Avenue in 1857. The following year flames destroyed the Bridge Street Bridge and several factories. In 1860 most county records and the post office went up in smoke.

Development of a police force lagged behind fire protection. Prior to 1850 no money was allocated for law enforcement. The City Charter of 1850 provided for up to five untrained part-time constables. The city did not acquire a full time police force until 1871. Local banker Harvey J. Hollister recalled a representative 1855 experience. When jeweler Aaron Dikeman attempted to deposit some cash, Hollister identified a $5 bill as counterfeit. Dikeman remembered receiving it from a ruffian named Cook. Later that day Hollister received a subpoena to testify before Justice of the Peace Thompson Sinclair. Upon arriving at the justice's office he found the court in session with Dikeman, Cook and a crowd of spectators present. Hollister proceeded to testify about the bogus bill when he "was suddenly seized by the prisoner and nearly strangled, and when the courtroom was turned into confusion by the act, the man seized the bill and escaped down the stairs, got into his wagon, the horses being hitched at the door, and started for the open country. The constable, the court, indeed, all who

Austin (standing) and George Bidwell left their Grand Rapids candy business for a life of crime.

witnessed the affair, were so upset by the suddenness of the man's performance that no effort was made by anyone to prevent his getting away." The next day a posse set out after Cook, but he had fled to parts unknown and never was brought to trial.

Western explorer John W. Gunnison was killed by Paiute Indians in 1853.

Coincidently, the year 1855 links Grand Rapids with another set of counterfeiters who would not be as successful in their escape from justice. Six years earlier Austin B. Bidwell and his sons, George and Austin, had moved from Toledo to Grand Rapids where they opened the community's first candy store on Monroe Street. Fire destroyed that small store shortly afterward, but the Bidwells persevered and opened up a larger establishment on Canal Street. Bidwell's bon bons, fudge and taffy sold well. George Bidwell had a particular knack for merchandising and he began sending out salesmen in wagons to supply dealers in surrounding towns with wholesale candies.

But the increased overhead, in conjunction with the financial panic of 1855, proved disastrous. The Bidwell Candy Company went bankrupt due largely to the machinations of a shyster lawyer they had hired to help liquidate assets. The family left Grand Rapids and wound up in New York City. The brothers got in with a bad crowd, began petty gambling and embezzling small sums from employers. By the 1870s the Bidwell boys had become hardened criminals specializing in forgery, bunco and assorted con games.

They shifted operations to Europe where in 1873 they attempted the biggest caper of their career — a $5 million forgery on the bank of England. They might have gotten away with it had they not failed to date one of their expertly forged bills. They led the bobbies and a set of Pinkerton detectives on a merry chase half-way around the world before getting nabbed. Following a spectacular trial in England they were sentenced to life imprisonment. Released after 15 to 20 years in jail, the Bidwells turned to a literary life, each publishing books detailing their Grand Rapids days and ultimate fall from grace.

Other Grand Rapidians of the 1850s achieved prominence through more respectable pursuits. Thirty-two-year-old John W. Gunnison bought a 120-acre tract of government land south of West Fulton Street in 1844 and made Grand Rapids his family home. A career soldier, Gunnison had graduated from West Point in 1837. He became a topographical engineer with few peers, served in the Florida campaign against the Seminoles as an Everglades scout and assisted in the unfortunate Cherokee "Trail of Tears." He explored and mapped parts of northern Wisconsin and for seven years labored on the Great Lakes mapping surveys. In 1849 Gunnison ventured into the far west as a member of Captain Howard Stansbury's exploratory expedition to the Great Salt Lake. He spent a winter among the Mormons and returning on leave to Grand Rapids in 1852 wrote a classic account of his observations, *The Mormons or Latter-Day Saints in the Valley of the Great Salt Lake.* While in Grand Rapids he also delivered popular lectures to local organizations. In 1853 Gunnison won promotion to captain and was selected to lead one of four surveys to determine the route of the projected Pacific Railroad. He performed his mission with his usual competency until the morning of October 26, 1853, when a band of Paiute Indians attacked the captain's camp. Gunnison and eight other explorers fell bristling with arrows. A river, national park and city in Colorado as well as Gunnison Street in Grand Rapids honor the brave captain's name. Delony Avenue was named after his son, Delony.

Another who achieved cartographic immortality in Grand Rapids was Henry L. Ellsworth. He originally became associated with Grand Rapids as a member of Lyon's Kent syndicate. Prior to his death in 1858 Ellsworth led a varied life as a lawyer, inventor, Indian commissioner and commissioner of the U.S. Patent Office and is best remembered as "the father of the U.S. Department of Agriculture." Ellsworth Avenue perpetuates his local connection and Goodrich and Bartlett streets commemorate two of his successive wives' maiden names.

4 TRAIN WHISTLES & CANNON'S ROAR

The year 1858 proved an important one for the development of Grand Rapids' transportation facilities. To replace the Bridge Street Bridge that burned earlier in the year, local subscribers formed a company to construct a covered bridge at Pearl Street. The venture was intended to turn a profit via a toll booth on the west end. Pedestrians utilizing the four-foot-wide walkway paid one cent for the privilege while wagon traffic on the 16-foot-wide roadway paid four cents a trip. Those fees remained in effect until the city purchased the bridge in 1873.

An event of greater significance came on June 27, 1858, when the shrill whistle of a steam locomotive emptied Grand Rapids stores, factories and even taverns. Five days later the locomotive *Empire* steamed and

A. C. Verhees.

Beginning in 1858 with the construction of the Pearl Street Bridge, covered bridges carried traffic across the river at Pearl, Bridge and Leonard streets.

snorted past the new Detroit and Milwaukee Railroad Depot at Plainfield Avenue and Leonard Street to the Pearl Street dock where it was loaded on a barge, ferried across the river and placed on the tracks that led to Grand Haven. Regular passenger service to Detroit began on July 13. On August 26 workmen pounded the last peg in the wooden railroad bridge across the Grand River and in September, service to Grand Haven began. At that port a Benton Harbor-based Goodrich Line steamer conveyed passengers and freight to Milwaukee. Two months later a telegraph operator first tapped out the dots and dashes that sped over wires strung along the track to Detroit.

The Detroit, Grand Haven & Milwaukee Railroad carried passengers to Grand Haven for further travel by steamship across Lake Michigan.

With the completion of the long-awaited rail link with eastern markets, the last obstacle to Grand Rapids' economic success had been eliminated.

The census of 1850 had pegged Grand Rapids' population at 2,686, nearly the same as that of Kalamazoo. The 1860 census counted 8,085 Grand Rapids residents, 25 percent more than its rival 50 miles to the south, and each succeeding decade of the 19th century would see its population double. The railroad spurred a boom in construction as well. In 1859 alone, local carpenters built business structures and residences valued at $136,000.

Citizens paused from their labors the summer of 1859 to enjoy a week of performances by a traveling troupe of actors. Staged in Squier's Opera House on Canal Street, the play, Harriet Beecher Stowe's *Uncle Tom's Cabin,* was of timely interest. Stowe's heartrending story of the evils of slavery had thrilled northern readers since its appearance in 1852, and the audiences that packed the galleries wept over Little Eva, mourned for Uncle Tom and wiped their eyes for poor Eliza. "They hissed Simon Legree and somebody threw a cat at Lawyer Marks," recalled Belknap, who as a boy had passed out handbills advertising the performances.

Michigan, where the Republican party had been founded in Jackson in 1854, had become a bastion of the

Grand Rapidians thrilled to the pathos of *Uncle Tom's Cabin*. This print appears as a frontispiece of a 19th-century Dutch edition "De Negerhut."

abolitionist movement and Grand Rapids was no exception. Following Abraham Lincoln's election in 1860, sectional attitudes hardened. With the bombardment of Fort Sumpter on April 12, 1861, the United States were at war. Nevertheless, "the secession at the South and precipitation of the War for the Union," wrote historian Baxter in 1891, "was to the people of this valley like a peal of thunder from a clear sky."

It did not take the citizens of the "Valley City" long to recover. On April 15, 1861, within hours after the telegraph brought news of Lincoln's plea for 75,000 soldiers to serve three months and end the rebellion, Grand Rapidians overflowed Luce's Hall in response to patriotic addresses. Other meetings followed fast and furious, the local ladies began crafting "housewives," little rolled up sewing kits, and "havelocks," hat covers to protect the neck from sunburn, for the soldier boys. On April 20 the local militia unit, the Valley City Guards, formed the nucleus of the 3rd Michigan Infantry.

Grand Rapids' young men served in numerous Michigan regiments, and some in their eagerness to be mustered joined units from other states such as Company K of the 1st New York Cavalry. But it was the 3rd Michigan Infantry that became known as distinctly a Grand Rapids regiment. As volunteers, primarily from Grand Rapids and Kent County, rushed to join the colors, the 3rd Michigan camped and drilled at "Cantonment Anderson" located south of the city at the present South High School. On June 13, 1861, its full contingent of 1,040 men, led by Col. Daniel McConnell, boarded the train amidst a cheering crowd to join the Army of the Potomac near Washington D.C. A month later the unit "smelled the enemy's powder for the first time" at Blackburn's Ford, Virginia. Then came the disaster of First Bull Run and the retreat to Washington. McConnell resigned in October 1861 to be succeeded by Col. Steven G. Champlin.

The regiment bivouacked for the winter at Alexandria, Virginia, and the following spring engaged in Gen. George B. McCleland's Peninsula Campaign. The unit fought bravely at Williamsburg, Virginia, on May 5 and earned special commendation for its part in the Battle of Fair Oaks. The regiment suffered 169 casualties in that bloody engagement, including Champlin who died two years later in Grand Rapids as a result of his wounds. The 3rd Michigan went on to participate in many of the major battles in the east including Malvern Hill, Second Bull Run, Chantilly, Chancellorsville and Gettysburg.

On May 5, 1864, the 3rd Michigan found itself in the center of the three days of butchery known as the Battle of the Wilderness. The engagement would claim 25,000 casualties but end in a tactical draw. Color Sgt. Daniel G. Crotty, a 21-year-old Irish immigrant who enlisted in the regiment in Grand Rapids in 1861 and survived four years of campaigning to return to the city and write a colorful account of his experiences, captured the horrors of the Wilderness: "The order comes to forward, and we go in, thinking to surprise the Johnnies, but they are up and waiting for us in the thick chaparral. They pour a volley into our ranks and the ball has commenced once more. Both sides stand and take the fearful fire, and the whole line seems to be one vast sheet of flame in the early morn. The number that fall on both sides is fearful, for we are fighting at very close range. We charge on their lines with great

Grand Rapids men of Company B, 1st Michigan Infantry, stood in ranks after the Battle of Lookout Mountain in 1863.

odds, but they stand their ground like a solid wall of masonry. The roar of musketry, the dying groans of the wounded, the hellish yells of the rebels, and the shouts and cheers of the Union men, mingle together, all making a noise and confusion that is hard to describe. Nothing is thought of but load and fire. The wounded must take care of themselves, and every man must stand and fight till either killed or wounded. The rebels fall in their line but those who fall have their places filled with a man in the rear. So they fall on one another. Pretty soon those in the rear make breastworks of their dead comrades. We don't like this kind of fighting much, and forward a charge in four or five line deep. The rebels now give way and we chase them through the dense forest. We have to be very careful or we step on their dead and wounded, which lay around in thousands. We drive them nearly a mile, when they fall behind some works for shelter. We now halt, for their artillery begins to fire into us. We hear them forming their broken lines, and their officers lead them forward again. About this time both armies, nearly two hundred thousand strong, keep up a rattle of musketry like the boiling cauldron of hell. My beautiful flag that looked as bright as a dollar when we started, is fit now, after nearly two days of fighting, to send home, for it is completely riddled with bullets and torn by bush. Nothing is done on this day but perfect slaughter on both sides, and at last night puts an end to the sickening carnage. The stench on this night is fearful, for the weather is very hot and the dead bodies, which lay around in thousands, commence to mortify. We suffer fearfully, too, on account of the scarcity of water, and sight of a mud-puddle is pleasant indeed — we go for it like a drowning man catching at straws. Oh, how tired we are, after these two fearful days. We stretch ourselves down, but are too tired to sleep, and spend the night in the greatest misery."

The desperate charges and counter charges resumed the next morning and thousands more bodies littered the battlefield. Crotty survived that day's fighting only through a lucky accident. While struggling to keep his unit's colors from falling into enemy hands, he tripped and pitched forward face down just as a volley of bullets whistled through where he had stood. Despite the terrific slaughter on both sides and the failure to gain ground, the Battle of the Wilderness would prove a strategic victory for Gen. U.S. Grant who on May 7, 1864, headed south unimpeded by Gen. Robert E. Lee's Army of Northern Virginia.

Israel Canton Smith rose from private to brigadier general during the Civil War.

Ultimately losing more than half its original roster to casualties, the 3rd Michigan continued to see action in Virginia battlefields until June 20, 1864, when many of its members, who had volunteered for three years only, were mustered out. Some, including Crotty, re-enlisted and were assigned to the 5th Michigan Infantry, which remained on active duty until the war's end.

Grand Rapids could be rightfully proud of the 3rd Michigan Infantry's conduct during the war and especially so of the exploits of Israel Canton Smith who enlisted as a private in the unit in 1861 and in less than four years advanced to the rank of brigadier general. The son, oddly enough, of Quaker parents who had immigrated to Grand Rapids from Rhode Island two years before his birth in 1839, Smith attended Grand Rapids schools and Albion College for two years. Then he lumbered on the Muskegon River, toured the south, studied to be a lawyer, traveled overland to California in quest of gold and worked on a Mississippi River steamboat before returning to Grand Rapids in 1860 to complete his law studies. When the war broke out, he traded his law books for the pack and musket and enlisted in the 3rd Michigan Infantry. Smith developed a flair for the military life and before the regiment left for the front he had won promotion to second lieutenant. His bravery during the First Battle of Bull Run earned him another promotion and six months later he got his captain's bars.

While leading a charge during the Second Battle of Bull Run, Smith took two minnie balls in his shoulder. He carried one to his dying day. Smith left his Grand Rapids unit in March 1863 to accept a brigade staff position. At the Battle of Chancellorsville two months later he

Captain James D. Robinson (third from right) of Grand Rapids posed with part of his company atop Lookout Mountain in 1863.

"gave his horse spurs and dashed away at full speed to rally the regiment, when a cannon ball tore off the top of the horse's neck just in front of the saddle. It was a close call, but instantly dismounting, he rallied the regiment back to line." At the Battle of Gettysburg, Smith remained in the thick of the fight until a bullet smashed his leg below the knee. He narrowly escaped its amputation and he carried that second ball in his tibia for the rest of his life. He recuperated on crutches in Grand Rapids until August 1863 when he was appointed major of the 10th Michigan Cavalry, which was then being organized in the city. In the fall of 1863 the 10th Michigan Cavalry joined the Army of the Ohio in Kentucky and east Tennessee. During an attack on a rebel fort at Watauga Bridge, Smith led the cavalry charge and was the first Union soldier to jump the parapet as the Confederate defenders streamed out the opposite side. Shortly after, he led his troopers in a charge against General John Hunt Morgan's cavalry and drove the Confederates from the field.

His audacity, however, sometimes landed him in trouble. In command of 100 cavalrymen on a scouting mission to ascertain General "Fighting Joe" Wheeler's position and strength, Smith encountered an enemy ambush. Rather than retreat from the terrific volley, he charged directly into it. The rebels broke and ran and Smith's force pursued for three miles, capturing 60 of their number. In the midst of the excitement Smith spotted a rebel artillery unit limbering up its guns to his front and cavalry units on three sides. He had blundered into the heart of Wheeler's camp and was nearly surrounded by 5,000 Confederates. Smith and his command retreated, pursued closely by the enemy for five miles. He came out of that engagement with only 18 of his men. Nevertheless, he had accomplished his reconnoitering mission and soon after was promoted to lieutenant-colonel.

In November, 1864, Smith found himself in another precarious position. While leading a night raid of 400 men with an artillery piece on a railroad flat car near Morristown, Tennessee, he encountering a superior rebel force. When Smith opened fire, the engineer panicked and steamed off, leaving Smith and his command unmounted, 40 miles from Union lines and facing 3,500 of Gen. John Breckenridge's Confederate cavalrymen. Smith's men held their position for several volleys, then managed to escape into the woods and after an 18-hour forced march reached Union lines unscathed.

Two weeks before Lee's surrender at Appomattox, the 10th Michigan Cavalry participated in Maj. Gen. George Stoneman's raid into North Carolina and Virginia. Near Salisbury, North Carolina, Smith led 20 men on a daring foray that resulted in the capture of an enemy battery and 1,100 prisoners. For "gallant and meritorious service during the war" Smith was breveted a brigadier general on March 13, 1865.

Not mustered out until November 1865, Smith returned to Grand Rapids to manage the National Hotel. He married two years later and moved to Kansas City where he operated another hotel for three years. Then came five years of adventuring as a miner and cattle rancher in Colorado and New Mexico. He returned to Grand Rapids in 1875 and reorganized the fire department, served as police and fire commissioner and in 1889 as brigadier general of the state militia. Tragically, the heroic soldier who had narrowly escaped death so many times during the Civil War was killed by the accidental discharge of his gun while hunting near Reeds Lake in 1899.

Civil engineer William Power Innes organized the 1st Michigan Engineers.

While Smith and the 3rd Michigan Infantry earned martial glory for Grand Rapids, another unit contributed to the Northern war effort in the less glamorous task of building bridges. William Power Innes, a 27-year-old civil engineer, had moved to Grand Rapids from New York in 1853 to work for the Detroit and Milwaukee Railroad. On September 10, 1861, a group of Grand Rapids men, including civil engineer Wright L. Coffinberry, merchant James L. Sligh, architect and contractor Barker Borden and bridge builder Perrin V. Fox, met with Innes to discuss the formation of a Michigan regiment of engineers. Innes telegraphed Secretary of War Simon Cameron and received prompt approval. Michigan Governor Austin Blair also backed the venture and designated the unit as the 1st Michigan Engineers and Mechanics. Ten companies comprising 1,032 men were rapidly recruited and the regiment was mustered on October 29, 1861.

Innes served as its colonel and Coffinbury, Sligh, Borden, Fox and another Grand Rapidian, Herman Palmerlee, each commanded a company. The first Michigan Engineers proceeded to Kentucky in December and began rebuilding railroad bridges destroyed by the Confederates. In June 1862 alone, the regiment constructed 3,000 feet of bridges as well as miles of corduroy roads through swamps.

On December 31, 1862, at the start of the bloody Battle of Stone River near Murfreesboro, Tennessee, Innes received orders from Gen. William Rosecrans to take position to the rear of the main army at Lavergne, on the road between Nashville and Murfreesboro, to protect supply trains. With only 391 men and expecting an attack at any minute, early on New Year's morning Innes circled his wagons. The engineers quickly fashioned breastworks of logs, brush and construction materials and the men huddled inside their primitive fort. Soon 3,000-4,000 Confederate cavalrymen and several batteries of light artillery under command of Gen. Wheeler galloped up. Wheeler sent in a flag of truce demanding the surrender of the little force. Innes replied, "We don't surrender much."

From 400 yards the Confederate artillery opened fire and continued to blast away for more than an hour, slamming shells into wagons and blowing skyward scores of mules and horses. Then Wheeler's cavalrymen attacked on three sides at once. The Michigan men met their charge with volley after volley of musket fire. The cavalrymen made it to the brush piles before being forced back. Seven times the Confederates attacked until darkness fell and they retreated, leaving the ground strewn with more than 100 dead or wounded. The Michigan engineers lost only one dead and six wounded. When the Confederates retreated, Sgt. Charles T. Woody from Grand Rapids and a crowd of engineers carried Innes on their shoulders around their makeshift fort shouting over and over, "We don't surrender much!"

The Michigan engineers earned more accolades on October 26, 1863, when they constructed a 900-foot pontoon bridge across the Tennessee River at Brown's Ferry while under intense sniper and artillery fire. For three hours the engineers sweated and strained to complete the bridge as artillery shells struck all around, throwing

Grand Rapids soldiers built this 460-foot-long bridge over the Elk River, Tennessee, in eight days.

clouds of sprays over them. One shell drilled a hole through one of the boats used as pontoons and a torrent of water gushed in. Pvt. Adrian Musty of Grand Rapids quickly stuffed his hat and coat into the hole and the boat made it to shore for repairs. The bridge opened up the "cracker line" that supplied the besieged Union forces at Chattanooga.

When their three years' enlistment expired on October 31, 1864, many of the unit's officers, including Innes, returned to civilian life. Others from Grand Rapids and elsewhere took their places and the regiment remained on active duty throughout the war.

The 4,214 men from Kent County who served in the war fought with many other famous units, including the 1st, 5th, 8th, 13th, 14th, 21st, 25th and 26th Michigan Infantry regiments. Grand Rapids also served as a northern training center, particularly for cavalry units. While training and awaiting the arrival of enough recruits to fill the rosters, the regiments garrisoned in rough wooden structures at Camps Lee and Kellogg located on the hill near the current site of Grand Rapids Community College. There, the 2nd, 3rd, 6th, 7th and 10th Michigan Cavalry units practiced horsemanship, sabre charges, marksmanship and the other martial skills that would earn Michigan's cavalry volunteers the reputation as some of the Union's finest. The 6th and 7th Michigan Cavalry won particular fame as part of Gen. George Armstrong Custer's Michigan Cavalry Brigade, which repeatedly distinguished itself in combat.

Another contingent of Grand Rapids men served with honor in the 1st Michigan Colored Infantry, mustered into service February 17, 1864, ironically and belatedly to allow the state's black citizens a chance to participate in the war being waged to end slavery. Some two dozen Grand Rapids area men enlisted, including William H. Ash, Isaac Bailey, Charles Chinn, Amos Cisco, Aaron Davis, Benjamin F. Guy, Leonard Harrod, David Ingham, George W. Jefferson, Charles Jones, Henry Letts, John Manning, Foster Morley, William Overton, Alvin Reed, Elijah Reed, Jeremiah Reed, Thomas Spriggins, Amos Swanagan, Jesse Taylor, Shadrick Valentine, James Walton and Andrew Washington. Brothers Elijah and Jeremiah Reed died of disease within weeks of each other in South Carolina. Shadrick Valentine took his final resting place in Arlington Cemetery in 1864.

Some other Grand Rapids citizens who won fame in the Civil War include Col. George Lee who served as Gen. Philip Sheridan's adjutant and Adm. John L. Worden who commanded the *Monitor* during its dramatic battle with the *Merrimac*. And one woman with a Grand Rapids connection became with Belle Boyd the only Civil War-era spies to be enshrined in the *Dictionary of American Biography*. She was born Harriet Woods or Du Bois (the record is conflicting) in New Orleans in 1835. Soon after, her father moved his large family to Grand Rapids where he worked as an Indian trader. Harriet grew into a beautiful Kent County teenager described by contemporary biographer Ferdinand Sarmiento as "lavishly endowed with the wealth of nature, her form so perfect that the sculptor's imagination would fail to add a single point, or banish a single blemish... The outlines of her face are of exceeding beauty, and the perfect features are set off to the best possible advantage by a pair of large, flashing black eyes."

Unfortunately for local admirers of such pulchritude, the teenager fled the Valley City for the allure of New York City sometime prior to the Civil War. She changed her name to Pauline Cushman and launched a stage career. March of 1863 found her playing at a theatre in Louisville, Kentucky, and that was the beginning of her great adventure. A pair of paroled Confederate troublemakers offered Cushman $300 to deliver a pro-Southern toast during a performance. When she dutifully reported this to the local provost marshall, he suggested she take the opportunity to serve as a Union spy.

Cushman toasted Jeff Davis that night, promptly got fired from the cast and thereby gained a reputation as a southern sympathizer. Then she was commissioned as a secret agent with orders to penetrate as far south as possible, collecting all available military information but not to write anything down. However, at Shelbyville and Tullahoma, Tennessee, the temptation became too great and she made detailed drawings of rebel emplacements and hid them in her shoe soles. Having that incriminating evidence made her nervous, so nervous that when routinely questioned she panicked and ran. Quickly captured, she was searched and the papers discovered.

Her captors led her to Gen. John Hunt Morgan, who though reputedly enamored by her beauty, passed her on

As illustrated in her 1865 biography, Union spy Pauline Cushman experienced many thrilling Civil War adventures such as this "fearful midnight flight."

to Gen. Nathan Bedford Forrest. He confronted her with her probable guilt and sent her to Gen. Braxton Bragg who told her brusquely, "You'll be hanged — that's all."

During her court martial she sickened and when the court found her guilty and sentenced her to be hanged as a spy, she collapsed. Before hanging her, the Confederates, always gallant, nursed her back to health — but before the sentence could be carried out Bragg suddenly evacuated Shelbyville before Rosecrans' advancing army and the spy was left behind. She related her intelligence report to the first Union officers who found her and that information proved of value to the Army of the Cumberland as it moved through Tennessee.

Cushman returned north, to be lionized as a symbol of patriotism, "the lady spy of the Cumberland." Lincoln commended her, she was formally proclaimed a major of cavalry and permitted to wear the symbols of her rank. She returned to the stage wearing an officer's uniform and toured the states lecturing on her deeds. But this acme of her life proved brief — inevitably audiences wearied of the lady spy. After the war she headed west, still lecturing in uniform and embellishing her exploits with every telling.

Her life went rapidly downhill. She married a succession of Californians, became a drug addict and died from an overdose of morphine in 1893. The San Francisco Grand Army of the Republic post escorted her flower-laden casket to the veteran's section of the city cemetery, a squad fired a volley over her grave and a bugler sounded taps for the most flamboyant of several Michigan Civil War heroines.

War-weary Grand Rapidians scanned the casualty lists for names of loved ones and read the *Enquirer* and *Herald* if they were Democrats or the *Daily Eagle* if Republican for latest news from the battlefields as Grant pounded away at the remnants of Lee's army in April 1865. On April 9 came the surrender at Appomattox Courthouse. Three days later the final major city of the Confederacy fell with the surrender of Mobile, Alabama. On April 14, exactly four years since the stars and stripes was lowered at Fort Sumpter, the American flag once again flapped in the breeze. But the joyful news was soon eclipsed by the assassination at Ford's Theatre later that evening of the man who had led the Union through its worst crisis.

Not unlike the assassination of another beloved president a century later, few Grand Rapidians ever forgot

Leonard Street Bridge, built in 1857 and rebuilt in 1879, was similar in construction to the Pearl Street Covered Bridge where the city staged a grand feast for Civil War veterans.

where they were or what they were doing when they first heard the terrible news. Angie Gilbert had been out trying to learn the details of the tragedy and was walking slowly and sadly back to her home on Lafayette Street while holding her little nephew by the hand when she encountered *Eagle* editor Aaron B. Turner. As they stood discussing the event at the little triangle that would become the Civil War Memorial Park, a farmer came running across Fulton Street crying out, "Oh! Mr. Turner, is the old ship drifting?" Turner's face went white as he replied, "I am afraid it is," and breaking into tears, "covered his face with his hands and sobbed aloud like a child," and the others too "joined in the chorus of tears."

On the Fourth of July, 1865, citizens determined to show their appreciation for what the returning boys in blue had done by hosting a grand banquet. The only site in the city large enough to accommodate the throng was the Pearl Street covered bridge. Belknap, who had enlisted in the 21st Michigan Infantry as an 18-year-old sergeant in 1862 and rose to the rank of captain, remembered the gala more than half a century later: "The cobwebs and dust of six years were swept into the river and two long rows of tables placed end to end of the driveway. They were loaded with all the good things the country and city afforded, roast pig, turkey, duck, chicken, cake, pie, jellies and preserves and would you believe it, beans, beans, beans, rations enough to feed an army corp."

One of Belknap's comrades from the 21st Michigan, Samuel Mapes of Salem Township, arrived at the festival with his wife and a brood of children in tow. The guards, however, would only allow the veteran to enter. But, as Belknap recalled, "he was equipped with canteen and haversack and being the champion forager of Company B, 21st Michigan, he fed up and came back with rations for five days — some bits of everything on the table except beans, including a roast pig that had not been carved and a hat full of cookies." After the feast, the tables were cleared and a dance held on the bridge.

On August 30, 1865, Philip Mason, an Indiana physician intent on a genealogical tour of southern Michigan, arrived at the Detroit and Milwaukee Railroad Depot on Leonard Street near the Plainfield Avenue intersection, having taken the steamer across from Milwaukee to Grand Haven. At the depot he boarded the horse-drawn streetcar that had been placed in operation a few months before and rode to the National House hotel at the corner of Monroe and Ionia, then the office for the stagecoach that left each morning for Kalamazoo. Mason left a detailed description of how the city of 1865 appeared to a stranger: "On arriving at the depot at the city I expected to find a broken, uneven country, and falls tumbling along a considerable descent, with sawmills, lumber yards and a few cheap buildings, such as would accommodate a population of lumber men, etc.; but instead of that, we saw a street a mile long within but a few rods of the river, with fine buildings from one story up to five, a fine woolen factory, gristmills, planing machines and all the modern improvements and fixtures in the shape of machinery for doing most of the work in the finishing of a fine house."

Although the thermometer read 88 degrees in the shade that afternoon, Mason decided to take a stroll: "In our walk we reached the bridge, that spanned the river nearly midway of the rapids, and crossed over to the opposite side. Here is a small town, and the land runs back from the river in a fine plain, while on the opposite it commences rising within a few rods of the river, and continues until it attains a considerable elevation. For some distance down the rapids from the depot there is only a single street (Monroe). This is the one on which the street railroad was built. A fine church had been commenced on the west side of the river a few squares above the bridge and there had been another large one begun some few years before, but one end had nearly tumbled out. It had been put up with brick with a veneering of slabs sawed from variegated plaster of Paris, a material which is found in great abundance two miles below, but on trial it seems that this veneering when first finished looks beautiful, but age turns it a dingy color. On the west side, not far from the end of the bridge, there was a large boarding house in a rather dilapidated condition. We recrossed the river and turned our course back to the hotel. The road soon made a turn up a gentle slope to where the street was well built up on each side and now and then a cross street coming in, which sometimes crossed the main street. This street seems to be the center of business, and had the best buildings on it. After we had ascended the first slight hill from the river there was a considerable plain, with a fine street as well as a cross street."

Early the next morning Mason climbed aboard a stage and set out for the bone-jarring 48-mile trip to Kalamazoo. Mason noted that the plank road was "considerably worn." Ten years of traffic and minimal maintenance had taken their toll on the once elegant plank highway. A few years later during a lecture tour to Grand Rapids Mark Twain rode on the same road. When someone asked how he liked the ride, the humorist replied, "It would have been good if some unconscionable scoundrel had not now and then dropped a plank across the road."

The need to "brave the peril, dare the danger of a journey on the Plank," as Asa Stoddard, the farmer poet of Kalamazoo County's Cooper Township, termed it, diminished on March 1, 1869, with the arrival of the first Kalamazoo, Allegan and Grand Rapids Railroad locomotive. Over a thousand cheering citizens greeted the puffing engine that offered the first rail connection to the south. The following September that line became part of the Lake Shore and Michigan Southern Railroad. The year 1870 brought two more southern routes. The Grand River Valley Railroad, later a branch of the Michigan Central, linked the city with Jackson in January 1870. The Grand Rapids and Indiana Railroad, which had begun service between the west side of the city and Cedar Springs in December 1867, began running the first through trains to Fort Wayne, Indiana, on October 10, 1870. Twelve years later the G.R. & I. finally reached Mackinaw City and began promoting itself to sportsmen as "The Fishing Line."

In 1891 the Grand Rapids and Indiana Railroad train sheds stood at the corner of Ionia and Oakes.

This woodcut of Monroe Street appeared in John Barber and Henry Howe's 1867 travel guide to the western states.

5 SWEET SINGERS & SCARLET LADIES

The federal census taker strolled the city's wooden sidewalks and dusty streets in 1870 and "enumerated" 16,507 Grand Rapids citizens, nearly double the 1860 population. In his *Directory of Kent County* editor Dillenback counted the city's commercial establishments: "15 hotels, 20 dry goods stores, upwards of 50 groceries, eight hardware stores, nine drug stores, 12 clothing stores, 16 boot and shoe stores, six photograph galleries, seven watchmaker and jewelers' establishments, seven printing offices, three book-binderies, upwards of 50 lawyers, upwards of 40 physicians, 14 dentists, six banking houses, eight machine shops, five flouring mills, four breweries, six furniture manufacturers, three large brick manufactories, one fanning mill manufactory,

A Chicago firm of lithographers executed this bird's-eye view of the city as seen from the west side in 1874.

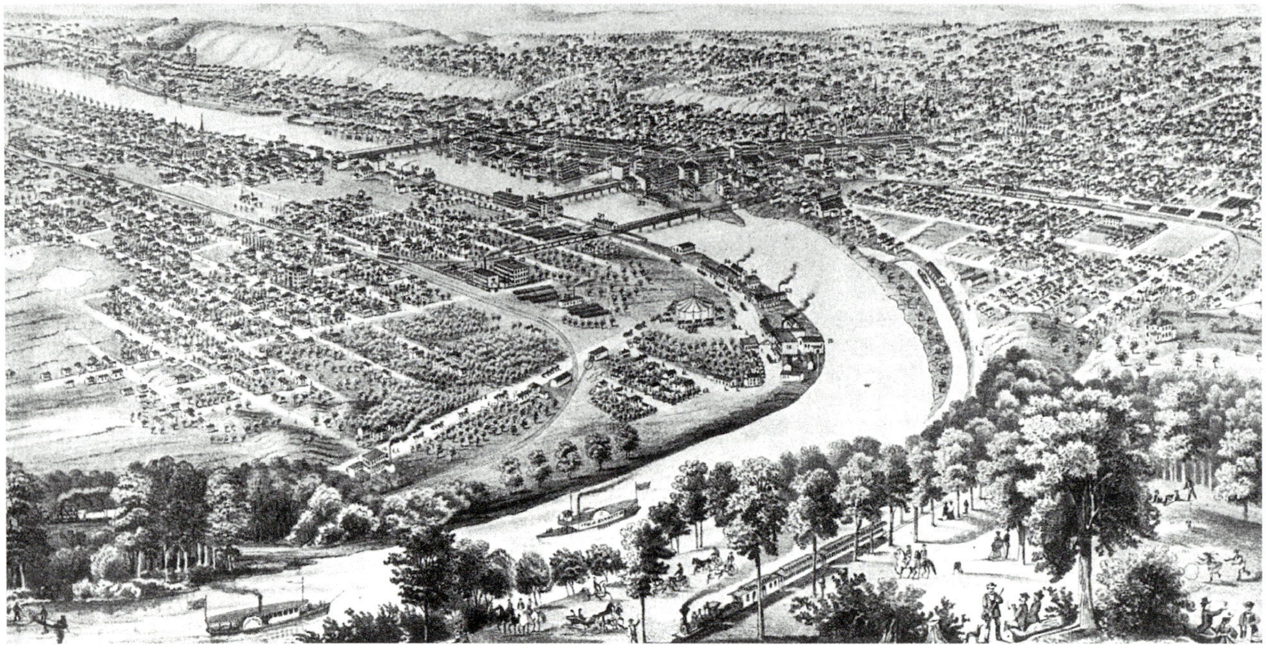

(Far right) "Grab Corners" looked like this in 1873, just before the jog was straightened to create Campau Square.

Stewart Edward White's 1908 lumbering novel featured illustrations by N.C. Wyeth.

one file manufactory, one mammoth box factory, one axe factory, two hub factories, two marble cutting establishments, one wagon factory, two woolen mills, seven planing mills, eight saw mills, one immense factory for the manufacture of Water's patent barrels, 14 wagon and carriage manufactories, etc., etc."

Among the etceteras that Dillenback thought not appropriate to mention were the more than 25 saloons that lined downtown streets. Four years later, Arthur S. White, then beginning his long journalistic career, felt no similar compunction to slight the city's burgeoning barrooms when he wrote the promotional pamphlet *Grand Rapids, A.D. 1873*. White cited the presence of no less than 70 saloons, five wholesale liquor stores and 20 billiard halls, which in those days usually dispensed alcoholic drinks as well. Three years later the number of saloons, taverns,

bars and gin mills within the city limits had mushroomed to an incredible 185. With a population pushing 25,000 then, Grand Rapids supported a whale of a lot of places to wet a dry throat. And perhaps not coincidentally, the city's industrial roster included six coffin manufacturers.

Many of those taverns owed their survival to the hordes of thirsty lumberjacks who descended on the Valley City during slack times or at the end of river drives. Stewart Edward White in *The Riverman* (1908), arguably the best novel written about Michigan lumbering, described a typical bar in 1872 Redding's (Grand Rapids) notorious "Hell's Half-Mile" tavern district. The novel's hero, Johnny Orde, leads a gang of "river hogs" into town

Rindge, Kalmbach and Co., whose officers included William Logie, an ancestor of Grand Rapids' popular mayor John Logie, made a specialty of the calked boots favored by "river hogs."

to settle a score with a saloon proprietor whose crooked three-card monte operation had fleeced the camp cook the night before:

"Facing the street stood a three-story wooden structure into which led a high arched entrance up a broad half-flight of wooden steps. This was McNeill's... McNeill's lower story was given over entirely to drinking. A bar ran down all one side of the room. Dozens of little tables occupied the floor. 'Pretty waiter-girls' were prepared to serve drinks at these latter — and to share in them, at a commission. The second floor was a theatre, and the third a dance hall. Beneath the building were still viler depths. From this basement the riverman and the shanty boy generally graduated penniless, and perhaps unconscious, to the street. Now, your lumber-jack did not customarily arrive at this stage without more or less lively doings en route; therefore McNeill's maintained a force of fighters. They were burley, sodden men, in striking contrast to the clean-cut, clear-eyed rivermen, but strong in their experience and their discipline. To be sure they might not last quite as long as their antagonists could — a whiskey training is not conducive to long wind — but they always lasted plenty long enough. Sand bags and brass knuckles helped some, ruthless singleness of purpose counted, and team work finished the job."

White knew the life of the shanty boy well. One of five sons born to Mary and T. Stewart White, young White grew up with the cry of "timber!" and the smell of newly cut pine a part of his everyday life. His father, a second-generation Grand River Valley lumberman, operated a log booming company that over a 20-year period supplied nearly three billion board feet of timber to the hungry mills at Grand Rapids and Grand Haven. Born in Grand Rapids in 1873, young White grew up in a northern Michigan sawmill town and accompanied his father to lumber camps and among his rivermen employees. His formal education began at Grand Rapids High School when he was 16. Two years later he graduated as class president and subsequently earned a bachelor's and a master's degree at the University of Michigan.

White wrote his first novel about Michigan lumbering, *The Blazed Trail* (1902), in the depth of winter while working in a northern lumber camp. He scrawled away for four hours early each morning before heading out to the woods to fell trees. The volume established his literary career. His other books containing Michigan lumbering episodes include a collection of short stories originally appearing in magazines, *Blazed Trail Stories* (1904), a juvenile novel, *The Adventure of Bobby Orde* (1908), and its sequel *The Rules of the Game* (1909). Among the most successful of the "red blood" school of fiction which glorified the heroic qualities of laboring men, White produced nearly 50 volumes of fiction, travel, biography and spiritualism prior to his death in 1946.

George Edward Lewis wrote his 1916 novel about Michigan lumbering under the pseudonym Alaska Blacklock.

Shanty boys worked from dawn to dusk "making light in the swamp."

Other Grand Rapids writers also chose as a theme the colorful life of the lumberjack. George Edward Lewis, a grandson of artist James Otto Lewis who painted portraits of Indian chiefs while a member of the 1826 Lewis Cass and Thomas McKenny expedition along the south shore of Lake Superior, was born in the Fife Lake vicinity in 1870. As a teenager he labored in northern Michigan lumber camps prior to moving to Grand Rapids. Sometime after 1910 he migrated to Alaska and later Portland, Oregon, where he published his novel about Michigan lumbering, *Nick of the Woods,* (1916) under the pseudonym Alaska Blacklock. The book offers apt descriptions of camp life, river drives and the felling of the pine:

"The most interesting and entertaining part of the loggers' life was seen amid the tall and waving pine where they were the masters. Sawing, chopping, skidding, loading and swamping was their delight. Each was proud of his dexterity, many a feat of skill and strength was exhibited. McQueen, with his timber cleaver weighing as it did two ounces over seven pounds, hung on a handle he had shaven from the trunk of a rock elm tree, would step up to a pine and darken the sun with chips, not an axe mark could be found on either stump or butt so accomplished was he in his craft. The ply of that mighty axe, the magic of the deepening notch, made one feel that the tree was but wax and the axe-man a giant from some other world. The champion gang with the cross-cut were equipped with a seven-foot Atkins saw, and on a wager for a new hat, pulled at the rapid rate of three strokes a second, and cut a thousand feet of logs in fifteen minutes."

Grand Rapids poet Francis Lacy penned a 200-page epic in 1881.

Before he moved from Grand Rapids, Lewis paid a poetic tribute to a lumberjack who had saved his life 27 years before while the two were cutting pine on the Manistee River. Published in Grand Rapids in 1909, the slim pamphlet *Jim* began:

"Bow-Legged Jim was a corker in camp.
He would drink like a fish and eat like a tramp.
He chewed tobacco, smoked Killikinich,
Played Seven-up and Sixty-six.
He could joke like Crockett, swear like Kidd
But he never would do what the rules forbid.
When the fellows quarreled, Jim would joke,
The argument passed like a whiff of smoke.
When the boss was angry, Jim kept mum,
He was a favorite lumberjack chum."

Lewis wrote four other volumes of poetry, including *Heart Echoes* and *The Poet's Idle Hour,* published in Grand Rapids during the 1890s. *Heart Echoes* contains a salute to "The City on the Grand:"

"We have temples of worship for prayer and for praise,
And schools where our children are taught modern ways;
We have a home for the orphan, the mangled and old,
No mortal may suffer with hunger and cold.
We have a grand home for old Masons to rest —
'Twas a love fraternal put the thought in their breast;
Our hall and our courthouse are built upon rocks,
We have long streets of asphalt and towering blocks."

If Lewis' verse seems less than Walt Whitmanesque, in all fairness he was merely following in the wake of a long tradition of terrible local poetry. Minerva Kutz of Bostwick Lake early contributed to the genre with her *Wab-Ah-See, Legend of the Sleeping Dew; and Other Poems,* privately published in Chicago in 1868. The lead poem, loosely based on a local half-breed Potawatomi chief named Wabasis who was murdered while returning from a green corn dance on the Grand River sometime in the 1860s, promoted the legend that the old chief had hidden a pot of gold, thereby inspiring generations of treasure hunters. Kutz also included in her volume numerous "poems for funeral occasions" which befit the Victorian passion for melodramatic death scenes. Many described in pathetic detail the demise of Kent County infants. Another titled, "Lay Me to Rest," she penned for the funeral of a lady burned to death:

"Lay my charred frame in the cold, cold ground,
And weep ye, but not in despair;
For sweetly it sleeps in this low swelling mound,
Unvexed by affliction or care."

In 1881 the Rev. David D. Peterson, pastor of the Scribner Avenue Messiah Temple of the Children of Zion, published in Grand Rapids his *Casket of Poetical Treasures,* aptly named because so many of the poems are funereal. Also in 1881, the same year that Rose Hartwick Thorpe, author of the popular ballad "Curfew Shall Not Ring Tonight," took up residence in Grand Rapids, Peterson's publisher, Welcome W. Hart, printed on his steam press another handsome volume. It was full-bearded rhymer Francis D. Lacy's *Star Lake Romance: A Modern Poem of Love and Rivalry,* a 200-page epic about the amatory adventures of the beautiful daughter of a wealthy Grand Rapidian. After narrowly escaping drowning in Star Lake near Baldwin, the heroine returned home to chortle:

"Sweet singer" Julia Moore's likeness appeared in her 1876 volume that brought mirth to generations.

"O, Valley City! noble, grand,
With records bold and true;
With men of enterprise and wealth,
We hail thy bluffs in view.
O, may you still in glory stand,
In beauty ever grow;
Till thy Grand River fountain dries,
And waters cease to flow."

Another volume of local interest, Alta Isadore Gould's *The Veteran's Bride,* was published by the Grand Rapids firm of P.D. Farrell and Company in 1894. The tear-jerker relates in 300 pages of fractured verse the story of a Civil War soldier's return to his remarried wife 18 years after he was reported killed in battle

But the achievements of all other local poetasters pale in comparison to the life work of the area's most illustrious bad poet, Julia Moore. Born December 1, 1847, in a log cabin in Plainfield Township, Julia A. Davis received but little formal education. Nevertheless, as a teenager she began to compose verse about everyday occurrences. As she explained in an autobiographical poem:

"It was my heart's delight,
To compose on a sentimental subject
If it came in mind just right."

She married Fred Moore at the age of 18. The couple lived on a farm near her family home for a while and then moved to the Algoma Township hamlet of Edgerton where they operated a general store. The hubbub over the centennial celebration of 1876 inspired Julia to assemble her favorite pieces for publication by Grand Rapids job printer Cassius M. Loomis. The book sold well, running through six editions in two years. Moore, soon sarcastically dubbed "the sweet singer of Michigan," garnered national publicity after her publisher sent review copies to various newspaper editors.

Humorists across the country lampooned her work. Bill Nye included a chapter on her verse in his popular volume *Bill Nye and Boomerang.* He suggested her poetic license be revoked. Mark Twain parodied her verse and wrote in 1897 that she had given him joy for 20 years. Hoosier poet Eugene Field thought her book so entertaining that he had printed a facsimile of the first edition for his friends. Other members of the literati found the sweet singer's technique so woeful, her subjects so morbid and her naivete so disarming that they lauded her poems as gems of American humor.

Except for occasional odes in honor of the Grand Rapids Cricket Club, local politicians and temperance, the majority of Moore's output dealt with death, that of children in particular. Nye counted 21 killed and nine wounded in her slim volume. "Julia is worse than a Gatling gun," he concluded.

No less than three separate pieces, for example, chronicle the tragic fate of Kent County's William House family. The unfortunate six-year-old Hattie House, who dropped dead amid her playmates, was the first to go:

"Those little girls will not forget
The day little Hattie died,
For she was with them when she fell in a fit
While playing by their side."

Hattie's teenage sister, Lois, caught some dread disease and expired following a quick kiss from her boyfriend:

"She gasped for her breath once or twice more, When lo! her spirit left her, and Lois is no more."

The remnants of the once numerous House family moved from Kent County to seek a healthier environment, but to no avail:

"They once did live in Edgerton,
They once did live at Muskegon,
From which they went to Chicago,
Which proved their fatal overthrow."

On May 1, 1877, a group of Grand Rapids pranksters convinced Moore to conduct a recitation of her poetry to a packed crowd at Powers' Opera House. Each time she

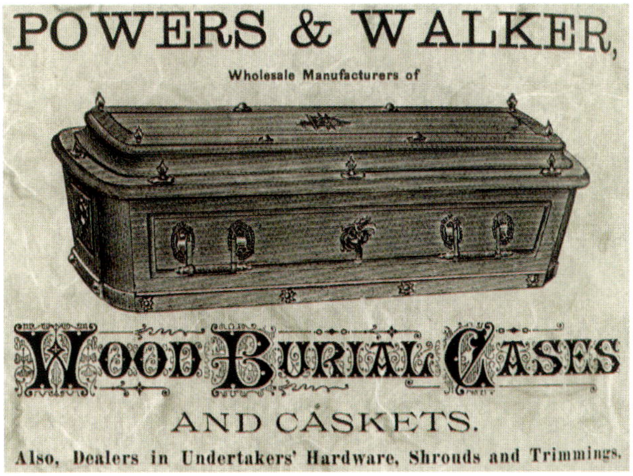

A fitting complement to Moore's murderous poetry, this product was advertised in 1883.

finished a stanza such as her tragic ballad of "Little Libbie" who choked to death on a piece of beef, pandemonium broke loose in the galleries as the crowd shouted and stamped its feet. Interpreting the interruptions as compliments, she continued her repertoire of deathly lyrics.

Moore apparently was the only one there who failed to catch the joke. The whole performance, including much advance publicity, was a burlesque, and she was the butt of the humor. Accompanied by a three-piece band that played off-key and in discord, Moore closed the recital by singing a tribute to Washington's birthday. At its conclusion, a group of young men presented her with a fragrant bouquet of cabbage blossoms.

During a return engagement on December 23, 1878, Moore got the last laugh. At the close of the reading she faced her hecklers and announced, "You people paid 50 cents each to see a fool, but I got $50 to look at a house full of fools."

Foolery aside, Grand Rapidians of the 1870s had plenty of other diversions to spice their workaday lives. Those, for example, who thrilled to the clang and clatter of horse-drawn fire engines racing to the scene got more than they bargained for. On April 11, 1871, five months before fire would claim much of Chicago, Holland and Manistee as well as millions of acres of Michigan forests, a conflagration destroyed all the mills, shops, factories and stores between the river and Canal Street (Monroe) for some distance above and below Erie Street. On May 8, 1872, the huge Squier's Opera House on Canal Street burned to the ground and the following October 30 fire raced through stores on Pearl and Canal streets with a loss

(Far right)
The big fire of July 13, 1873, left 130 families homeless.

The firemen of Engine House No. 4 at Crescent and Bond posed with their horse-drawn equipment in 1899.

of $200,000. New Year's Day 1873 brought the fiery destruction of the recently constructed Kent Woolen Mills.

These fires were but a prelude to the devastating inferno of July 13, 1873. A particularly hot summer had rendered the city with its numerous wooden structures and boardwalks tinder dry. About 4 p.m. fire started in the stable of the Bridge Street House at the corner of Canal and E. Bridge streets. Fanned by high winds, flames quickly leaped into the adjacent poor immigrant housing district. The city's three steam fire engines and a 200-man bucket brigade fought the blaze to little avail. It burned its way to the foot of Lookout Hill when the wind shifted to the east. Later that night heavy rains finally extinguished the fire. A 15-acre tract bounded by Michigan, Ionia, Trowbridge and Monroe lay in blackened ruins. Nearly 100 buildings, hotels, stables, factories, a massive brewery and the homes of 130 immigrant Dutch and German families had gone up in smoke. Miraculously, the six-and-one-half-hour-long inferno claimed no lives. Two years later another huge fire on the west side destroyed 62 structures from the Bridge Street Bridge west to Turner Street.

Tragic as those repeated conflagrations were they did little to stem the growth of the vigorous city. For every building destroyed by fire, 10 took its place. In the first nine months of 1874 alone, 624 new business blocks, schools, churches, factories, stores, depots and dwellings graced city streets. Another major event of 1874 came in June with the seemingly incredible engineering feat of raising all the brick buildings on Canal Street, from Pearl to Lyon, four feet higher. The need to do so arose from the city's acquisition and razing of downtown buildings during the previous four years to partially realign the labyrinth caused by Campau's and Lyon's platting feud. Another stage of the project involved the laborious mining of fill from Prospect Hill (which ultimately disappeared) and transporting it to raise the level of Canal Street even with Monroe, an improvement which left the existing structures four feet below street level.

The city hired the veteran Chicago house-moving firm of Hollingsworth & Coughlan to accomplish the task. James Hollingsworth arrived with box cars of equipment including 1,800 screw jacks and proceeded to lift the structures one by one. The massive five-story Sweet's

The massive five-story Sweet's Hotel was raised four feet in 1874.

Hotel, covering a half acre at the northwest corner of Canal and Pearl streets, offered the greatest challenge. Using all 1,800 jacks and 217 workmen who scurried to turn each jack exactly one-quarter revolution every time a steam whistle sounded, in four days' time the hotel stood four feet higher. Most of the numerous guests had not even been aware of the process.

No challenge seemed too great for Grand Rapids of the 1870s. One that tested the city's will to succeed, however, came in 1873 with a spirited contest to become the site for the state fair, which at that time annually rotated to various cities. The weeklong event drawing thousands of visitors from across the state would naturally prove a boom to the local economy. By February, 1873, the State Agricultural Society committee charged with deciding the location of the fair had narrowed it down to two contestants — Grand Rapids and East Saginaw (not until 1889 would the two Saginaws merge into one city).

Henry Fralick, a Grand Rapids realtor and insurance agent, headed up a Citizen's Committee organized to secure the plum. Fralick touted the city's advantages including the 70-acre fairgrounds located just south of the municipality in Paris Township. The site boasted numerous exhibition halls and barns, 30 refreshment booths, 10 wells of pure water and a half-mile race track with grandstand. Furthermore, citizens had pledged $1,500 worth of improvements to the grandstand, halls, and track and use of the facility would be absolutely free. But the committee voted in favor of East Saginaw's smaller fairgrounds because a large fair had never been held there.

Grand Rapids booster Henry Fralick won the site of the state fair for the city in 1873.

Fralick refused to give up without a fight. At the next meeting of the state committee in Eaton Rapids, he upped Grand Rapids' ante. The city would pay for a switch and siding of the Grand River Valley Railroad to the fairgrounds, provide all the hay, straw and ice used on the grounds for free as well as pay $1,500 in cash. East Saginaw countered that proposal with additional allurements. Whereupon Fralick tossed in another $800 and the game was over. The committee voted 18 to 2 for the Valley City.

That September tens of thousands of fairgoers stepped gingerly through the horse, hog, cattle and sheep barns, past the 128 coops of chickens and along the glittering displays of needle, wax and shell work. They viewed the untutored paintings and the best furniture entries, including local undertaker Allen Durfee's award-winning caskets. They packed the grandstands to cheer on the local favorite winner of the one-mile horse race, "Dick Lewis." They strolled among the numerous games of chance, food booths and amusement rides. They ogled the bearded lady, the strong man, the giant and the midget and they left many a nickel, dime and quarter in the hands of the itinerant "carnies" who flooded the fair.

Not all innocent rural youths who attended the state fair emerged unscathed. Take the case of Georgie Young, for example. Born in South Creek, Pennsylvania, in 1858, Georgie and her five siblings suffered a harsh childhood owing to the death of their father. In 1872 the family found itself eking out an existence in Sand Lake. Entranced by the publicity over the gala state fair, an older brother squirreled away every penny he could earn the following year and managed to save enough to take his sister with him. Arriving in Grand Rapids, the wide-eyed girl experienced her first ride on a streetcar. When they reached the fairgrounds, her brother told her to wait on a bench for him and went exploring. Attracted by a carousel, she left her seat and got lost in the maze of strange faces. She was befriended by a seemingly kind woman who took her home. Unfortunately, she turned out to be a hard-hearted pandress who linked her up with a fellow "sharper" named Charlie Young. The street tough wooed the naive 15-year-old under false pretenses, convinced her to lie about her age and married her before a justice of the peace. Charlie and his mean-spirited mother starved and abused Georgie, and her attempts to escape and find work only landed her in the Grand Rapids lock-up. Weakened from her ordeal she took sick and wound up in the only available facility — The Kent County Poor House.

Ultimately she fled on a train to Jackson and then Kalamazoo where she walked the final mile on her road to ruin. In company with a streetwise painted lady she caught a hack to a run-down section of town where they got lodging at what Georgie thought a boarding house. But she wondered when the proprietor, Miss Alice, greeted them in "a long white wrapper and no sleeves." Her suspicions were confirmed later that night when Miss Alice called: "Come girls; gentlemen are in the parlor!" Georgie met the rest of the staff after breakfast the next day as the ladies of the evening cut cards to see who would buy their morning cigars.

Fairgoers inspect a pomological display at the Kent County Agricultural Society grounds where the Michigan State Fair was held in 1873.

Georgie tried futilely to escape the red-light routine and after a series of misadventures with Irish Annie, Old Mother Thompson, a certain traveling man from Toledo and a stint in the Detroit House of Corrections she returned to Grand Rapids. She found employment at "Mate Elliott's," the best house of its kind in the city where the girls "did not drink nor swear and nothing but champagne was sold." Georgie spent 10 years at that "first class house" until she eventually worked her way up to become madame of her own operation on Almy Street, on the other side of the tracks south of Fulton. According to the autobiography Georgie published

Ladies of the night enjoyed their morning stogies.

in 1889, *A Magdalen's Life,* she ultimately renounced her career as a "hooker," but contemporary newspaper evidence suggests her redemption was not permanent.

The Grand Rapids *Evening Leader* gave a favorable review of the book. The reviewer, it seems, had known her quite well for 10 years, in his capacity as a reporter, that is. He wrote: " Georgie Young is one of the best known young women of Grand Rapids. For many years she was one of the most dashing and one of the most wicked of the members of the scarlet sisterhood. She was one of the queens among the cyprians who flaunted their shame in the face of the public and allured men to her gilded place for debauchery and bacchanalian revelry. Miss Young has not a handsome face, though she has always been an attractive woman because of her dash and spirit and bright and intelligent manners. She has been a favorite among men and carries in her mind secrets that would cloud more than one home if they were made public."

A few days later, the Rev. Peter Moerdyk, pastor of the First Reformed Church, offered a less glowing critique. He thought the volume would "excite a widespread curiosity that, alas, in many cases will be prurient." Furthermore, he was disappointed in Georgie's failure to narrate how "the divine help of a Saviour" had caused her to "arise out of the depths."

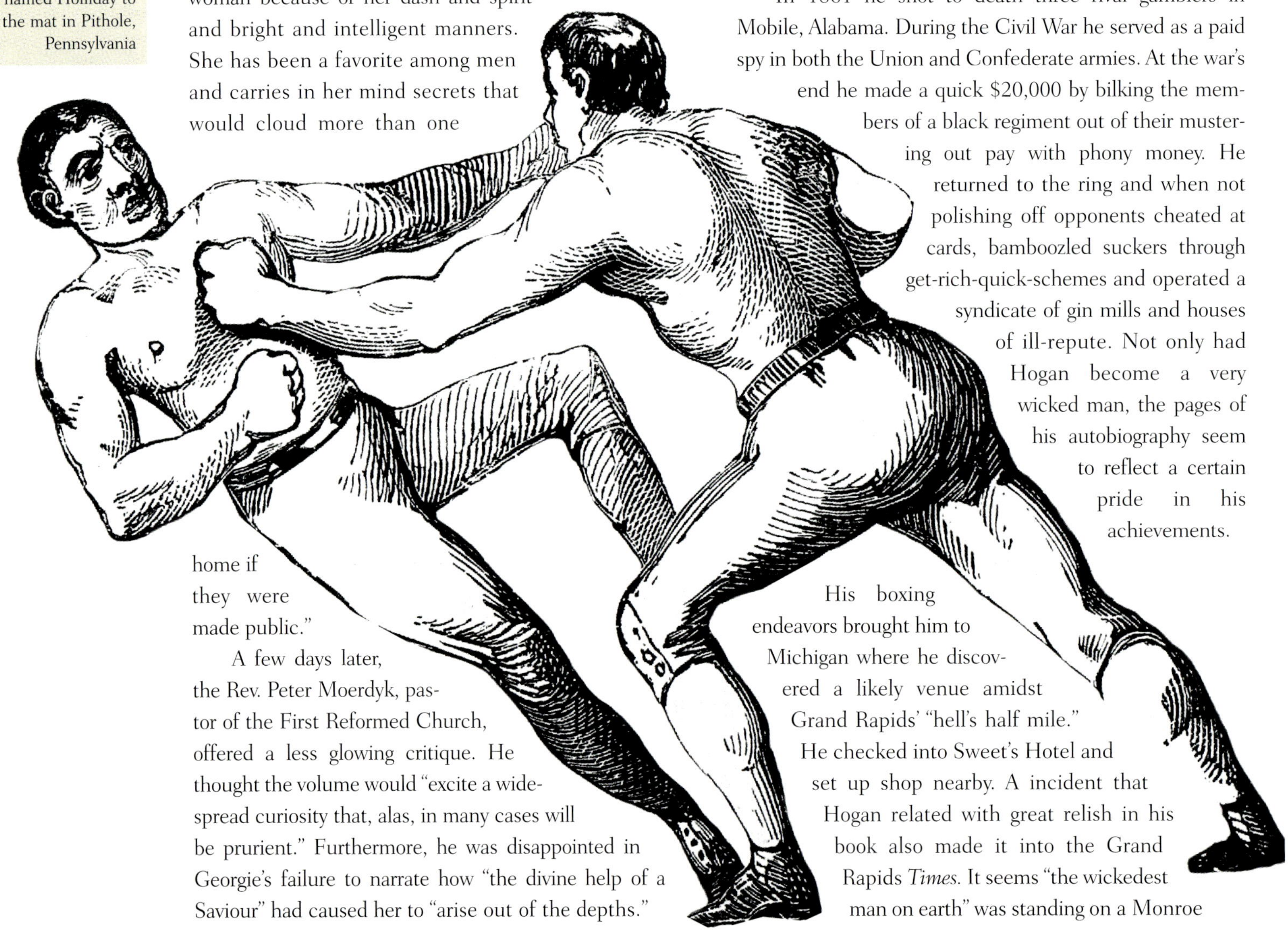

Ben Hogan battered a pug named Holliday to the mat in Pithole, Pennsylvania

Young's literary apologia vies in interest with volumes written and hawked by several other reformed scoundrels. Ben Hogan, "the wickedest man in the world," opened a gymnasium in the city in 1875 and delivered lectures on physical culture. As described in an autobiography he published three years later, he had launched his wicked career shortly after emigrating as a youth from Germany to New York City when he burgled a minister's home. A series of similar offenses landed the young hooligan in prison where, out of necessity, he learned to use his dukes rather well. When released, Hogan took the ring name "The Sailor Boy" and toured the country, earning his livelihood via his fists, gambling and assorted con-games.

In 1861 he shot to death three rival gamblers in Mobile, Alabama. During the Civil War he served as a paid spy in both the Union and Confederate armies. At the war's end he made a quick $20,000 by bilking the members of a black regiment out of their mustering out pay with phony money. He returned to the ring and when not polishing off opponents cheated at cards, bamboozled suckers through get-rich-quick-schemes and operated a syndicate of gin mills and houses of ill-repute. Not only had Hogan become a very wicked man, the pages of his autobiography seem to reflect a certain pride in his achievements.

His boxing endeavors brought him to Michigan where he discovered a likely venue amidst Grand Rapids' "hell's half mile." He checked into Sweet's Hotel and set up shop nearby. A incident that Hogan related with great relish in his book also made it into the Grand Rapids *Times*. It seems "the wickedest man on earth" was standing on a Monroe

Street corner one day dressed in his usual black suit and high collar with a textbook on gymnastics under his arm. Mistaking him for a fellow clergyman and his book for the Bible, a minister introduced himself to Hogan and asked whether the good reverend might entertain him, a hungry visitor to the metropolis, in his home. Hogan went along with the blunder as a practical joke and escorted the divine to his gymnasium where he proceeded to give an exhibition of weight lifting and boxing. The bewildered minister was only too happy to seek his free lunch elsewhere.

A genuine brother of the cloth, to Hogan, that is, Joseph F. Hess "the converted prize fighter and saloon keeper" arrived in Grand Rapids in 1882. As outlined in his 1890 publication, *Out of Darkness Into Light,* Hess had "got in with evil companions" as a 15-year-old, and soon became a drunk. He took time out from his debauchery to learn the "manly art" while working on a construction job in Toledo. Armed with his new skill, he wandered about the country for several years stopping whereever he could line up a prize fight. But as more and more of his opponents hit the canvas, Hess hit the bottle with his increasing frequency. At a standing-room-only match in Grand Rapids, he slugged Thomas Kanear to unconsciousness in four rounds. He continued trading punches for money and blowing every cent he made on wild sprees for three more years until a bout with delirium tremens inspired him to take a pledge. Whereupon he launched a new career as a pulpit reformer and book vendor.

Books by reformed drunks were a popular genre in the Victorian era and a surprising number of their authors visited Grand Rapids. Samuel W. Shockey, according to his 1892 treatise, *Twenty-five Years Fighting Fate,* had led a checkered career as a door-to-door bookseller, evangelist, school teacher, lumberman, phrenologist, palm reader and U.S. Cavalry deserter. All the while he guzzled increasing quantities. Inevitably there came the "jim-jams" and delirium tremens. In 1890 he got spiflicated in one of Grand Rapids' numerous saloons and created such a spectacle on the street that a crowd gathered to watch his antics. Whereupon a passing patrolman escorted him to the city lock-up to sleep off his jag. After 10 years as an alcoholic, Shockey found Jesus again, renounced his low-down ways and became a temperance crusader.

Alcoholic prizefighter Joseph Hess enjoyed spiffing up in a top hat.

None of the numerous tosspots who visited Grand rapids, apparently, realized that they could have found salvation from demon rum by simply walking upstairs to the Canal Street office of the good Dr. Clark Cummings. In his full-page advertisement in the 1867 *City Directory,* Cummings promised a "cure of which he has been wonderfully and particularly successful" for drunkenness. What is more, he could achieve this miracle "without the knowledge of the party." Of course Cummings' cure was not without its drawbacks. A standard procedure of the era was to dispense opiates to the patient's wife or other loved one who would surreptitiously add them to his morning coffee, thus ridding him of the taste for liquor by substituting a drug addiction.

Cummings, a walking panacea, also promised speedy cures for a wide variety of complaints including asthma, fits, cancer, kidney disease, ulcers, hysterics, all female complaints and "piles of long or short standing" as well as catarrh, salt rheum and scald head, which, whatever they were, sound bad.

6 PILL PUSHERS & CHAIR MAKERS — WHEEL RIDERS & ROUGH RIDERS

The final third of the 19th century proved a divisive era for the American medical profession and a confusing one for patients in Grand Rapids and elsewhere. In opposition to the so-called regular physicians whose primitive procedures often proved worse than the complaint, imaginative medics developed an array of exotic theories. Homeopathic practitioners prescribed drugs that produced on a healthy person effects similar to the patient's complaints. Allopaths dosed their victims with drugs that had the opposite effect. Eclectics let the patient, or next of kin, choose from either category. Thomsonians used only vegetable-based or "botanic" remedies in conjunction with vapor baths. Hydropaths relied solely on the beneficial effects of copious drafts of water

The south side of Monroe Street looked like this in 1858.

(Below, center) The city's first homeopathic physician, Dr. Alvah Botsford, arrived in 1850.

Typical of turn-of-the-century medical shenanigans was the panacea promoted by the Egyptian Manufacturing Co.

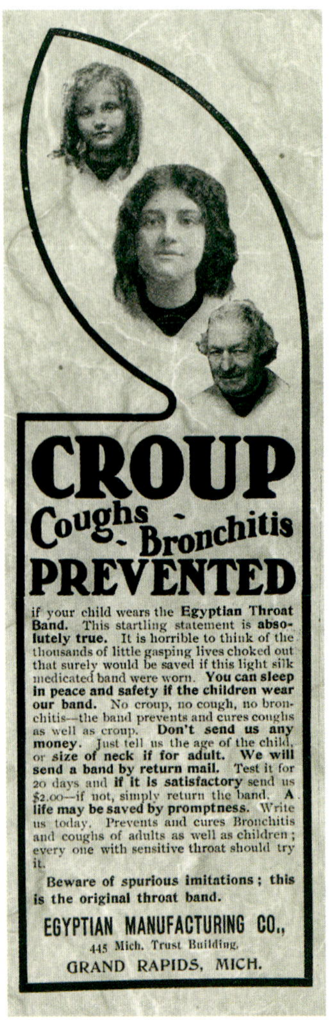

and various baths, showers, douches and enemas. Periodically other humbugs, usually itinerant, employed magnetism, electricity and clairvoyancy to dupe the ill.

The 1867 *Grand Rapids Directory* listed the city's 28 physicians by their respective disciplines. Most were "regulars" including dipsomania specialist Cummings and Dr. Frederick Christ, a Berlin-trained surgeon and accoucheur, as obstetricians were then called. But by 1890 more than 22 homeopathic physicians had practiced in Grand Rapids. The local dean of the profession, Dr. Alvah Botsford, had arrived in 1850 to begin dosing patients with the powders he ground in his pestle and mortar. The year before, Dr. H.R. Seeley had established a hydropathic hospital near the corner of Division and Fountain streets.

Hydropathy developed a new wrinkle in 1869 with the discovery that the water flowing from an artesian well in the little Gratiot County lumbertown of St. Louis seemed to possess magnetic qualities capable of healing everything from rheumatism to "softening of the brain." As St. Louis enjoyed a magnetic water boom, lo and behold if Richard Butterworth, who had earlier made a fortune in Grand Rapids gypsum, did not discover his own magnetic water supply. He put up a "plain but comfortable bath-house of 20 rooms" and soon scores of invalids, particularly those suffering from "torpid secretions of the liver" splashed in and imbibed the output of Butterworth's Magnetic Spring.

Unfortunately, the water proved "so highly charged with chemical properties" that it dissolved the iron piping of the well and, diluted with other waters, lost its marvelous powers. The spa closed within two years. But Butterworth's foray into the health care industry may well have motivated him to donate land and money in 1887 and 1888 that made possible a more legitimate institution — Butterworth Hospital.

Others, too, began analyzing their springs for medicinal qualities. By 1873 four Grand Rapids entrepreneurs bottled curative mineral waters. In nearby Cascade, proprietors discovered mineral springs reputedly capable of curing St. Vitus Dance. An elegant three-story hotel erected over the springs enjoyed a thriving business until the flow undermined its foundation and the structure came crashing down.

Dr. Bliss Sexton, the area's first Thomsonian practitioner, arrived in 1847 and later founded a little community near Sparta he dubbed Sextonville. Another botanic physician, Dr. Elmer Woodruff, hung out his shingle on Canal Street in 1861. Thirteen years later he claimed to have dosed over 18,000 patients with his selection of some 200 kinds of roots, barks and herbs "without losing one of them." He did not say, however, if he cured any of them. Periodically a clairvoyant healer set up shop in the city. Usually women, these mediums professed to diagnose and prescribe remedies via communication with the spirit world. Beginning in 1863 and until she joined that "invisible world" herself 20 years later, Mrs. Mary J. Squires offered medical advice from the hereafter at her Bridge Street parlor. In 1889 Dr. J.C. Kennedy opened his "New Method Cure" at the corner of Bridge and Canal streets. There he treated patients to jolts of his electro-chemical apparatus as well as remedial sniffs of the ozone he generated.

And then there were the sundry entrepreneurs who compounded the pills, potions and panaceas known as patent medicines, whose active ingredients generally included as much as 80 percent alcohol, narcotics or both. As early as 1835 Dr. Charles Shepard merchandised the "cure alls and kills alls" he formulated. By 1870 from its office and depot on Canal Street the firm of McConnell, Lacey and Company had begun a national campaign to alert sufferers of "the greatest discovery of the age," Snow's Great Catarrh Remedy. John Snow had invented his marvelous cure for catarrh, a generic term for any sort of head cold or sinus infection, some years before. The firm offered testimonials by a long list of Grand Rapidians including newspaper editors Aaron Turner and Ezra Burr.

Competition emerged when Dutch immigrants George Steketee and Martinius B. Kimm teamed up to market Kimm's Anti-Bilious Root and Plant Pills, a cure for all liver complaints, bad blood and general debility of the system. Conditions the pills did not improve could be bettered by generous swigs of Steketee & Kimm's Holland Stomach Bitters. The proprietors recommended before each meal a dosage of a half wineglass full of the substance mixed with two parts liquor. "You will have a pleasant drink," they assured. Junior partner Kimm, who came to Grand rapids with 30 years experience as a chemist in the Netherlands, was particularly proud of Kimm's Holland Worm Cakes, "a safe and pleasant remedy" that "children love as well as they do candy."

In the 1880s the Grand Rapids Medicine Company began bottling the patent medicine panacea Hoptonic. In 1883 George Rhodes opened a Universal Dispensary on Lyon Street where his patent treatments promised cures for rheumatism, dyptheria, cancer, scarlet fever, malaria, nervous prostration, pneumonia, varicose veins, brain fever and "dethroned manhood." "Why," Rhodes asked prospective patients in a full-page advertisement, "when the joint command was given to preach the gospel and to heal the sick, is there so much preaching and so little or no healing?"

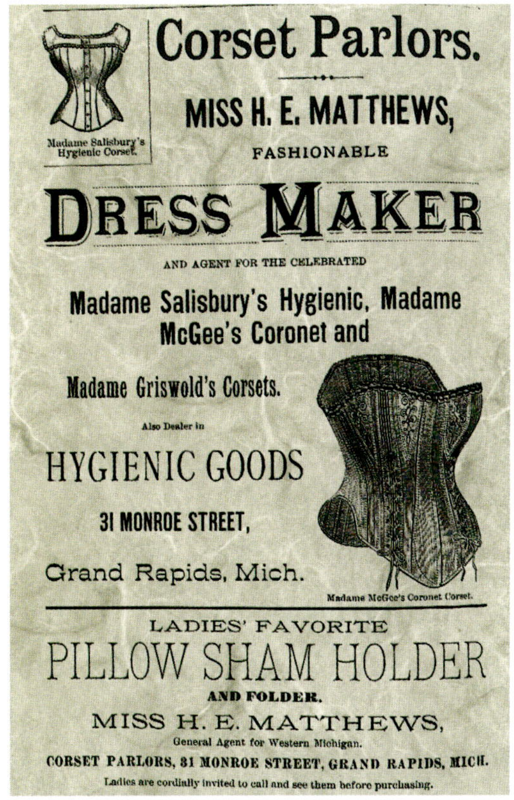

The fashionable instruments of torture offered by Miss Matthews in 1883 sent many a woman to the patent medicine shelf.

Well, he was right about the preaching anyway. With a population in 1883 of approximately 35,000, some 50 places of worship lined Grand Rapids streets. By way of comparison, that is 40 percent more religious organizations than were present in Kalamazoo when it reached that population level in 1905. And the denominations identified Grand Rapids' ethnic diversity. Greatest in number were the Reformed and Christian Reformed

This view from the top of Bridge Street Hill c. 1856 shows the newly constructed Immanuel Evangelical Lutheran Church that catered to the city's German residents.

Harper's Weekly carried an illustration of Professor Donaldson's ill-fated Chicago launch in 1875.

churches, 14 in all, marking the schism that had sundered Van Raalte's people. At least six of them offered services only in Dutch. St. Adalbert Catholic catered to Polish speakers and St. Mary's Catholic and two Lutheran congregations to Germans. A Norwegian Lutheran church, a Swedish Lutheran church and the Temple Emanuel Synagogue served their respective worshipers. Two Methodist churches offered services for black citizens.

As more and more spires defined the horizons of this city of churches, Grand Rapidians had an opportunity to look skyward for another reason in 1875 — the arrival of ace "aeronaut" Professor Washington A. Donaldson. Amiable, athletic and known as a man who "could do anything he undertook to do and would undertake anything that came his way," 35-year-old Donaldson had early in life taken to the stage as a gymnast, ventriloquist and magician. He toured the continent performing daredevil feats, appearing some 1,300 times during the period 1857-1871. That final year he discovered ballooning, and he brought his typical daring to that dangerous sport. Numerous brushes with death in the ungainly and unreliable contraptions failed to stem his enthusiasm. In 1874 he joined P.T. Barnum's traveling circus.

Barnum's "hippodrome" set up its big tent in Grand Rapids on July 4, 1875. Donaldson's balloon ascensions were part of the side show. Never one to miss a chance at publicity, Donaldson invited local press representatives to go for a flight. Sidney Stevens, Robert Wilson, Frank Jeffries and Ed Clark, each a reporter for one of the city's newspapers, volunteered. Clark recorded his experience in the Grand Rapids *Democrat:* "We went up slowly, surely, majestically up, as high or higher than Elijah did in his chariot of fire, bidding a fond adieu to our tearful creditors. Barnum's big tent looked like a lifeless buckwheat cake griddle. Choking sensations overpowered us. Donaldson, who held the rudder of our craft, laughed at our distress and bade us to break pieces from the big cake of ice that lay at our feet and chew them."

Wilson pulled out a cigar and was about to light it when Donaldson climbed the rigging, brandished a knife and warned, "You do that and I'll cut the rope; You'll go down, I'll go up." Wilson postponed his smoke. The airship descended near Ada and all survived, although Jeffries and Wilson landed in tree tops. The newspapermen probably did not realized how fortunate they had been. Ten days later in Chicago while making a similar flight with a reporter, a storm blew the balloon out over Lake Michigan. Donaldson jettisoned the journalist to gain height and his body washed up on shore near Whitehall a month later. The professor and his balloon were never seen again.

Balloon ascensions, circuses, spirited baseball games, battle re-enactments and parades of weirdly clad "horribles" made 19th-century Grand Rapids

On July 4, 1871, a parade of "horribles" marched down Lyon Street.

Independence Days memorable. The grandest celebration came in 1876 when the city staged a three-day extravaganza in honor of the nation's centennial. Flags flew from every conceivable location and colorful decorations festooned downtown buildings, highlighted by a massive Centennial Arch constructed on Campau Square. Eighty-four feet high, 44 feet wide and completely covered with sprigs of evergreen, the arch bore six 8 by 12-foot paintings of "Washington Crossing the Delaware" and other patriotic scenes. The keystone of the structure proclaimed "The People of Grand Rapids to their Country."

On July 4 carriages and pedestrians thronged every road leading to the city, and many more arrived via reduced-fare train tickets to more than double the community's 25,000 residents. Police platoons, brass bands and drum corps, marching militiamen and the fire brigade led a two-mile-long parade. The city's various fraternal and ethnic organizations marched in force as did Father Patrick McManus' contingent of 100 children of the Holy Angels Society. The procession continued for nearly two hours, halting at the park on Fulton Street where orators addressed "a living sea of faces." In the afternoon came a burlesque "parade of horribles" led by Gen. Isaac Smith, bareback on his steed and dressed as an Indian. A massive fireworks display on Island Number Two that evening concluded the gala Centennial Fourth.

But for the nation as a whole the Centennial Celebration was far from over. For six months beginning on May 10, 1876, Philadelphia hosted the Centennial Exposition, an unprecedented effort to showcase

America's finest products. Michigan Governor John J. Bagley appointed Fralick, who had marshaled Grand Rapids' campaign to secure the state fair three years before, as one of four members of the State Board of Centennial Managers charged with coordinating Michigan's role in the exposition. On July 6 the Michigan Building, a gothic mansion built on the fairgrounds to offer a resting place for the more than 30,000 Michigan citizens who attended the exposition, opened amid much fanfare. Its interior featured polished gypsum paneling from Grand Rapids. The Berkey and Gay Company furnished the parlor and upstairs bedrooms with the choicest products of its Canal Street factory. The furniture was "very handsome and elegant and called out the highest praises from all visitors."

Berkey and Gay also exhibited its wares elsewhere at the exposition, as did Grand Rapids competitors, the Phoenix Furniture Company and Nelson, Matter and Company. All three firms won medals for their efforts, but Nelson, Matter and Company stole the show with its "Centennial bedstead." Constructed of slabs of elaborately

(Far left)
Grand Rapidians erected an 84-foot high Centennial Arch on Campau Square in 1876.

The Michigan Building at the 1876 Philadelphia Centennial Exposition featured Grand Rapids-made furniture.

Thousands of fairgoers scrutinized the furniture exhibits at the Centennial Exposition of 1876.

carved Michigan black walnut inlaid with French burl, its massive backboard rose more than 10 feet. Ebony pillars supported what resembled a medieval altar occupied by a large statue of George Washington. A huge wooden eagle with widespread wings surmounted the Victorian masterpiece. Columbia, flanked by Gutenberg and Columbus, stood within the footboard and classic bronzes with uplifted arms posed atop each bedpost. Hundreds of thousands of furniture fanciers from across the country gazed in awe at the huge bedstead and matching dresser and bureau. The suite carried a price tag of $10,000 at a time when furniture factory workers earned an average $1.25 for an entire 10-hour work day.

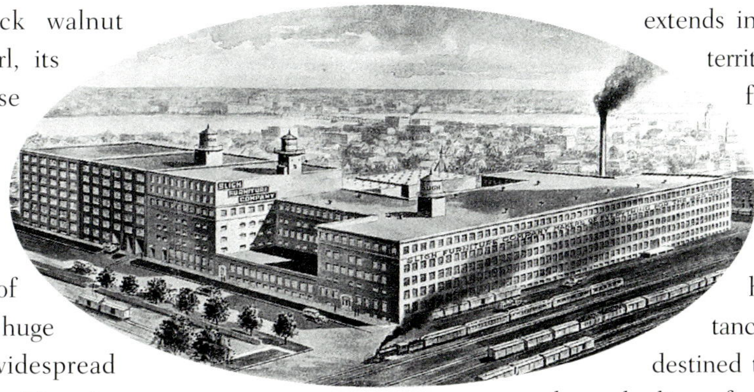

From humble beginnings in 1880 the Sligh Furniture Company grew to become one of the city's largest employers by 1924.

The Centennial Exposition is often credited with first attracting widespread interest in Grand Rapids furniture. In reality, the factors that won it the title of "Furniture City" to the nation — abundant supplies of cheap furniture-grade lumber, transportation routes offering ready access to a wide and seemingly insatiable market, locally produced high-output woodworking machinery and especially the presence of skilled entrepreneurs who would parley those advantages into furniture empires — had already created a thriving industry.

In his promotional booklet, *Grand Rapids in 1874,* Dillenback outlined with an optimism that proved prophetic, the state of affairs: "The furniture manufactories that have sprung up so rapidly within the past ten years and assumed such gigantic proportions, are now only in their infancy and promise still greater things for the future. The building erected by the Berkey and Gay Furniture Company during the present year is one of the largest of the kind anywhere in the West; and yet that, in connection with their very extensive factory, will not afford them any more room than they can immediately occupy. The immense factory erected by the Phoenix Furniture Company in 1873 is by no means equal to the requirements of their business and will soon be greatly enlarged. The furniture trade of Grand Rapids now extends into nearly every state and territory in the union... The furniture factories of the city now employ nearly 1,000 men, most of whom are receiving high wages... It would be hard to overrate the importance which this interest is destined to assume, and if it were the only line of manufacture pursued, it would warrant us in expecting to see a continued and prosperous growth of the city."

By 1874 Nelson, Matter and Company, which evolved under various names beginning in 1855, had emerged as the city's leading furniture maker, specializing in bedroom, parlor, dining room and office products. At its five-story, 70 by 160-foot factory, approximately 200 woodworkers turned out $200,000 worth of furniture annually. The company's lumberyard north of the factory stocked more than one million feet of lumber. Business continued to boom. After the Centennial Exposition, the company and the other two Grand Rapids exhibitors leased showrooms in New York City. By 1890 Nelson, Matter and Company's employment reached 450 and the firm had won the reputation as "the largest and best known manufacturer of its day."

Another Grand Rapids furniture dynasty began with the arrival of the English craftsman George Widdicomb in 1856. His four sons later organized the Widdicomb Brothers Company, the William Widdicomb Company and the John Widdicomb Company. Other nationally known 19th-century furniture firms include: The Grand Rapids Chair Company, incorporated in 1872, The Luce Furniture Company, a descendant of the John Bradford Company founded in 1874, and The American Seating Company. The Sligh Furniture Company went into production in 1880 and grew to become one of the city's largest, employing more than 1,200 at its 16-acre plant during the 1920s. Stowe and Davis traces its heritage to the 1880s as well.

During the 1880s and 1890s some 85 furniture manufacturers went into production in Grand Rapids. The city's furniture industry gained additional fame through

In 1894 the nationally known Semi-Annual Furniture Expositions were held in the Blodgett Block at Ottawa Avenue and Louis Street.

award-winning exhibits at the 1884 World's Exposition in New Orleans and the Columbian Exposition of 1893. By 1928, when Grand Rapids celebrated its own 100th semi-annual furniture exposition (held sometimes four times a year), 365 different manufacturers including companies from New York, Chicago, Milwaukee, St. Louis and numerous Michigan cities capitalized on the Furniture City's good name to fill more than 2,400,000 square feet with displays.

Grand Rapids residents became painfully aware that theirs was "a city built on wood" in 1883 when the river heaved with "the greatest log jam in the nation's history." Monsoon-like storms that struck on July 22 and 23, coupled with logging operations that denuded stream banks thereby allowing an unabated run off, had swollen the Grand River. About noon on the 23rd the huge boom three miles upstream broke and some 80 million board feet of big logs churned into the city, slamming into the Detroit and Milwaukee Railroad Bridge. For two days the bridge held back the flood of timber, as railroad laborers worked feverishly to reinforce it while piling on 25 tons of rails for extra weight.

On the evening of the 26th, just after a long train had chugged across the bridge, the log jam won the tug-of-war. The surging mass of logs snapped off the middle span of the bridge and whirled it 100 feet downstream where it sank. For two hours the logs "like a monster demon mad and bent on destruction" tumbled and pitched in the current. At the south edge of the city the Lake Shore and Michigan Southern Railroad Bridge, where special booms had been built, brought most of the logs to a halt. Two weeks of skillful prying by "river hogs" finally released the jam to make its way to awaiting mills at Grand Haven.

The "Great Log Jam of 1883" proved the beginning of the end for the colorful era when pine was king in the Grand River Valley. The lumberjacks had done their work only too well and the drives grew smaller with each passing year. In 1893 with practically all the pine in the valley cut, the loggers and mill operators shifted operations to the north.

But when one industry died, Grand Rapids seemed destined to develop others to take its place. And while the furniture factories dominated the city's industrial roster,

(Far right) The 1883 log jam swept the Grand Rapids and Indiana Railroad Bridge downstream.

During the 1883 "Great Log Jam" thousands of logs piled up at the Detroit and Milwaukee Railroad Bridge before it gave way.

(Far left)
One of many collateral industries made possible by the success of the furniture companies was Dodds' dove-tailing machine advertised in 1894.

The Harrison Wagon Works shown here in 1891 had been rebuilt two years before.

employing more than 5,000 by 1888, a variety of other enterprises revealed industrial diversity. The 1880s witnessed the birth of some companies whose products catered to the needs of furniture makers, such as rattan for wickerwork, excelsior used in stuffing, and several furniture machinery manufacturers. Other heavy machinery producers included the W.T. Powers & Son Michigan Iron Works that made mill machinery, steam engines and brass castings. Adolph Leitelt's Valley City Iron Works specialized in boilers and steam engines. Harrison's Wagon Works, with its adjoining company town of "Harrisville," remained a major employer. Local competition came from Arthur Wood's carriage, cart and sleigh factory that specialized in the Wolverine Spring Buggy, John Mack's Pearl Street Carriage and Sleigh Manufactory and the big Belknap Wagon and Sleigh Company operation founded by the Civil War veteran and historian.

In 1876 Melville R. Bissell began producing a new type of carpet sweeper he had invented. By 1889, the company had grown to a massive complex of six factories on Mill Street where hundreds of employees turned out "one and a half sweepers per minute." Following Bissell's death that year, his widow Anna succeeded him as president of the company. Another 150 artisans worked at Chase Brothers' Piano Company on South Front Avenue producing highly decorative rosewood, ebony, mahogany, oak and walnut upright pianos. Printing and engraving had also emerged as a Grand Rapids specialty due to the

In this c. 1905 view the Bissell factories that sprawled between Mill Street and the river filled the atmosphere with smoke as a sign of prosperity.

In 1904 the Bissell Co. promoted its avant garde "Cyco" model.

(Far right) Built in 1895, the massive Grand Rapids Brewery remained a landmark for decades.

demand by furniture makers for elaborate catalogs, and some of the leading firms of the 1880s included the Valley City Engraving Company, the Grand Rapids Engraving Company and the Grand Rapids Electrotype Foundry established in 1887.

A Grand Rapids tradition of notable German brewers began in 1844 when Christoph Kusterer established a small brewery on the west side of the river. Ten years later four big breweries operated by German families were bunging up thousands of barrels of beer, ale and porter annually. In the 1880s Anheuser-Busch and other national brewers offered intense competition to the local producer. In response the Kusterer family, Tusch Brothers, George Brandt, Veit and Rathman, Adolph Goetz and the Frey Brothers amalgamated into The Grand Rapids Brewery Company in 1892. Three years later they laid the cornerstone of a massive Richardsonian Romanesque plant on the corner of Bridge Street and Ionia Avenue. The success of its popular "Silver Foam" beer made the company the largest Michigan producer outside Detroit.

Many of those who lined bars to quaff big mugs of Silver Foam also puffed cigars, the dominant nicotine delivery system of the era, and like cigar makers in many other Michigan communities, local producers found a steady demand for their product. As early as 1867, five Grand Rapids firms, including J.B. Moon & Co., Edward Mohl & Co. and Henry H. Vanderstoop, hand rolled thousands of cigars annually. By 1883 the *Grand Rapids City Directory* listed 26 cigar makers. In the early 20th century, Grand Rapids cigar makers rolled more than 50 million stogies annually. Dutch immigrant Gerrit J. Johnson began a career in cigar making at the age of 12. In 1892 he opened a factory in Grand Rapids, employing 11 workers. By the decade's end his work force had grown to 210 and his El Portano, Exemplar and, later, Dutch Master brands sold from coast to coast.

In 1892 also, the Star Knitting Works moved from Niles to Grand Rapids to produce the "Perfect Gem Suit" of ladies long underwear. Three years later the Grand Rapids Knitting Company joined in production of "fashionable ribbed" long underwear. The knitting factories and the

In 1867 J.B. Moon appeared to promote his "segars" to a youthful clientele.

Joseph Tandler's three friends named Bill proudly posed for his 1901 advertisement.

cigar makers profited from the railroads' need to fill returning boxcars with cotton and tobacco from the south.

At the O. & W. Thum Company plant, founded in 1884 by the Thum family of druggists, some 150 workmen smeared special formula glue on mile after mile of sticky "tanglefoot" fly paper each 10-hour day in the 1890s. Other Grand Rapids laborers made ball bats, refrigerators, brushes, air rifles, felt boots, wire nails,

Hundreds of workers smeared glue on miles of sticky flypaper each day at the O. & W. Thum plant pictured here in 1910.

(All photos this page and opposite)
A colorful art form, boxes that housed turn-of-the-century Grand Rapids-made cigars, have become coveted collector's items.

10¢
PINZON

MASTERPIECE
HAND MADE 5¢
SELECTED LONG FILLER
MERIT WILL WIN
TITLE & DESIGN OWNED BY ANTHONY KLEINER, GRAND RAPIDS, MICH.
AS GOOD AS IT'S NAME

(Far right) Perry Whiting pictured his memorable high wheeler spill in his autobiography.

In 1894 the Grand Rapids Cycle Co. leaned its output against the front of the factory for customers to inspect.

portable houses, barrels, soap, fire ladders and trucks, electric railroad cars, wheelbarrows, burial caskets and embalming fluid.

Still other Grand Rapids manufacturers sought to satisfy the craze that had swept the nation in the 1890s — bicycles. In 1896 C.B. Metzger began marketing the bicycles he manufactured and the following year the Hamilton Kenwood Cycle Company of Ohio moved to Grand Rapids to consolidate with the bicycle manufacturing company of the Sligh Furniture Company. By then, according to the Grand Rapids *Herald,* the city's six bicycle factories had an annual output of 25,000 to 30,000 bicycles.

The bicycle fad had been made possible by the invention of the "safety bike," which replaced dangerous velocipedes with huge front wheels. Perry Whiting, who grew up as a teenager in Grand Rapids of the 1880s, recalled the dangers of riding his 52-inch-high wheeler on downtown streets: "I was homeward bound, riding on the plank sidewalk, going about as fast as I could make it go. The planks in this particular stretch of walk were laid lengthwise, and some of them were one or more inches apart. Without warning my wheel dropped into one of the cracks and stuck there. I kept right on going and landed about ten or fifteen feet in front on my head and shoulders."

Whiting survived that and several other bad spills, including one in which he slammed into a farmer's wagon on South Division Street then flew over the handlebars to land unhurt in the vehicle's bed. Despite his mishaps, Whiting and about 25 other pioneer Grand Rapids bicyclists formed a club and staged races on the dirt track at the fairground. In 1888 they also organized a local chapter of The League of American Wheelmen which campaigned for improved roads for cyclists. In 1896 a periodical published in Grand Rapids, *The Western Wheelman,* advocated bicycle racing. Four local enthusiasts constructed a one-third-mile concrete race course including a 5,000-seat grandstand on the north side of Fulton Street between Lane and Marion.

On June 4, 1896, Libbie Chesebro, who lived on the family farm extending from the southeast corner of

(Far right) In 1896 the Automatic Cycle Seat Co. advertised its novel seat that was adjustable to fit the vagaries of either cheek.

The famous trademark of the Sticky Fly Paper Co. featured a fly in dire distress.

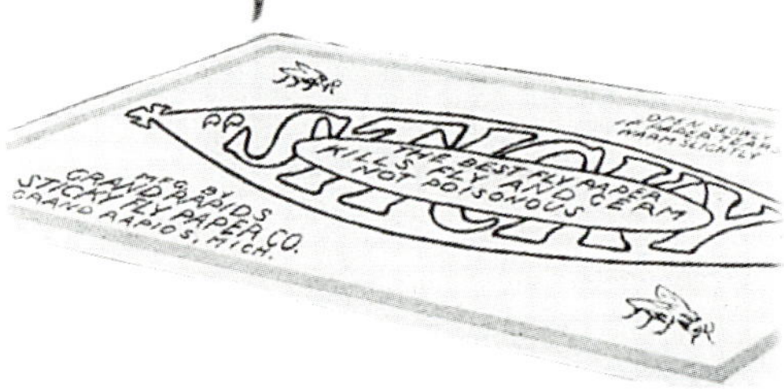

In the 1890s Mr. A. Smilde proudly posed before his Cass Avenue home with his two favorite things, his daughter and bike. *Calvin College Archives*

Burton and Eastern Avenue, wrote to her brother Frank: "The world moves on wheels hereabouts. Everybody has 'em. Folks who were never here before come now to call or rest or drink. Some get treated to pie and cream, some to plain cold water and some to nothing. Sunday there were five wheels here at once. Looked like a livery here."

But Grand Rapidians had a few things besides "wheels" on their minds that hot summer of 1896 — politics for one. The presidential election pitted Republican William McKinley against golden-tongued orator William Jennings Bryan. While McKinley waged a decorous contest from the porch of his Canton, Ohio, home and relied on the enormous campaign chest his party had raised, Bryan carried his battle to the people in the most vigorous presidential campaign America had yet seen. Gold vs. silver emerged as the dominant issue. Farmers and other have-nots reeling from a recent depression seized on silver as a panacea for their economic woes. Bryan rose up as their champion, calling for the free and unlimited coinage of silver at a radio of 16 to one gold. That would have inflated U.S. currency, making it easier for debtors to pay loans. Bankers, employers and most Republicans naturally favored the strict gold standard.

Bryan traveled 18,000 miles by rail to deliver more than 600 speeches to five million Americans in a 10-week whistle stop campaign. Beginning October 14, 1896, he launched a four-day whirlwind sweep through Michigan. Joined by a delegation that included Grand Rapids Furniture mogul Charles R. Sligh, an outspoken Democrat activist, Bryan sped through the Upper Peninsula to reach Grand Rapids the following day. He delivered an outdoor speech in Campau Square, a standing-room-only oration that evening and a special presentation to a female audience. Though banned from the ballot box, the ladies showed their support by presenting Mrs. Bryan with "a handsome badge made of 16 parts of silver and one of gold."

Grand Rapids enjoyed a long tradition of supporting liberal currency reform issues. Furniture maker Charles C. Comstock ran unsuccessfully as a Democrat for governor in 1870 and congressman in 1872 and 1878 before winning election to Congress in 1884 on a Democratic Greenback fusion ticket. The Greenback Party, organized to promote continued government issuance of paper money, ran its candidate in the presidential election of 1876. That year fellow furniture manufacturer William A. Berkey authored *The Money Question,* an ardent appeal for fiat money Greenback principles. Luther V. Moulton, a local patent solicitor, wrote a similar treatise, *The Science of Money,* in 1880. And in 1895 Grand Rapids lawyer Charles Howell published a pro-silver volume.

With its major Dutch population, traditionally hard-core Republicans, Kent County Democrats had long faced a losing battle. The disgruntled proprietor of a 65-acre farm on Grand Rapids' east side, Allen D. Chesebro wrote his son, Frank, on May 25, 1896: "Have hired (a teacher) for the coming year at $38. Reduce taxes. Don't pay to educate Dutch and have them vote the G.O.P. ticket like a lot of cattle and don't know as much about what they are voting for." McKinley won Kent County by an overwhelming majority in 1896. Bryan ran again in 1900 and 1908, loosing by greater margins each time.

In the meantime, Grand Rapids galloped toward the 20th century as a vibrant city adopting state-of-the-art technology. Electric streetcars replaced the horse-drawn

The horse-drawn Valley City streetcars were replaced by electric models in 1892.

(Far right) Grand Rapids militamen of the 32nd Michigan infantry paraded at Camp Desoto near Tampa, Florida, in 1898.

Scores of electric streetcars made turn-of-the-century Grand Rapids streets busy and dangerous places.

Grand Rapids' young men, such as the officers of the Park Congregational Church-sponsored Merriam Rifles, shown here in 1895, yearned for martial adventures in the "splendid little war" of 1898.

The sandstone arch built for the 1893 Columbian Exposition stood at the entrance of John Ball Park for decades.

models in 1892. All other vehicles remained equine powered until 1897 when Dr. Perry Schurtz's Woods horseless carriage became the first such contraption to putt around Grand Rapids streets. In 1899 the number of telephones in the city had reached 1,000.

The increasing technological complexity of life in the city made recreation all the more desirable, and in 1900 the city purchased an additional 40-acre tract adjoining the original 40-acre park willed to Grand Rapids citizens following Ball's death in 1884. Ultimately the popular park and zoo would grow to encompass 140 acres. At the close of the Columbian Exposition of 1893, the massive arch carved of reddish sandstone from Marquette designed for Michigan's mineral exhibit was moved from Chicago to serve as the entrance to John Ball Park.

The year 1898 brought the sinking of the *Maine* in Havana Harbor and America declared a "splendid little war" to free Cuba from Spanish tyranny. Eager for a chance to prove their mettle in battle, Grand Rapids youths again rushed to join the colors. The second unit raised in the state, the 32nd Michigan Infantry Regiment, contained four companies of Grand Rapids militiamen. Local volunteers also served in the other four state regiments mustered. Grand Rapids newspaperman Frank Knox joined Teddy Roosevelt's Rough Riders.

Former Grand Rapids resident Russell A. Alger served as secretary of war during the conflict. A self-made lumber baron who moved to Grand Rapids in 1859 and married a local girl two year later, Alger had compiled a brilliant military record in the Civil War. Enlisting as a captain of the 2nd Michigan Cavalry at Grand Rapids in 1861, he fought in 66 battles and skirmishes to rise to the rank of major general. He won election as Republican governor of Michigan in 1885. Prominent in the party hierarchy, Alger was appointed secretary of war by McKinley in March 1897. But when war broke out, Alger's department proved woefully unprepared. At the embarkation point in Tampa, Florida, soldiers received wool uniforms, Civil War mess equipment and obsolete single-fire trap-door Springfields. Rations included canned meat so bad the troops dubbed it "embalmed beef." Medical supplies were inadequate and the majority of the casualties of the war came from yellow fever and other disease. Alger suffered stinging criticism for his role, although in fairness, much of the fault for the debacle lay in the appointment of War Department personnel via the spoils system. Alger resigned in August 1899 to save McKinley further embarrassment.

Former Grand Rapidian Russell Alger, who served as secretary of war during the Spanish-American War, posed with Michigan Governor Hazen Pingree in 1898. Both suffered humiliation as a result of the war.

Humiliation also came to Michigan Governor Hazen Pingree as a result of a scandal involving a pair of Grand Rapids men during the aftermath of the war. In 1897, Pingree had appointed 36-year-old Grand Rapids pharmacist William I. White quartermaster general of the state military board. Another Grand Rapids native, Harold A. Smith, served as White's assistant. During the war the state purchased more uniforms than, as it turned out, were needed. So White, Smith, State Inspector General Arthur F. Marsh of Allegan and possibly several other officials hatched a scheme to feather their own nests. The surplus uniform were sold for next to nothing to the fictitious Illinois Supply Company and shipped to the Kalamazoo-based Henderson Ames Company. Henderson Ames, which specialized in masonic regalia, merely changed the labels on the uniforms, the military board bought them back and the schemers split a tidy $35,000 profit.

Rumors of the crooked deal surfaced and a grand jury indicted White, Smith and Marsh. Whereupon, White skipped town and hid out in California. Smith pleaded guilty and was fined, Marsh went to trial and was convicted and Henderson Ames escaped prosecution by paying restitution. White returned to Grand Rapids in 1900 after more than a year on the lam, just in time to review the glowing three-page account of his career that appeared in the biographical "mug book" of Kent County published that year. Prosecutors were not impressed. White pleaded guilty and received a 10-year prison term. He spent only one day in Jackson, however, before Pingree pardoned him and Marsh because the other guilty parties had gotten off so lightly. White returned to counting pills at the East Fulton Street pharmacy he operated with his brother. Sharply criticized for his leniency in the matter, Pingree failed to secure his party's nomination for governor in 1900.

Another reminder of Grand Rapids' role in the war in Cuba spans the river at Fulton Street. Private William H. Dean had been an itinerant Grand Rapids house painter before enlisting in the cavalry during the war. August of 1900 found him serving on occupation duty in Cuba where he reported for sick call because of venereal disease. Major Walter Reed, then seeking to discover the cause of the yellow fever that had claimed so many lives in the tropics, offered Dean an opportunity to stay in the hospital longer if he volunteered to be bitten by a mosquito. Dean agreed, contracted yellow fever and thereby helped confirm Reed's hypothesis that the insects transmitted the disease. Dean's role in the experiment remained a military secret for the succeeding 27 years. But in 1927 the city named the newly constructed Dean Bridge in its inadvertent home town hero's honor shortly after he succumbed to the effects of the recurring bouts of yellow fever he had suffered.

Corpulent Gov. Pingree (second from right) sat with his military staff in 1898. White, seated on the right, and Smith, standing behind White, immersed his administration in scandal.

LABOR WOES AND WATER FLOWS 7

Despite the formation of numerous local trade unions during the post-Civil War decades, Grand Rapids did not enjoy a reputation as much of a union town, thanks largely to the efforts of the Board of Trade and other booster groups. So on the first Labor Day of the new century the local Trades and Labor Council intended to make its presence felt in a big way. The huge parade began on West Bridge Street at 10 a.m. sharp that Monday and crossed the bridge to Front Street. The 36-member Evening Press News Boys Band led the procession drumming and blowing cornets, piccolos, trombones and tubas to the tune of the "Evening Press March," halting every few blocks to rend the air with their "association yell":

"Jimmy got de pants,
Molly got de dress,
Hi, there!
Buy there!
Eve-nine Press — See!!!"

The Grand Rapids Evening Press Newsboys Band appeared on the cover of the c. 1900 sheet music written in its honor.

Then strode Mayor George R. Perry, waving freely, head held high, yet to be sullied by his role in the forthcoming "Great Water Scandal." Phalanx after phalanx of union members followed, representing the pattern makers, theatrical stage employees, broom makers, glass workers, teamsters, window trimmers, upholsterers, book binders and the typographical union.

The Furniture City Band led the second division, then the Letter Carriers Band followed by Postmaster Bishop and all the postmen. The Iron Molders' Union marched briskly as did contingents of bakers, coopers, horse shoers, metal polishers, brewers, beer bottlers and bottle wagon drivers, barbers and bricklayers. The Musicians' Union Band proved a crowd favorite. The parade concluded with the cigar makers', furniture workers', tailors' and amalgamated sheet metal workers' unions.

That afternoon the celebrants convened at Reeds Lake for a picnic followed by the awarding of cash prizes to the prettiest babies. The tallest, shortest, lightest and heaviest union members present each won $3 cash awards. While not much of a prize by contemporary standards, in 1901 it was well worth vying for.

The standard workday then ran a full 10 hours, and for that Grand Rapids furniture makers earned from $1.30 to $1.65 per day. As revealed in the annual reports of the Michigan Bureau of Labor, the cigar rollers at the G.J. Johnson Company earned $1 per day. Tanglefoot employees took home 84 cents for their sticky 10-hour shift. Other occupations were rewarded according to the complexity of the task and/or the generosity of the employer and presence of a strong union. Broom makers earned $1.40 a day, brushmakers $1.01, Automatic Dust Pan Company employees 90 cents, shoemakers $1.75 and at the top of the scale the average brewer got $2.33 plus certain fringe benefits. Jobs filled by women paid the least. The Grand Rapids Knitting Company's female employees earned 75 cents a day for turning out ladies "fashionable underwear" and they

These employees of the Grand Rapids Brass Co. earned 15 cents per hour during their 10-hour workday in 1901.

earned 68.5 cents at the rival Simmons Knitting Company. The women laborers at the Mosley Brothers Seed Company, half of whom were less than 16 years old, earned a mere five cents per hour.

For workers unfortunate enough to be injured on the job, no state or federal law required disability payments. Whether or not a disabled worker received any compensation remained strictly up to the conscience of his employer. In 1900 and 1901 the state factory inspector recorded 34 accidents in Grand Rapids factories. The majority involved the loss of several fingers or an entire hand while operating a saw. Injured employees lost as many as 50 of days work during which only half received any wages or benefits whatsoever.

The city population stood at 87,505 in 1900. Ten years later it reached 112,571. A promotional pamphlet from 1911 smugly noted: "It would be a deception to deny that people emigrate from Grand Rapids, from time to time. They do. It is seldom, however, that those who go are of the stamp which causes regret to those who remain." Booming industrial growth provided jobs for the increased population. Furniture making remained the dominant occupation in 1910 but by then the city's industrial diversity had expanded exponentially. That year the Grand Rapids Board of Trade compiled an alphabetical list of more than 300 products manufactured in the city ranging from adding machines and automobiles to washing machines and wooden shoes.

As the decade wore on, more and more women found employment in Grand Rapids factories. The G.J. Johnson Cigar Company, for example, employed 75 men and 46 women in 1901. Nine years later its work force stood at 17 men and 293 women. Statewide, the Michigan Bureau of Labor estimated the number of women "engaged in gainful occupation had increased 200 percent from 1900 to 1910." A major reason for the growth of the women's work force lay in the fact that employers could pay them less than men — often far less than a living wage.

In 1913 the Michigan legislature created a commission to look into the controversy over minimum wages for female employees. U.S. District Attorney Myron H. Walker of Grand Rapids was appointed one of three commissioners. On March 16, 1914, he convened a public meeting in his home town to seek local input. Gerritt J. Johnson, president of his cigar company, offered testimony concerning the cost of living for a "girl." Itemizing laundry at 75 cents per week, room rent $2 per week, meals 50 cents per day, car fare $1 per week, etc., he came up with a minimum annual expenditure of $538.20. Yet, Johnson's experienced female employees earned about $100 less per year than he had computed as their minimal needs.

Of course, a major disadvantage in hiring a woman, as Johnson explained, was "that she is liable to get married at any time and quit work." Women beginning the cigar trade at his factory, Johnson continued, earned only $4 - $5 per 60-hour week. After six months, they might progress to $6 - $7 and with a full year's experience reach the $9 per week rate. Personally, Johnson felt badly about the situation but as he rationalized, "competition compels me to buy labor as cheaply as possible."

Johnson, a Dutch immigrant who had built up his cigar empire by repeatedly lowering his employees' wages in the 1890s after winning an 1894 strike, continued his explanation: "Now a girl come to our doors, and the first question we ask is 'Do you live at home?' If she does not live at home, we do not take her. Now, it is not fair to the girl; it is not fair to the girl without parents, who lives out of town. And yet we have to do it to protect ourselves. We know that a girl at $4 a week cannot support herself. I realize the injustice of that thing as much as anybody, but competition compels us to act that way — it makes us inhuman."

The workers' plight further deteriorated around 1910 with a dramatic surge in the inflation rate. Labor unrest

In 1910, when this view of the G.J. Johnson Cigar Co. appeared, the proprietor's 293 women employees earned $9 or less per 60-hour work week.

The classically pillared Union Depot constructed in 1900 fell to the wrecking ball in 1961.

had occasionally jolted Grand Rapids, despite the fact that the Christian Reformed Church attended by numerous Dutch workers took a dim view of unions. In 1911 the furniture industry earned a well-deserved strike and it proved a long and violent one. The Grand Rapids employers had banded together to form the Furniture Manufacturers Association in an effort to combat unionization efforts. The manufacturers insisted on open shops and "the liberty of every man to sell his labor freely, independently and at the best price obtainable."

Nevertheless, the United Brotherhood of Carpenters and Joiners made progress among the workers. A proposal by 4,900 workers in October 1910 calling for a nine-hour workday, a 10-percent pay increase and the end of piecework, was dismissed outright by management. As the situation worsened, the employers flatly refused an offer to arbitrate by Mayor George Ellis. Union members overwhelmingly passed a strike vote on March 25, 1911, and on April 19 at least 3,000 workers walked off their jobs.

By 1910 more than 32,000 trains a year arrived at the Union Station, "The Gateway to Western Michigan."

The big furniture factory owners refused to budge. They imported outside strike breakers and goaded the strikers with sarcastic rhetoric. Harry and William Widdicomb, proprietors of the huge factory that bore their names, had been particularly provocative, waving handguns in the air and transporting "scab" workers to and from the plant in their own automobiles. Violence broke out the evening of May 15 as thousands of strikers and their families milled around the Widdicomb factory and stoned Harry Widdicomb's car. Police fired shots into the crowd and battered stone throwers with billy clubs — scores on both sides were injured. Widdicomb succeeded in making his getaway but the mob hurled rocks through every window in his plant. The riot lasted for five hours, ending only when fire hoses drenched strikers.

As seen in this 1901 view, the Grand Rapids streetcar lines featured special postal cars for rapid transit of mail.

The Grand Rapids mourners at this 1906 immigrant funeral prepare to escort the deceased to his final resting place. *Calvin College Archives*

This 1910 map of the city's railway system illustrates the recreationist-oriented "triangle" linking the major parks.

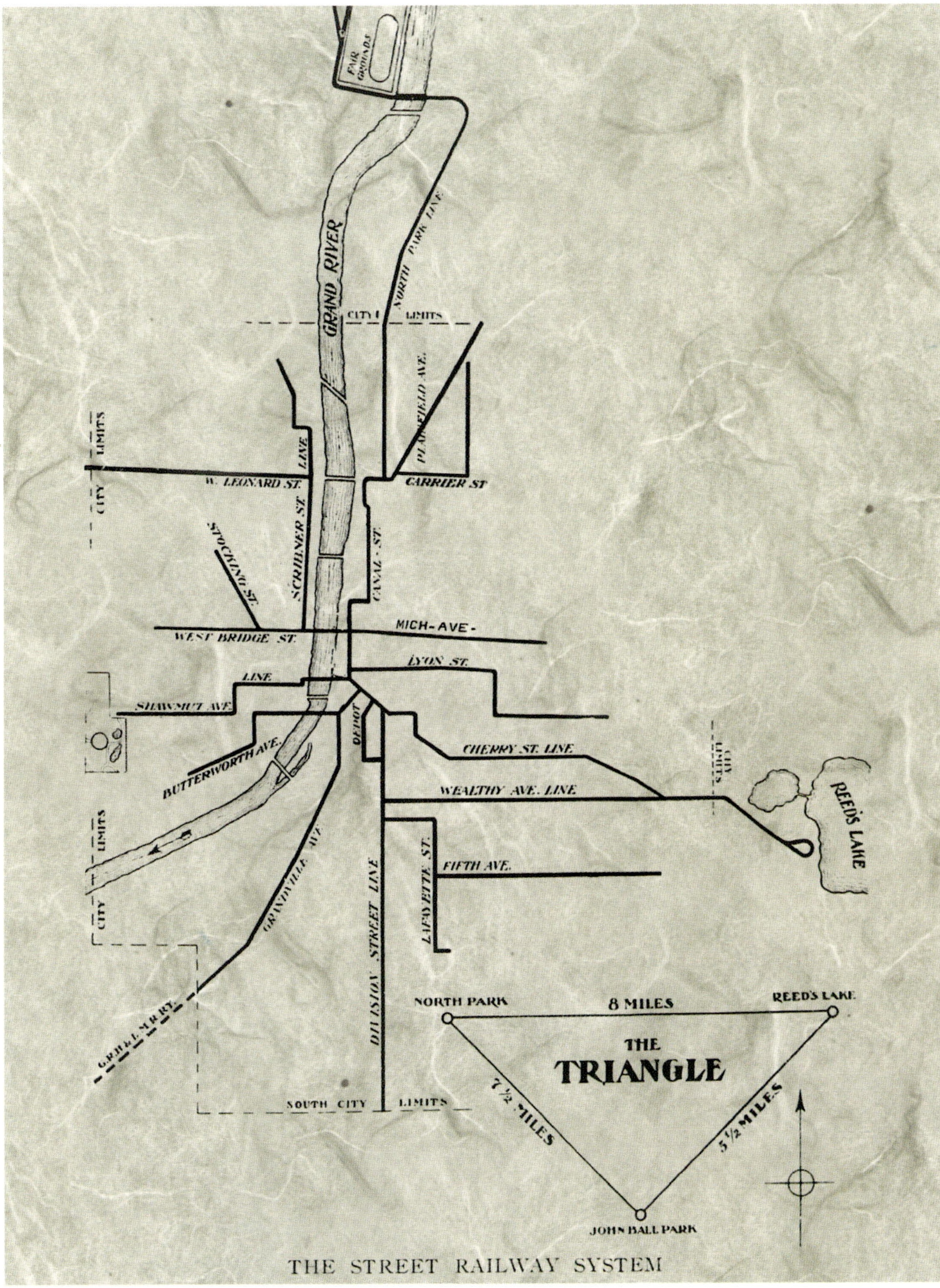

The new St. Mary's Hospital opened in 1911.

(Far right) In 1910 Butterworth Hospital was housed in this Romanesque structure built in 1890.

The Union Benevolent Association Hospital constructed in 1886 served the city until it was replaced by Blodgett Hospital in 1916.

The owners maintained a solid front for four months, refusing to negotiate with strikers. Finally, the national leadership of the union realized the futility of the situation and withdrew. The Christian Reformed Church hierarchy announced that union membership was incompatible with its doctrines and a week later, on August 18, 1911, the strike ended. Those workers who were not blacklisted went back to their jobs having gained little but simmering bitterness. Nevertheless, over the following

Constructed in 1916, Blodgett Hospital honors the name of the major donor's mother, Jane Wood Blodgett.

decade most employers gradually granted what had been sought by the strikers.

The city that returned to its regular routine of 60-hour workweeks in 1911 had grown to encompass 17.5 square miles where 112,571 citizens lived in 19,873 residences. Five railroads connected the city with its far-flung markets. In 1909 alone 31,755 trains chugged in and out of the Union Depot. Electric interurbans linked Grand Rapids with Holland and Muskegon and in 1915 the western Division of the Michigan Railroad Company reached Kalamazoo. More than 63 miles of electric streetcar lines within the city carried as many as 15 million passengers annually. Some 22,000 employees worked in 508 factories.

The city's medical facilities had also improved vastly since the beginning of the century. The new five-story, 75-bed St. Mary's Hospital opened in 1911. That same

By 1914 the Burleson Sanitarium had become the seat of a specialized medical industry.

year Butterworth Hospital received the first of many bequests from Butterworth's grandson, Edward Lowe, when he bought and remodeled three houses adjoining the hospital. In 1911, also, the Mary Free Bed Guild was established and in conjunction with Blodgett Hospital began funding various clinics to benefit children. The new 125-bed Blodgett Hospital, named in honor of the mother of the donor, lumberman John Blodgett, opened in 1916.

Grand Rapids also gained a national reputation for its specialty treatment centers. After receiving his diploma from the Saginaw Valley Medical College, Dr. Willard M. Burleson moved to Grand Rapids in 1899 where he established a proctology practice. His brother, Dr. John F. Burleson, joined him in 1906 and within eight years the Burleson Hospital had become "the largest institution in the world for the cure of Piles." Grand Rapids became the seat of a similar industry in 1929 when Doctors Ward and Lynn Ferguson and James Droste opened what would evolve into the largest institution in the nation for the surgical treatment of diseases of the colon and rectum.

Unfortunately, not all medical practices that brought Grand Rapids national attention were as legitimate. Take Anthony W. Van Bysterveld, for example. Unable to earn a genuine medical degree, Van Bysterveld coined his own title, "Expert Inspector of Urine." The quack, whose portrait reveals a curly-haired, middle-aged gentleman with a rather villainous uplift to his moustache, boasted he had "spent a lifetime examining human urine," an average of 25,000 specimens a year.

This colorful quack left Grand Rapids for parts unknown in 1914.

Van Bysterveld alerted clients of his exotic services via advertisements in nationally circulated journals. Patients suffering from any and all medical complaints simply mailed in a vial of their urine labeled with their name, age and sex to his Sheldon Street address. The expert inspector posted back a speedy diagnosis and supplied weekly doses of his patent medicines at a healthy fee.

Van Bysterveld's expertise, he informed clients, came from a "careful and secret process handed down generation after generation, and most carefully guarded by the old families of Europe." In 1910 Dr. Arthur J. Cramp, director of the American Medical Association's special investigative task force, decided to give the litmus test to Van Bysterveld's methodology. Cramp sent him identical vials of a mixture containing tap water, a trace of pepsin and ammonia and a little yellow dye for color from addresses in Illinois, Iowa and Michigan. Back came the following analyses:

Diagnosis one: "Careful examination of the urine shows there is too much acid in the blood, which will cause a rheumatic condition, the back is weak, and you will have a tired nervous feeling most of the time."

Diagnosis two: "Careful examination of the urine shows the circulation of the blood to be very poor, the liver is not working properly, which will cause gas in the stomach and bowels and will effect (sic) the heart. You have caught a little cold which has settled in the back and stomach, and you will a have a nervous feeling."

Diagnosis three: "Careful examination of the urine shows you are losing too much albumen in the urine, which will cause the back and kidneys to be weak and there is a catarrhal condition of the stomach and bowels, and you will have a tired nervous feeling most of the time."

William Harrison promoted his wagons as being so light running they could be pulled by bunnies in 1890.

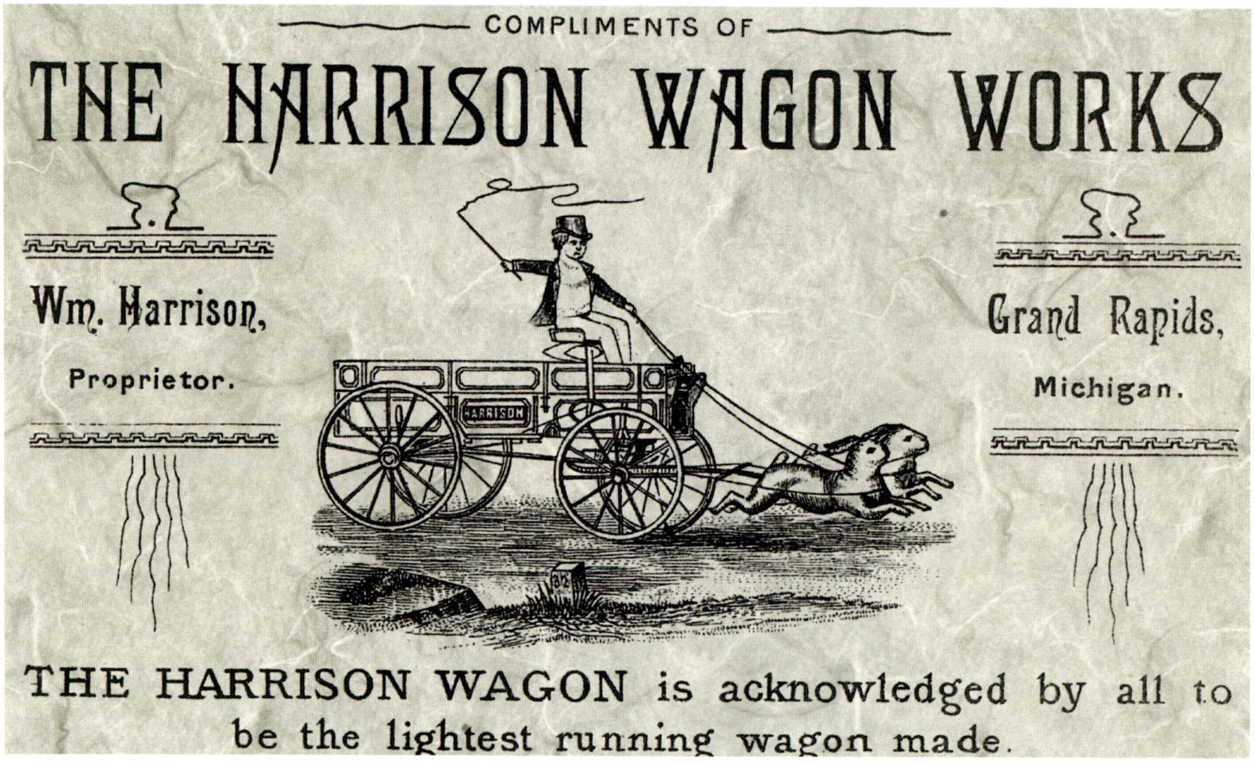

Evidently, Cramp noted with interest, the only condition common to three individuals secreting a mixture of water, pepsin, yellow dye and a trace of ammonia was a nervous feeling. Then again, a certain degree of nervousness seemed advisable for anyone dealing with Van Bysterveld. By 1914 the "urine expert" had received his third conviction under the 1899 Michigan Medical Act and his name soon disappeared from the *Grand Rapids City Directory*.

The year the city lost its picaresque humbug, 1914, set a record for the number of building permits issued. A total of 1,983 new structures went up that year. Grand Rapids boomed despite some disappointments and losses over the decade. In 1909, for example, the Michigan Stove and Castor Company moved its 86 jobs to Battle Creek where it became the renowned A-B Stove Company.

In 1905 old William Harrison decided to compete with the newfangled contraptions that were rapidly replacing the wagons he manufactured. He produced a big automobile with a 10-foot wheelbase. The Harrison featured a four-cylinder engine with a self-starting system. But Harrison lacked sufficient capital to compete against the big manufacturers in Lansing, Detroit and elsewhere, went bankrupt in 1907 and died the following year. Other early horseless carriages produced in Grand Rapids included the Lorraine, the Sintz, the ephemeral

This c. 1910 caricature parodied Walter Scott Austin, manufacturer of the automobile named after him.

Matheson and the Austin, known as "the highway king" and produced for 20 years beginning in 1901. Ultimately the Furniture City's automotive dreams went the way of the more than 2,500 other short-lived models produced nationwide.

Another disappointment came in 1903 when, despite the efforts of State Representative Henry B. Vandercook of Grand Rapids, the city lost its bid as the site for the new Western State Normal School to Kalamazoo. Although Grand Rapids did not win the institution destined to evolve into Western Michigan University, it remained a city of readers and writers. In 1901 Chicago industrialist Martin A. Ryerson gave his hometown an initial $150,000 to build a new library. The classically pillared Ryerson Library opened in 1904. Within two years it boasted a collection of 73,573 volumes.

The Romanesque Ryerson Library that opened in 1904 underwent an extensive renovation beginning in 2000.

That collection contained a growing number of books by local authors. Horace Barnaby had moved to Kent County from Gratiot County as a 5-year-old in 1875. After graduation from the University of Michigan Law School in 1902, he started a practice in Grand Rapids. In 1908 Barnaby published his one and only novel, *The Decade: A Story of Political and Municipal Corruption,* a thinly veiled account of an actual Grand Rapids case that made local headlines for five years beginning in 1901. The scandal began in the late 1890s when City Attorney Lant K. Salsbury conspired with Stilson V. McLeod, a bookkeeper at the Old National Bank, to embezzle $30,000 to cover a series of investment blunders. The two intended to replace the funds before the misappropriation was discovered with their share of the proceeds of a scheme dreamed up by a New York City syndicate of con men. The plan was to convince the city to issue bonds far in excess of the actual cost of constructing a pipeline and pumping station to bring Lake Michigan water to Grand Rapids. The extra funds would be pocketed by the schemers. To ensure the success of the venture, Salsbury bribed the city clerk, 16 of the city's 24 aldermen, Mayor George R. Perry and other city and state officials. The plot went awry in 1901, however, when rumors of malfeasance surfaced. A grand jury indicted Salsbury and the New York syndicate and they were tried and convicted. Faced with the prospect of several years in Jackson Prison, Salsbury named the various government officials involved. Convoluted court proceedings, lasting from 1903 until 1906, resulted in the conviction and fining of 10 aldermen. Others involved, including Perry, managed to escape punishment.

The frontispiece of Horace Barnaby's 1908 novel about the great water scandal depicts an actor (right) who bears a strong resemblance to the actual culprit.

The man behind the great water scandal, Lant K. Salsbury, bribed city officials.

Amid court proceedings concerning a project to bring water to the city, ironically, Grand Rapids residents got more water than they bargained for in the spring of 1904. A cold winter with no thaw had resulted in a heavy snow pack on the ground and a thick ice jam on the river. Mid-March brought a heat wave and heavy

During the 1904 flood this big bob-sleigh floated two blocks down West Leonard Street before crashing into the storefront.

(Opposite page, top) Elton R. Shaw published his diatribe against alcohol in 1909.

Curious spectators inspect the remains of a Grand Rapids grocery store toppled during a fierce 1904 storm. *Calvin College Archives*

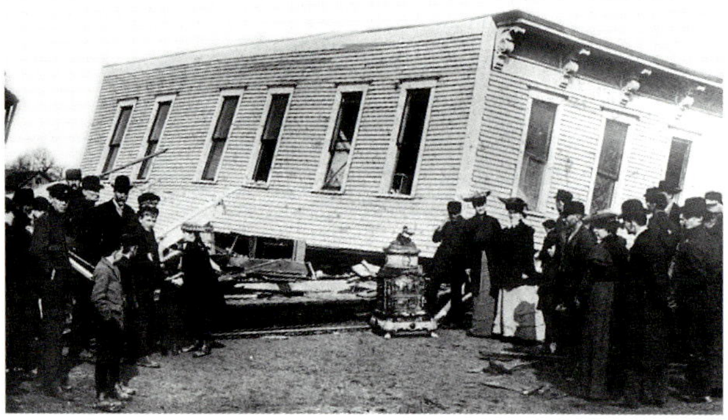

(Far right, below) A fire hose cart forded Bridge Street during the 1904 flood.

Melvin Trotter's novel about the redemption of some street toughs appeared in 1904.

rains. By March 25 the river reached flood stage and continued to rise. Three days later the water stood at more than five feet above flood stage at Pearl Street. The foul smelling water and mud completely inundated the west side neighborhoods and the lower areas of the east side, rising over the roofs of some homes. Factories closed and hundreds of residents retreated upstairs as the dark waters continued to swirl. Police Chief Albert A. Carroll secured 50 boats from Reeds Lake and elsewhere and patrolled the flooded streets to rescue stranded families. The water finally receded a week later, leaving a thick casing of mud within homes and causing some $1 million damage. The city began construction of concrete flood walls along the riverbanks in 1905 following a lesser flooding that spring. The year 1907 brought another damaging flood and finally in 1911 the flood walls stood complete.

A slum neighborhood located on a low tract of land along the river, south of the downtown core, pejoratively nicknamed "Bucktown" because about one-third of its residents were black, had taken the brunt of the big flood of 1904. Coincidently, that year also marked the publication of Melvin E. Trotter's novel, *Jimmy Moore of Bucktown*. A moralistic tract about the redemption of a gang of "street Arabs" by an evangelist temperance crusader, the book would become a best-seller and remain in print for more than a half a century. Based on actual characters, the volume also charted the beginnings of Trotter's famous City Rescue Mission. A reformed drunk who took the pledge through the influence of a Chicago evangelist in 1897, Trotter came to Grand Rapids three years later when a group of local businessmen including Myron Walker chose him to run the rescue mission they had founded. Despite never having delivered a temperance sermon before, Trotter proved a natural organizer. Over the decades he successively enlarged his facilities and when the "Great Drink Saver" preached, crowds sometimes jammed all 1,834 seats in the mission while 1,000 more stood outside.

In 1909 another literary temperance crusader, Elton R. Shaw, compiled and published at his Pearl Street company *Stories of Hell's Commerce or the Liquor Traffic in its True Light,* a 544-page compendium of anti-alcohol stories, poems and songs. A volume that took a lighter approach to the problems of society, Roy K. Moulton's *The Blue Jeans of Hoppertown* appeared in 1908. Moulton, a reporter for the Grand Rapids *Evening Press,* had begun publishing his witty, down-to-earth stories about local characters in the newspaper in 1903. Judging from some of his bon mots he was clearly not a teetotaler: "John D. Rockefeller says he never touched whiskey in his life, and, by jing, if he had, the rest of us wouldn't have got much."

Myrtle Koon Cherryman, whose verse also appeared in the *Evening Press,* published her first collection of poems, *Songs of Sunshine,* in 1908. Her sentimental poems about "hearth, heart and home" reminiscent of those written daily by Detroit newspaper poet Edgar A. Guest include such "gems" as "What's the Use" from her 1916 collection, *Rhymes for Rainy Days:*

"What's the use o' bein' snippy?
Makes you seem so queer an' dippy,
For it really is a joke —
Patronisn' other folk.
Think you seem superior, eh?
Well, it's quite the other way."

Another local poet, Ida Putnam Tubbs, published *A Book of Poems* in 1913. Much of her verse, a la Julia Moore, lamented the premature death of area people. When Albert Jennings, principal of the Union High School, passed suddenly in 1912, Tubbs penned, "We Miss Him:"

"Your work here was completed
When you finished last year's term
You stayed to spend vacation
But the Saviour for you yearned
So when vacation was ended,
He claimed you for His own..."

Other Grand Rapids rhymesters wrote lyrics to songs they hoped would strike the public's fancy. In 1909 Walter F. Miles took time from his job at the Desoto Coal Yard to team up with Newel H. Carrier and compose "You're the One I Dream About," an artfully illustrated piece of sheet music that began with the rather boastful lyrics "I've been in love a hundred times, and each time I would vow, that my sweet-heart is quite the best." Fortunately, neither songwriter gave up his day job. The two also collaborated on another less-than-successful piece, "Love is Like a Game of Cards."

That song might well have served as a requiem for a man fond of both ladies and gambling, the great boxing champion Stanley Ketchel. Born in Grand Rapids on September 14, 1885, of German and Polish ancestry, Ketchel (actually Stanislaus Kiecal) grew into a scrappy west side hooligan. At the age of 12 he hopped a freight train and landed in Chicago. When an ex-pug saw the young hobo knock the stuffing out of a bigger street tough he took Ketchel under his wing and give him his first real boxing lessons. Two years later Ketchel hopped another freight and ended up in Butte, Montana, where he found work as a barroom bouncer. Soon he was boxing for money and as the "Michigan Assassin" knocked out better and better opponents, his fame and the prize money grew.

Newel Carrier and Walter Miles' ballad was published in Grand Rapids in 1909.

Stanley Ketchel inprudently knocked heavyweight champion Jack Johnson down in a 1909 match. Seconds later Ketchel was out for the count.

Nat Fleischer, editor of *Ring Magazine,* described his style: "I've never seen a fighter who staged such an attack as Ketchel. He got his punches away from all angles, always was 'cocked' and in shooting position. If he missed with one hand he would nail his opponent with the other. He was game as a bulldog and tough as a bronco. There was no stopping him. He always was on top of his man, blazing away with both hands."

The five-foot-nine-inch,154-pound pugilist battled his way to the middleweight title in 1908. He lost it to Billy Papke on September 7 of that year and miraculously regained it seven weeks later by knocking out Papke in the 11th round. In 1909 he made the mistake of taking on heavyweight champion Jack Johnson in Colma, California. In the 12th round he knocked the huge black fighter to the mat for a count of eight. A few seconds later, however, he lay flat on his back as Johnson picked two of Ketchel's teeth out of his glove. Ketchel knocked out three opponents in rapid succession in 1910 when, debilitated from the high life of champagne and women he led between bouts, he took a vacation at a friend's ranch near Conway, Missouri. There, on October 15, 1910, the jealous boyfriend of a ranch waitress Ketchel had dallied with shot the boxer in the back. Ketchel died hours later. Some 7,000 to 8,000 mourners showed up at his funeral service in St. Adalbert's church — the largest Grand Rapids crowd that had ever assembled for such an occasion.

Nearly as many Grand Rapidians attended an event of a different kind six years later — an attempt to put "demon rum" in the grave. On November 6, 1916, former baseball player turned hellfire and brimstone evangelist, the Reverend Billy Sunday, roared into Grand Rapids as part of his month-long campaign to buoy the state drive to prohibit alcohol. Seven thousand men came to Sunday's colorful performance and when he asked who would vote for prohibition they all stood up. The following day they got a chance. On November 7, 1916, Michigan voters overwhelming approved the adoption of Prohibition effective May 1, 1918. Grand Rapids went "dry" by 3,000 votes, making it the largest city in the nation to do so at that time. Nearly two years before national Prohibition took effect, Grand Rapids' 160 saloons, 50 clubs that served liquor, seven wholesale liquor dealers and three breweries faced the bleak prospect of the "dry decades."

It did not take long for bootleggers and speakeasies to fill the void. Within months the first bootlegger was fined $100. In 1920 investigators unearthed evidence of a lucrative underground market, citing the case of "the factory mechanic who made whiskey at home nights, while his wife carried on the manufacture during the day. Between them they produced four or five gallons every 24 hours, which they put into bottles and jugs and sold to people who called at the house for $5 a pint." The following year, Grand Rapids police made as many arrests for intoxication as had been usual before the advent of the "noble experiment."

In an attempt to reduce the mayoral powers that had been flexed in support of labor during the 1911 strike, Grand Rapids also launched an experiment in civic reform. In August, 1916, voters passed a new charter that adopted the commission-manager form of government. The first commissioners were elected in April 1917, and the following month City Manager Gaylord C. Cummin began reorganizing departments. Cummin only lasted one year before resigning, citing "commission meddling," a trend that would mar several more decades of city government.

This 1920 map plotted the city's 160 saloons that closed following Prohibition. It also identifies the ethnic neighborhoods of the era.

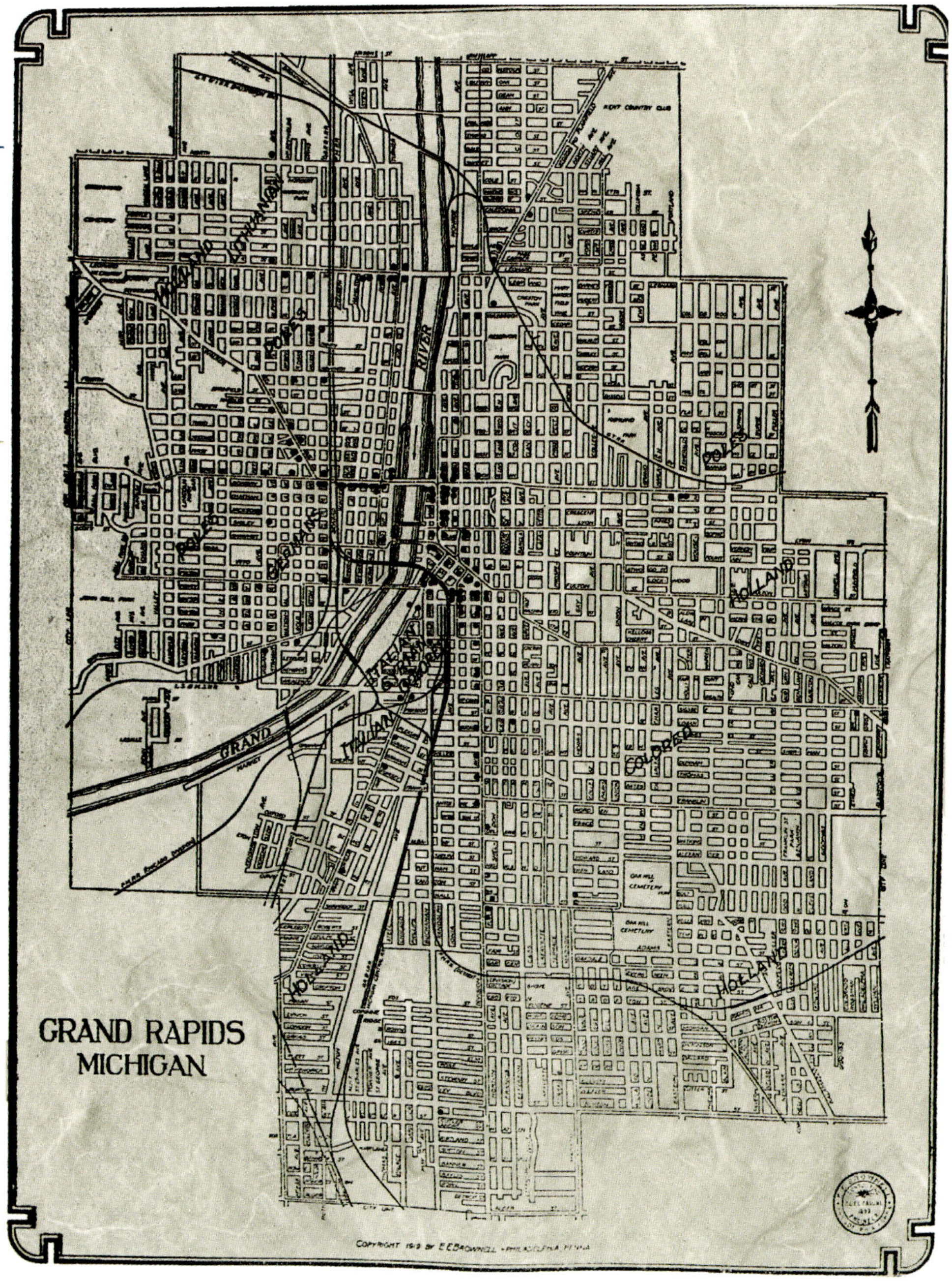

8 GRAND RAPIDS — A GOOD PLACE TO LIVE

Following the outbreak of violence in Serbia in 1914 that triggered a world war, the United States had inexorably been drawn into the conflict. And on April 6, 1917, the United States declared war on Germany. Prior to that, Grand Rapids citizens had not been of a single mind about entering the war. A significant pacifist movement existed, spurred perhaps by Homer L. Boyle's *History of Peace* published in 1902 and Daniel Roy Freeman's 1915 volume *God and War.* Another local author, Central High School English teacher Cornelia Steketee Hulst, published an anti-Woodrow Wilson article in 1916 that cost her her job two years later. But when war broke out, most opposition vanished to be replaced by intense anti-German sentiment.

HERPOLSHEIMER CO.

Men of the 32nd Division enjoy their first warm meal in 11 days near Mont St. Martin, August 8, 1918.

Sauerkraut became "liberty cabbage," frankfurters became hot dogs and later the Ottawa County town of Berlin changed its name to Marne in honor of the battle. Grand Rapids *Herald* editor Arthur H. Vandenberg, who ironically, would emerge as one of the country's leading isolationist politicians prior to World War II, led a successful campaign to eliminate German language courses from the Grand Rapids school curriculum, demanded that German-American newspapers close down and applauded local citizens of German heritage who changed their names. Homefront patriotism ran high as Grand Rapidians endured wheatless and meatless days, grew victory gardens and purchased millions of dollars worth of bonds during five Liberty Loan drives. City girls became "farmerettes" to replace the farm laborers who went to war. Martin F. Schram took time off from weaving rush furniture to pen the militant song, "For the Honor of the USA."

> "When the Star Spangled Banner is waving
> In battle whenever it be
> We'll be proud of our boys who are fighting
> With our Allies way over the sea"

During a patriotic rally at the Michigan Avenue Armory within a week after war was declared, 100 Grand Rapids young men volunteered for service. Ultimately 9,856 men and women from the county would serve in uniform. Companies I,K,L, and M of the Grand Rapids-based 32nd Michigan Infantry became part of the 126th Infantry U.S. National Guard that joined other Michigan and Wisconsin units to form the famous 32nd Division. Following training at Camp Grayling and Camp McArthur, Texas, in February 1918, the men of the 32nd Division embarked for France from New York on troop ships for a tense two-week long voyage under threat of submarine attack.

During the spring of 1918, a massive German offensive launched by Gen. Erich von Ludendorff had punched a bulge in the Allied lines that reached to within 50 miles of Paris by mid-July. French Gen. Ferdinand Foch, supreme commander of the western front, began a counter attack known as the Aisne-Marne Offensive on July 18. As part of that campaign, the men of the 32nd Division would earn the combat experience they craved — against battle-hardened German divisions — at a terrific cost. At the end of their first day of battle, one out of every five of the doughboys in the 126th Infantry would lie dead or wounded, a total of 460 casualties.

On July 30, the 126th moved into the front line trenches along the Ourcq River. The next day, the Michigan men came under intense artillery fire while

Seconds after a photographer snapped this picture of 32nd Division men snatching a moment of rest, a machine gun bullet pierced his hand.

advancing northeast toward their objectives, the village of Cierges and the dense Jomblets Woods. The unit dug in for the night and at 3:30 the next morning went over the top in bloody bayonet charges against entrenched German machine gunners. By nightfall the 126th had forced its way 500 yards into the Jomblets Woods, a strategic coup that forced the Germans to retreat.

The intense hand-to-hand fighting continued over the succeeding four days as the 32nd served as an elite shock division, to be hurled at the enemy "every time the Huns became obstinate." By August 6, the Aisne-Marne Offensive had resulted in an Allied victory with the German bulge pushed back to a line that stretched from Soissons to Reims. The Division, dubbed by the Germans "Les Terribles," rested a few days after the Aisne-Marne action before engaging in the Battle of Juvigny. Following that fierce struggle, the division remained in the thick of battle until the war's end. It compiled one of the most notable records of any of the 41 other American divisions that went to war. Fighting on five fronts in three major offensives, it vanquished 23 German divisions. The 32nd Division adopted a red arrow as its shoulder patch, signifying "that the division shot through every line the enemy put before it."

During the six months it served under fire, the division suffered 14,000 casualties. Over 800 of its men received decorations for valor from the American, French and Belgian governments. Five members of the 126th from Grand Rapids, Charles E. Cunningham, Dougald Ferguson, Alexander Salik, Nicholas Smith and John J. Zeldan, were awarded the distinguished service cross, the nation's second-highest award for bravery in combat. Grand Rapids men in other units who received distinguished service crosses include: John G. Emery, Chester C. Kromer, Henry D. McNaughton, Frank S. Marek, Walter J. Steede and Bernard Van't Hof. A total of 244 servicemen from the city paid the supreme sacrifice during "the war to end all wars" as well as six members of the "Polar Bear" division that fought the Red Russian Army in Siberia after the war had officially ended.

As terrible as the World War proved to be, its waning months brought a menace that would kill many more than died in battle — the Great Influenza Pandemic of 1918. Transmitted in March 1918 to Europe from China, where it had raged since 1910, the viral disease raced through the armies. The Germans called it *Blitzkatarrh*. The Allied forces named it the Spanish influenza because of a particularly virulent outbreak in Spain. Its symptoms included fever and chills, sinus infections, pneumonia and encephalitis. The disease proved particularly fatal to pregnant women, children under two and, strangely, those between 20 and 40 years of age, who were slaughtered by the millions.

In America it hit like a biological bombshell. Ultimately, one out of every four citizens fell ill. The plague reached Michigan at the end of September 1918. The first death in Grand Rapids occurred on October 2. By October 18 nearly 2,000 new cases across the state were being reported daily. On that date, Dr. R.M. Olin, commissioner of the Michigan Department of Health, issued an order closing churches, dance halls, poolrooms and all places of amusement, and prohibiting funerals or public gatherings of any kind.

The death toll in Grand Rapids remained low until in early December it increased dramatically. Butterworth and the other local hospitals overflowed with patients and even the student nurses found themselves working seven days a week, giving tepid baths to patients and repeatedly changing perspiration-soaked bedding. By Christmas Eve the outbreak had run its course in Grand Rapids, leaving 266 residents dead. Nationwide, the pandemic claimed

At this delousing station the Red Arrow doughboys bid goodbye to their "cooties."

This view of Monroe Avenue from Campau Square shows a bustling Grand Rapids of the 1920s.

Calvin College Archives

(Far left)
In 1920, The La More Agency on Division Avenue used a big blackboard to market to "the city of homeowners."

The clubhouse and new concrete runway of the Kent County Airport looked like this in 1928.

the lives of more than half a million, and some 20 million perished across the globe.

When the doughboys returned home to Grand Rapids, they found a city struggling to cope with a rapidly changing society. Prohibition and women's newly won suffrage vied with disillusion over the horrors of the war to end all wars to usher in the "Roaring 20s," a decade of exuberance — bobbed hair and bathtub gin, the Charleston and Charles Lindbergh, flagpole-sitters and goldfish-swallowers, flappers, sheiks and raccoon coats, as well as the abandoned hopes and morals of a "lost generation."

Nationally, the war had triggered a dramatic rise in inflation. In Grand Rapids between 1917 and 1920 the cost of living rose by 70 percent. Fortunately, average local wages rose faster than prices, doubling their prewar levels and resulting in an unprecedented level of prosperity. In 1921 the slogan coined by the Advertising Club, "Grand Rapids, a good place to live," rang true. Traditionally a city of homeowners, by 1920 Grand Rapids ranked 34th among all American cities in its annual number of building permits and second in the nation in per capita home ownership. In 1925 alone, 2,000 new homes went up.

Many of those new homes sported garages as the automobile became an integral part of American culture. In 1915, only 6,672 passenger cars were registered in the city. Five years later that figure had risen to 15,101. In 1925 residents drove more than 53,000 automobiles about the city's 380 miles of streets, and 208 service stations pumped 25 million gallons of gas. That year the state legislature passed the first gasoline tax at two cents per gallon.

As more automobiles crowded city streets, accidents increasingly became a grim statistic. The Grand Rapids Department of Public Safety produced a pamphlet in 1926 that analyzed the leading causes of accidents. It noted, "792 persons in Grand Rapids left their homes in 1925 after bidding cheerful farewells to their dear ones only to return injured or maimed or to be returned cold in death." Nearly 6,000 automobile accidents were reported to police that year.

The 1920s also witnessed the practical development of another mode of transportation — flight. A primitive

This c. 1925 view of the Pantlind Hotel, now the Amway Grand, portrayed a busy street scene of cars, trolleys, pedestrians and an occasional horse-drawn vehicle.

As scrawled by a former owner on this sheet music cover, Charles Lindbergh visited Grand Rapids on August 12, 1927.

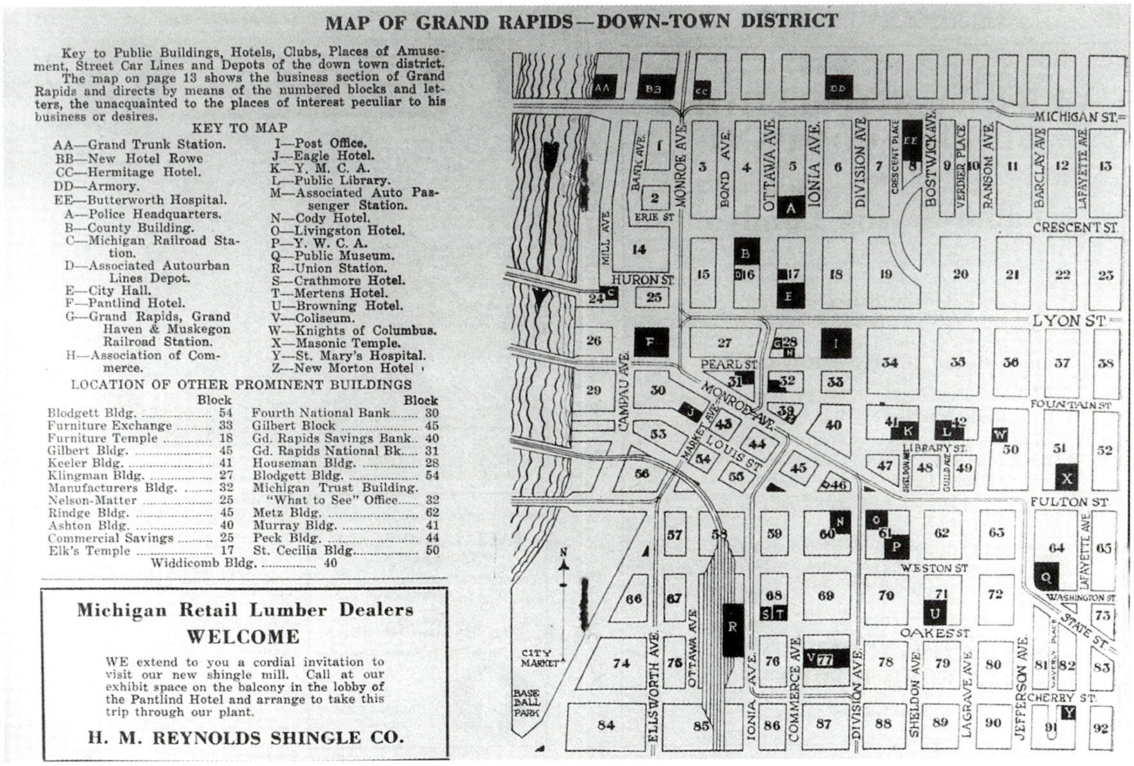

This 1922 map, prepared for a lumber dealers' convention, identifies what were then the key features of the downtown district.

airfield had been constructed by the Grand Rapids Aero Club in 1919. Six years later Detroiter William B. Stout addressed the Grand Rapids Rotary Club to promote the concept of regularly scheduled inter-city airline passenger service. The idea caught on and a community fund drive resulted in an upgraded airport complete with a passenger terminal. On July 31, 1926, a huge crowd cheered as a Ford-Stout monoplane christened *Miss Grand Rapids* glided down the runaway to inaugurate daily Grand Rapids to Detroit flights, giving the city claim to "the first strictly passenger airline in the United States."

On August 12, 1927, another crowd of 100,000 lined the road from the airport to John Ball Park to welcome "the lone eagle of the air," Charles Lindbergh. A national hero and symbol of the potential of aviation since his daring trans-Atlantic flight the previous May, "Lucky Lindy" touched down in Grand Rapids in his *Spirit of St. Louis* as part of a cross-country tour promoting air travel. At John Ball Park Lindbergh gave a speech touting the teaching of aviation in public schools.

While the city was not quite ready for aviation training in grade schools, Grand Rapids could pride itself on the calibre of its educational system in the 1920s. As early as 1916, a survey of the city completed by Charles H. Judd had noted: "In general, Grand Rapids shows itself a leader in the extent to which it taxes itself for schools. Furthermore, although it spends less for general city departments than most cities of its class, it gives a larger per cent of its municipal revenue to schools than any other city of the same size." The 1920s witnessed hectic high school and junior high construction programs, including the avant garde Davis Vocation and Technical School begun in 1922.

During the 1920s city engineers continued to grapple with a long-standing problem — pollution of the Grand River. As a result of a suit brought against the city by Wyoming Township in 1913, the Michigan Supreme Court had mandated "Grand Rapids cease pollution of the river with sewage and industrial waste." Studies by city engineers and consultants dragged on until 1922 when the filing of a preliminary report brought a pre-emptory order by the state board of health to install a modern sewage disposal plant. The following year voters overwhelmingly passed a $5 million bond issue to fund "a complete plant for the disposal and eliminating of all noxious waste matter." Despite completion of the project during the late 1920s,

the system proved incapable of jointly handling sewage and storm sewer runoff during rain storms and periodically pollutants continued to pour into the river to the detriment of downriver communities and Lake Michigan.

The city paused briefly from its frenetic pace of development in 1926 to celebrate the centennial of the arrival of the fur trader that it considers its founder. Held September 23-26, the Campau Centennial Celebration featured a pioneer pageant recreating the landing of Campau, the first marriage and an "Indian pay day;" historical style show held at the Armory; a huge display of pioneer and Indian relics at the Klingman Building and a massive pageant of progress "spectacle extraordinary" with 6,000 participants. A fleet of 27 spanking new streetcars were featured in the parade, which ended with a huge bonfire of the old streetcars.

(Above) Visitors to Grand Rapids in the 1920s sometimes took home as souvenirs beautiful hand-painted plates depicting local scenery.

Partly as a result of Charles Garfield's planning, beautiful trees shaded the city's boulevards in the 1920s. Pictured are the famous Bostwick Avenue elms.

New York sculptor Pompeo Coppini's bronze statue of John Ball welcomes visitors to the zoo that Ball donated to the city.

The year 1926 also marked a celebration of its heritage by the Herpolsheimer Company. Since its founding by William G. Herpolsheimer and Charles G.A. Voight in 1870 as a small dry goods store, the firm had grown into a Grand Rapids institution complete with a fashion salon and huge furniture galleries. Dean of local newspapermen Arthur Scott White wrote a pamphlet for the occasion delineating the city's progress. He noted that Grand Rapids in 1926 had grown to 165,000 residents, 35,000 of whom worked in industry. Other businesses included 428 grocers, 52 furniture outlets, 57 clothing stores, 100 drug stores, 100 bakeries and more than 1,200 retail outlets. The city supported 1,500 teachers, 200 lawyers, 200 doctors, 125 dentists and 125 ministers preaching in 204 churches. Of 600 factories, 72 made furniture. Grand Rapids boasted the largest factories in the world, producing refrigerators, carpet sweepers, show cases, gypsum products, window sash pulleys, cardboard boxes, metal belt lacers, sticky fly paper, excelsior, woodworking machinery, home furniture, school seats, opera chairs and church pews.

And beyond its booming industrial success, "Grand Rapids, a good place to live" prided itself on its civic beauty, particularly the numerous trees that lined its streets. Much of the city's natural beauty came through the efforts of Charles W. Garfield, banker, legislator, conservationist and "nature lover supreme." Over the course of a 40-year career beginning in 1894, Garfield shaped the city's physical appearance. As head of the Board of Trade, precursor to the Chamber of Commerce, Garfield spearheaded a drive to plant tens of thousands of seedlings along streets in the 1890s. A 1920 article in *Survey Magazine* noted that because of those verdant shade trees, tidy lawns and flower gardens: "it would be difficult to find another city in America of its size with the same degree of civic pride — a pride very different from mere boasting and boosting — which has its origins in a real participation of each home in the effort to make the city beautiful and liveable."

In 1924 Stewart Edward White returned to the scene of his youth to use Grand Rapids as the model of the town "Little Falls" in his novel *The Glory Hole*. He echoed similar sentiments: "Every one of the sixty-odd thousands who made up the population of Little Falls believed that Little Falls was the most beautiful city in America. Nor was this entirely the judgement of inexperience. One met Little Falls people all over the world: probably no city of its size could produce as many assiduous travelers. They would tell you that themselves very soon after they had met you. In three seasons of the year there was something to be said for their opinion of the place. It occupied a bend in the river and the low hills on either side. Its streets were wide; and bordering them all, down to the very edge of the business district, stood double rows of broad-leaf maples. All the residential section was set in lawns. Even the workmen's small cottages had their little plots of green; and some fortunate tradition had almost eliminated fences between them. It was pleasant of a warm day to walk or drive beneath the deep continuous mottled shade, with the close-clipped green grass on either side, and the mingled sound of cicadas and whirling sprinklers. Most of the houses, especially of the well-to-do, were set back from the street. You saw wide verandas and glimpsed dark cool interiors through open doors. Then as you gained the heights and could look down, you saw beneath you apparently an almost unbroken forest. Here and there a roof or a chimney showed, or the spire of a church thrust forth; but save for these and the tall electric light towers, you could never have imagined a city below you."

White was at the height of his career in 1924 when he published *The Glory Hole*. The successful author of 26 novels, travel stories and biographies, rich and happily married for 28 years, White had settled down in California. There, he came under the influence of one of that state's many outre movements. It started in 1919 when he and a number of partygoers tried their hands at a ouija board using an inverted shot glass as the indicator. When the device repeatedly spelled out "Betty," a young woman of that name was urged to participate. The glass went wild when she touched it. Among the cryptic messages spelled out, the phrase "Get a pencil" repeatedly occurred. Several days later, Betty did get a pencil and found herself scribbling a message from beyond the grave. She shared her newfound psychic powers with her friend, White, and thus began a 17-year relationship during which the two explored the mysteries of the hereafter.

The Rev. Eli W. Sprague wrote widely read spiritualist books in Grand Rapids during the early 1930s.

Following his beloved wife's demise, White began writing a series of spiritualism books, beginning with *The Betty Book* in 1937, based partially on material dictated by his departed wife through a medium. To many, spiritualism was no laughing matter and *The Betty Book* went through at least six large printings. Grand Rapids in 1937 supported no less than seven spiritualist churches.

Among the nationally known practitioners of the occult sciences who called Grand Rapids home in the 1930s, was the Rev. Eli W. Sprague. Born in North Boston, New York, in 1847, the year before three teenaged sisters launched modern American spiritualism via communication with a mysterious wall knocker, Sprague fell under the sway of the religion as a boy. In 1881 he and his wife, Clarissa, became spiritualist missionaries, touring practically every state to organize congregations of believers. The Spragues settled down in Detroit in 1907 and he served as pastor of the city's First Spiritualist Church. Following Clarissa's death Sprague moved to Grand Rapids where he published *The Science of Magnetic, Mental and Spiritual Healing* in 1930 and the following year *Letters From Heaven,* containing Clarissa's correspondence from the other world, "automatically written through his hand and mind." Sprague joined his wife in the "Spirit World" in 1933.

According to her husband's writings, Clarissa Adelia Sprague continued to inspire him after her demise via spiritual communication.

The Grand Rapids Sprague departed in 1933 was far from a heavenly place. The Great Depression, triggered by the stock market crash of 1929, had reached its nadir. The furniture industry, struggling since the mid-1920s due to overproduction and competition from southern

(Far right) Fruit vendors and horse-drawn milk wagons continued to clip-clop down neighborhood streets in the 1930s. *Calvin College Archives*

Kent County Health Department nurses posed with their fleet of automobiles in the late 1930s.

manufacturers, had been devastated. Grand Rapids firms began dropping like flies. Berkey and Gay, the city's largest manufacturer, stunned the community when it closed its doors in 1931. Of the city's 72 furniture manufacturing companies operating in 1928, nearly one-half suffered a similar fate by 1940. Employment in the industry dropped from more than 12,000 to less than 3,000. The average hourly wage slipped from 63 to 33 cents an hour in 1933.

Monroe Avenue seemed a somber place during the nadir of the Depression.

Bankers foreclosed on mortgages and evicted families before their institutions, too, went belly up. Unemployed and homeless, hundreds of desperate men milled before city hall. In May 1929 Grand Rapids' welfare role numbered 749 persons. By December 1932 it had swelled to 34,300 citizens in need of food, fuel and clothing. City manager George Welsh, who had taken the helm of a city with empty coffers in May 1929 and built up a surplus by the time the Depression reached serious proportions, faced an unprecedented challenge to local government's responsibility in time of need.

Welsh, a self-made man who had worked his way up from newsboy to successful printer and publisher, responded promptly and boldly. With city funds he purchased 30,000 bushels of potatoes in northern Michigan to feed the hungry. He established shelters for unemployed single men and developed municipal work projects to grade streets, improve parks, stabilize the river banks, shovel snow, tear down dilapidated downtown structures and recycle the debris. Needy workers were paid in scrip, with hours allocated according to the size of their family, redeemable in a city-run, nonprofit store that stocked food, clothing and even furniture.

Despite national acclaim for Welsh's success in making Grand Rapids, "a city where everyone has a job," local critics, led by the Rev. Alfred W. Wishart of Fountain Street Baptist Church, denounced governmental meddling in the free enterprise system, even when it was broken. An

Constructed in 1932-33, the George R. Welsh Civic Auditorium honors the name of Grand Rapids' prominent city manager and mayor.

(Far right)
The proprietor of this typical Grand Rapids neighborhood grocery store of the 1930s needed to be fluent in Dutch as well as English.
Calvin College Archives

Grand Rapids' favorite son, Gerald Ford, shown here in 1934, did not let the Depression prevent him from starring as a football player at the University of Michigan.

investigation by a "Committee of One Hundred" businessmen resulted in an adverse report and Welsh resigned shortly after. Ultimately, Franklin Roosevelt's New Deal "alphabet programs" removed much of the burden of public relief and make-work projects from local governments. Welsh returned to office in 1938, this time as mayor, and secured Public Works Administration (PWA) funding for construction of a 30-mile Grand Rapids to Lake Michigan pipeline. Hundreds of local unemployed worked on the project. When completed in 1940, it finally erased the stigma of the Great Water Scandal of 40 years before.

During the Depression, many Grand Rapidians took advantage of their forced idleness to read. In 1931 and 1932 the Grand Rapids Public Library experienced the largest annual increase in patronage in its history, as hundreds of unemployed desperately scanned out-of-town newspapers for help wanted ads. Local writers, too, catered to a growing national demand for literature. Born in the Netherlands in 1905, David Cornel DeJong immigrated with his family to Grand Rapids at the age of 13. Not knowing a word of English, he enrolled in a Grand Rapids grade school but quit to go to work two years later. At the age of 18 he began working his way through high school and Calvin College. He set his first novel, *Belly Fulla Straw,* published in 1934, in Grand Rapids. Based on his own family's experiences, it relates the story of Harmen Idema, a Dutch immigrant who arrived in Grand Rapids to "discover a clannishness among the Dutch-Americans for which he is not prepared, an acute consciousness that they are the very elect, and solid instances of chicanery mixed with apparent piety." The novel launched a national reputation for DeJong. He won a prestigious literary award in 1937 and prior to his death in 1967 published some 20 other books.

Many Grand Rapids citizens, of course, did not appreciate DeJong's indictment of Dutch-American culture. Constance Rourke wrote a less-than-glowing review of the volume. Rourke, a Vassar graduate who had grown up in Grand Rapids and continued to live there until her death in 1941, achieved a notable literary career beginning with the publication of an article about Michigan's mythical lumberjack, Paul Bunyan, in 1918. Credited with founding the American studies movement, Rourke wrote seven popular books, including biographies of Davy Crockett, James Audubon, Horace Greeley and Lotta Crabtree.

The city's self-esteem got another literary jolt in 1935 with the publication of Arnold Gingrich's *Cast Down the Laurel,* "the book that shook Grand Rapids." Set in the city where he was born and lived until graduating from the University of Michigan in 1925, Gingrich's novel about the local musical scene especially stung those who recognized themselves in the uncomplimentary, thinly veiled characters. Gingrich ultimately achieved more lasting success through editorship of the magazine he founded, *Esquire.*

The last of a trilogy of Depression-era novels that pilloried Grand Rapids society appeared in 1937. Irving J. Bissell's *A Sow's Ear* told the story of the local country club set through the exploits of the fictitious Jim Houlton, a wealthy Grand Rapids businessman who pursued numerous affairs with the wives and daughters of his associates, to the ultimate destruction of his marriage.

But fictional exposés of the city's foibles could not seriously detract from the recognized fact that even in the Depression Grand Rapids was a great place to live and work. A highly respected sociologist, Dr. Edward L. Thorndike of Columbia University, studied life in 310 American cities during the last years of the 1930s. He evaluated 37 factors, such as the infant mortality rate; per capita public expenditures for schools, libraries and museums; public park acreage; rarity of extreme poverty; average wages; and number of homes owned. When he tabulated his statistics, Thorndike found that Grand Rapids ranked first among Michigan cities and seventh in the United States in terms of general quality of life.

Nevertheless, the city's population, which had grown from 137,634 in 1920 to 168,594 in 1930, remained virtually unchanged through the succeeding decade. As the 1930s drew to a close, the American economy finally began to shake off the deadening effects of the Great Depression. Various metal working industries had replaced furniture making as the leading Grand Rapids employer. Federal government and Allied spending for war materiel spurred increased industrial production, and employment reached heights unattained since the bright days of the 1920s. But as the unsolved problems inherited from the previous generation's world war avalanched into another global conflict, fear of war replaced economic uncertainty.

Not unlike the U.S. response to the outbreak of World War I when Woodrow Wilson campaigned in 1916 under the slogan "He kept us out of War," initially the dominant American mindset favored neutrality, if not outright isolationism. Grand Rapids' Senator Arthur H. Vandenberg emerged as one of the chief national advocates of what he termed "insulationism."

Born in Grand Rapids in 1884, Vandenberg had pulled himself out of poverty by his own bootstraps to become the political voice of the Grand Rapids *Herald*. He entered politics in 1928, moving directly from the editor's chair of the *Herald* to the U.S. Senate when Michigan's Republican Gov. Fred Green named him to fill the unexpired term created by the death of Democrat Woodbridge N. Ferris. He won election on his own later that year and again in 1934. Initially ambivalent about Roosevelt's New Deal reforms — he voted against repeal of Prohibition and in favor of the Social Security Act of 1935 — he ultimately became one of the president's chief adversaries. He championed U.S. noninvolvement in Japan's war against China and Hitler's aggression in Europe. But when Nazi bombs began falling on Holland in May 1940, he suddenly wavered. Later that year he made an unsuccessful bid for the Republican presidential nomination. Then on December 7, 1941, with Japan's treacherous attack on Pearl Harbor, "a day that will live in infamy," the nation's tightwire walk over the abyss of war ended and America faced its greatest challenge since the days of the Revolution.

(Above)
Irving Bissell's racy 1937 novel pilloried the Grand Rapids country club set.

Senator Arthur Vandenberg championed isolationism prior to Pearl Harbor.

By the late 1930s Monroe Avenue had begun to reflect the city's recovery from the Depression.

EPILOGUE

THE TUMULTUOUS RUSH TOWARD THE 21ST CENTURY

Grand Rapids citizens soon shouldered their share of the load when their country entered World War II. More than 30,000 young men and women from Kent County served in uniform during the war and 1,022 died. Local industry rapidly geared up for the war effort, helping to win Michigan the title of "Arsenal of Democracy." The Fisher Body Plant turned to producing airplane parts, Hayes Manufacturing converted to production of torpedo bodies and bomb fins, and it hired 1,500 women to manufacture parachutes. The Irwin Furniture Company milled components of M-1 carbines and other local companies turned out helicopters, anti-aircraft guns and boat propellers.

The Grand Rapids homefront pitched in as never before, and increasing numbers of "Rosie the Riveters" replaced men in factories to perform labor of which they had never been thought capable. Families proudly displayed service flags with a star for every member in the service. Home guards drilled, factories and homes practiced blackout regulations and air-raid wardens scanned the skies for enemy planes. As price controls and rationing of food, tires and gasoline became a way of life, men patched up their old cars and women their nylons, and war gardens grew on vacant lots. Scrap drives collected iron, aluminum, rags and even kitchen grease; bond drives went over the top; and children bought war stamps and balled up tin foil.

The supreme effort paid off and by early 1945 victory was within sight. In January of that year, Vandenberg, who had a gradually swung away from isolationism, helped found the United Nations. That same month the Grand Rapids city chemist began dumping barrels of fluoride into the local water supply. Grand Rapids' pioneering experiment would pave the way for fluoridation of municipal water systems across the nation, thereby dramatically lessening juvenile tooth decay.

Even before the war ended, the Grand Rapids Chamber of Commerce began planning for postwar reconversion and recruitment of new companies to ensure a healthy diversified economy. When the veterans returned home they found jobs in new industries that had moved to Grand Rapids, including

Monroe Avenue bustled with traffic in 1950.

Lear Avia and the General Motors Diesel Equipment plant. Other established firms such as the Metal Office Furniture Company (later Steelcase), the Rapistan Company and the American Seating Company expanded rapidly during the postwar era. By 1953 General Motor's three Grand Rapids plants employed 8,900 and the automotive giant had become the city's largest employer.

The local construction industry also boomed in answer to pent-up dreams of home ownership. From July 1947 to July 1948 the city issued 6,286 building permits and more single-family homes went up than in any previous year. In 1949 householders found a new reason to stay home with the advent of the city's first television station WLAV-TV. Two years later it became WOOD-TV, and soon "Howdie Doodie," "I Love Lucy" and "Buck Barry" became an integral part of local popular culture.

Also in 1949 Grand Rapids received national attention for its postwar efforts when the National Municipal League named it an "All-America City." Grand Rapids would win that honor again in 1960 and 1981.

The dawn of the 1950s meant a lot of things to Grand Rapidians. For many veterans it meant pulling uniforms out of mothballs and marching off to fight another war, or "police action" — this time in Korea. More than 6,000 from Kent County served and 40 gave their lives. For Grand Rapids motorists the 1950s were a time when "a dollar's worth of regular" meant something as they nuzzled great gas-guzzling cars up to the pump — cars sporting shark-like fins which grew bigger and sharper as the decade wore on. Others remember the early 1950s as the McCarthy era with its communist witch hunts or the dawn of the Eisenhower-led Republican ascendancy.

The 1950s marked tremendous growth in suburban development, ringing Grand Rapids with mile after mile of new roads lined with cookie-cutter homes. To preserve its tax base, the city responded with numerous annexations to swell its size from 23.5 square miles in 1958 to 44 square miles four years later. The year 1958 also witnessed the beginnings of a trend that would dramatically alter the local landscape in the succeeding decades — the construction of the area's first shopping center, Rogers Plaza on 28th Street. Subsequent explosive commercial development would render 28th Street the busiest thoroughfare, exclusive of expressways, in the state.

In 1955, construction began on the region's first expressway, I-131, connecting the city with Kalamazoo. Over the next six years residents watched as bulldozers leveled more than 1,000 west side homes, as the S-curves snaked their way past the downtown core. The expressway opened in December 1961 to be followed three years later by the first 12-mile stretch of I-96. Other transportation

Grand Rapids' skyline of the 1950s would drastically change in the ensuing decades.

(Opposite page) Originally erected in 1926 to honor the city's World War I dead, the monuments and reflecting pool in Veterans Park were later modified to also pay homage to those who gave their lives in other wars.

This Hall Street residence of the William Massie family was one of more than 1,000 west side homes bulldozed to make room for the I-131expressway.

needs were met in 1963 with the opening of the new Kent County Airport.

The local economy boomed in the 1960s, spurred by plant expansions and the arrival of new companies lured by improved transportation facilities, tax abatements and platting of industrial parks. Area schools grew by leaps and bounds and hospitals staged massive fund drives for expansions. By the mid-1960s the city's "big four" hospitals accommodated 70,000 patients annually. A long cherished desire for a local four-year college became reality in 1963 with the opening of Grand Valley State College. The institution would grow to become a university with an enrollment of more than 15,000 students by the 1990s.

Completed in 1888, the magnificent Grand Rapids City Hall fell victim to urban renewal in the late 1960s.

The 1960s witnessed the continued emergence of outlying shopping malls: Breton Village in 1962, Eastbrook in 1969, followed by the Woodland Mall and the North Kent Mall the next year. As shoppers responded to the convenience of malls, the downtown retail core suffered. In an attempt to revitalize the downtown, the city launched an urban renewal project in 1962 which over the succeeding decade would see numerous architectural gems, including the magnificent Romanesque City Hall, fall to the wrecking ball. But from the rubble would arise the breathtaking splendor of Grand Rapids today.

Grand Rapidians who lived through the 1960s and 1970s remember an era that began with the bright promise of the Kennedy administration to deteriorate into one of the most turbulent times in American history. Assassinations, protest demonstration, race riots and the Vietnam War filled headlines. Grand Rapids citizens learned new geography: The Bay of Pigs and Da Nang, Woodstock and Kent State. Some rode in Mustang convertibles and Volkswagen vans, wore Beatle boots and miniskirts, listened to Bob Dylan, the Mamas and the Papas, the Beach Boys and Motown. It was a time of school desegregation, flower power, the women's movement, long hair, LBJ, Tricky Dick and Watergate.

By 1965 the draft had become a reality for the area's young men and over the succeeding eight years thousands would serve in the Vietnam War. That year Grand Rapids mourned the death of the first serviceman from Kent County and ultimately his and the names of 130 others would be enshrined on "the Wall" in Washington. As the war dragged on, some Grand Rapids citizens staged peace vigils and protested U.S. involvement in the war, culminating in a City Commission resolution in May 1971 calling for an end to the war.

In Detroit the hot summer of 1967 flared into an ugly race riot. The destruction and looting ended only with the arrival of the 82nd Airborne Division. Grand Rapids experienced a milder version of the racial strife that July as hundreds raged through downtown streets smashing windows and venting frustration. The two-day-long confrontation resulted in scores of injuries, the arrest of more than 200 and hundreds of thousands of dollars in property damage. The city's black population had grown from 4,000 in 1940 to more than 20,000 by 1967. Most lived in segregated ghettos and found employment largely in menial jobs at substandard pay. De facto school segregation was a reality. In 1968 the city launched a plan to improve the situation by integrating the school system through busing. It brought mixed results and actual racial equality has yet to be achieved.

Twin memorials to Kent County veterans who died in Vietnam joined the other monuments in Veterans Park in 1974.

The decade of the 1960s ended with the installation of a new symbol for the city, a huge modernistic public sculpture designed by Alexander Calder. In celebration of the first phase of downtown urban renewal, *La Grande Vitesse* was dedicated on June 14, 1969. Grand Rapids' own Gerald R. Ford, then minority leader of the House of Representatives, told the crowd gathered for the occasion that "this sculpture dedicated here today raises the quality of life in our community." That statement proved prophetic as the following decades brought renewed vitality to the city. In 1970 came the first downtown Festival of the Arts, a three-day celebration that would eventually draw 500,000 participants each June.

The following year concerned local preservationists helped create the Heritage Hill National Historic District to ensure survival of some of the city's most significant domestic architecture. The year 1978 saw the beginnings of another Grand Rapids tradition, the Old Kent River Bank Run, an annual May event that draws thousands of sweating contestants to attempt its 25-kilometer course.

Continued efforts to sustain the downtown resulted in the opening of the Monroe Avenue Pedestrian Mall in 1980. The experiment would prove of dubious value and work to reopen the street to vehicular traffic began in 1996. In 1981, the Ford Museum opened, a monument to the city's native son who had been appointed vice president in 1973 and upon the resignation of Richard Nixon the following year become president. In 1981, also, the remodeled Amway Grand Plaza Hotel (formerly the Pantlind) opened. In honor of those accomplishments and the dedication of the New Grand Rapids Art Museum, the city staged "Celebration on the Grand," which evolved into an annual end-of-summer festival.

This training capsule from the Apollo moon exploration program was transformed into a time capsule to cap the city's celebration of the nation's bicentennial in 1976.

The Gerald R. Ford Presidential Museum was dedicated in 1981.

The modernistic 29-story Amway Grand Plaza west wing opened in 1983.

The "flowering of the arts" would continue through the 1980s and 1990s with construction of DeVos Hall to house the local symphony, opera and ballet; the 1994 dedication of the magnificent new public museum; improvements to John Ball Park and its zoo; beautification of parks and walkways adjacent the Grand River and a complete renovation of the Ryerson Library slated to begin in 2000.

In the meantime the city's economic climate remained healthy as the mid-1980s witnessed the beginnings of an unprecedented era of prosperity. By 1995 the area boasted a diversified array of 27 manufacturing plants that each employed more than 500 workers. Steelcase led the roster with 8,100 employees followed by the Amway Corporation and General Motors. Since the mid-1980s both Steelcase and Amway had achieved annual sales of more than $1 billion. By 1990 Kent County had become the fastest growing region in Michigan.

The Plaza Towers dominate a portion of the city's eastern skyline.

As Grand Rapid moves toward the bright promise of the 21st century, problems relating to its heritage remain. The assumed superiority of one ethnic group over another that began with Indian-White relations in pioneer days continues. The crooked downtown streets resulting from the rival founders' stubbornness still baffle visitors. The lack of a living wage for all workers and the disparity in pay between the sexes that troubled turn-of-century social crusaders still occur as does the occasional raw sewage overflow into the Grand River.

Yet the same spirit of cooperation, determination and courage that has made Grand Rapids one of the nation's most vibrant urban success stories cannot fail to ultimately resolve even those ancient dilemmas.

In the summer of 2000, imaginatively decorated fish, as in this example in front of the Van Andel Museum, proliferated throughout the downtown.

PARTNERS IN GRAND RAPIDS

Table of Contents

BUILDING A GREATER
GRAND RAPIDS

Grand Rapids real estate development and construction companies shape tomorrow's skyline, providing and improving working and living space for area residents.

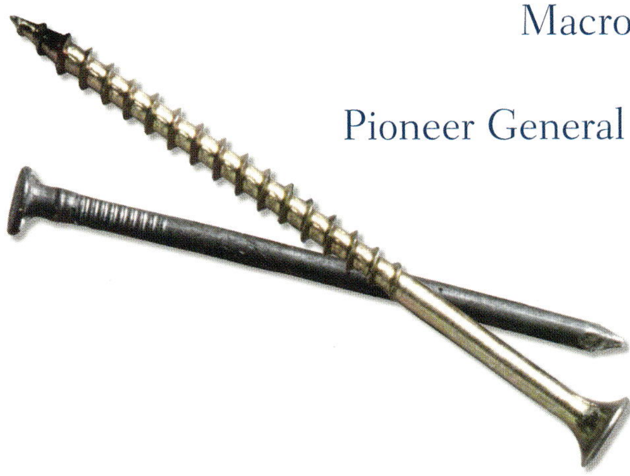

GRAND RAPIDS SASH & DOOR AND THE HAGER GROUP OF COMPANIES

As the first truck backed out of the warehouse, smiles on the watching faces grew, and several people clapped their hands. It was 1928 and this was a day to be remembered. It signaled the birth of T.W. Hager Lumber Company. As that first load of lumber went merrily on its way through the nestled, rolling hills of Grand Rapids making its first wholesale delivery, Titus W. Hager beamed with quiet contentment.

Titus W. Hager, founder of Hager Lumber Company

Hager, after a successful career in lumbering, set out on a mission. He had the burning desire to create a family-owned business that he could pass down to generations of his children and grandchildren. Hager was the type of man who remained humble and in the background of his accomplishments. He went about the business of creating innovative, successful companies with an eye on the future for helping family, the community and the environment.

Some time after Hager founded his first company, he saw another opportunity to serve the building industry that would create a full-service organization. He later purchased Grand Rapids Sash & Door Co., founded in 1924, and served as its president from 1946-1961 while growing Hager Lumber Company. Both companies still exist and fall under the corporate umbrella of "The Hager Group of Companies."

After Titus W. Hager's passing at the age of 76, the companies were passed down to the children and grandchildren, just as he had planned. Titus J. Hager took control of Hager Lumber Co. in 1955. Control of the company was passed to Timothy Hager in 1990, and Titus R. Hager assumed control following Timothy's death in 1998.

Grand Rapids Sash & Door was acquired by Titus J. Hager in 1961. Titus R. Hager assumed control in 1987 and is the current chairman and CEO; Titus J. Hager now serves as a co-chairman.

Seven great-grandchildren with a bright future are involved in varying roles within the company because of the gift their great-grandfather created for them.

With a focus on growing the entire entity as a whole, a dedication to family values and commitment to Titus W.'s dream, The Hager Group of Companies expanded rapidly and earned a priceless reputation. This progress encompassed new offerings that now include many products and services in demand in the building industry. As Titus R. says, "The company was founded on the basic principle to select and warehouse the best materials, accessories and products for the building industry and offer these items to the largest number of dealers compatible with good distribution — at the lowest possible cost." The companies are well known to dealers and retailers and yet Hager remains behind the scenes with the public — a philosophy that is in alignment with the history of the company.

The organization has a right to boast about its lumber production. Its dedication to wood preservation techniques upholds the highest ecological standards — chemicals and waste products never reach the ground, and internal processes exceed EPA requirements.

The Hager Group of Companies today is a multifaceted manufacturing/industrial distribution concern. The industrial division focuses on the distribution of panel products to the furniture industry, deck products and deck accessories. Lumber products include hardwood plywood, particleboard, medium-density fiberboard and other commodity lumber. Cutwork is compliant with customer specifications. Hager Lumber Co. also offers custom services such as temperature-controlled storage of specialty particleboard.

Excitement has grown as new quality products have been added to the manufacturing mix. The Hager Group of Companies collectively manufactures such products as fencing, lattice and accessories, interior/exterior door units, siding, windows, ceilings, floors and exclusive design products sold to retailers.

Hager Lumber Co. and Grand Rapids Sash & Door are keenly aware of the importance of timing and inventory — so much so that they hold a multimillion-dollar inventory in stock at all times. Customers appreciate this because it alleviates the pressures and expense of their own stocking issues and guarantees rapid response. The Hager Group of Companies is concerned with being in the forefront of changing market trends and uses valuable information to lower costs to dealers, which in turn pass on the savings to the individual purchaser.

Grand Rapids Sash & Door is the largest, oldest and most prestigious Andersen Window distributor and wholesaler in Michigan, an alliance that shapes Hager history. In keeping with a philosophy to "serve with quality," the organization has chosen product lines that are cutting edge in their respective industries. The firm has grown to eight wholesale distribution centers in four states — amazing resources that help customers earn a higher profit due to the streamlined processes.

Looking toward the future, The Hager Group of Companies established yet another company, Superior Steel Components, Inc., to meet the demand for light-gauge steel trusses and wall panels for the commercial, institutional and light-industrial construction markets. These three ventures — Hager Lumber Co., Grand Rapids Sash & Door and Superior Steel Components, Inc. — make up The Hager Group of Companies.

Today, four generations of the Hager family contribute to making The Hager Group of Companies market leaders. The family and dedicated staff are committed to responding to change through innovation and preparedness. Current employees describe The Hager Group of Companies as a family-owned organization with a good financial background that is generous in supporting community charities. It understands the importance of family and proves it by its loyal and genuinely caring attitude toward its employees. It functions with integrity, honesty and trustworthiness.

The Hager Group of Companies are superlative models to be held in high regard in the Grand Rapids community. Titus W. Hager would be proud.

Three active generations of the Hager Family

A building project demonstrating the use of Hager product lines

MACROE PROPERTIES

Build it historically preserved and technology-ready and they will come. That is what Sam Cummings, Macroe Properties visionary, believed and proved true to the naysayers of the downtown Grand Rapids community. In an era when people were escaping the city and heading for the suburbs to commute to work, Cummings knew

The downtown Macroe grid showcases beautifully restored buildings.

the near future was restoration, preservation and breathing a whole lot of life into a sagging city.

"We believe in the strength of the urban center. We believe that the urban center defines us, and that it's an exuberant part of the our culture," Cummings says.

Cummings has a booming business of property management, urban reclamation and development; to the Grand Rapids citizen that translates to seeing vacant buildings from the late 1800s transformed with restored wood flooring and sandblasted brickwork, open atriums and rooftop decks. Such beautiful architecture and design gives the downtown character and the feel of big-city living.

The interiors of the restored buildings at 15 Ionia, 16 Ionia, 25 Ionia, Tannery Row and the Brassworks Building, to name a few, include massive timber supports and beams, soaring ceilings with exposed duct work and the magic of retaining an aged beauty. This has attracted retailers and businesses of all kinds. The Foye McDonald Associates hair salon, an upscale up-to-the-minute style haven, jumped at the chance to rent property in a Macroe Building. The loft-style space, with floor-to-ceiling windows that provide plenty of natural light and draw the attention of pedestrians, has "exploded" their business, says owner McDonald.

"Being here is very energizing," he says. And he has nothing but praise for Macroe as a landlord. "It's a dream come true. Their standards, in fact, are as high as my own when it comes to satisfying customers."

Shopping downtown is a must now that Macroe has drawn retailers like A.K. Rikk's Menswear, which offers the designer lines Kenneth Cole and Giorgio Armani, and the specialty-order furniture store, Urban House. Shoppers treat themselves to fine dining at the Sierra Room, Sanchez restaurant and nightclub Opus 1894.

One of the biggest coups for Cummings is Tannery Row on SW Ionia Street, a vacant building that had been decaying for over 25 years in the middle of the Heartside Historic District.

"WE BELIEVE IN THE STRENGTH OF THE URBAN CENTER. WE BELIEVE THAT THE URBAN CENTER DEFINES US, AND THAT IT'S AN EXUBERANT PART OF THE OUR CULTURE," CUMMINGS SAYS.

The challenge was to transfer an 1890s structure that housed pigeons into loft-style apartments. Special amenities include a workout room, extensive storage, on-site parking and a rooftop deck.

Tannery Row was the result of extensive studies of the urban housing market, including trips to comparative projects in Chicago and Minneapolis. Floor-plan viability, storage needs, amenity surveys and cost controls were part of the process to evaluate the feasibility of the project.

TANNERY ROW WAS ONE OF THE FIRST WAREHOUSE PROPERTIES TO BE RENOVATED FOR HOUSING.

At Tannery Row the past meets the future. Builders included completely new mechanical, electrical and safety code upgrades in addition to preparing the building for future technology needs. The exterior work included brick repair, repairs to existing windows, sandstone sill replacement, new roofing and prepared cornice details.

The urban housing project was the antithesis of what most thought residents wanted. "No one wants to live in the city" was the refrain Cummings heard more often than not. But ultimately his vision proved correct — the project, which included condos, was completely occupied within six weeks after opening in July 1996.

Not only did he develop it, but Cummings turned it into one of downtown's most honored historic structures. The Kent County Council for Historic Preservation named Tannery Row as its outstanding commercial restoration project in the city. This project also received an award from the Historic Preservation Commission for preserving the historic architectural character of the building.

Kim Beyer of Constructors Inc. did the renovation work, and Tom Nemitz, president of Cornerstone Architects, designed the building's comeback. "It was incredibly well-built," said Nemitz, recalling his first response to Tannery Row. "But it was decaying essentially from the roof down. The upper floor, the fifth floor, was pretty much a basket case. But it was so structurally sound when it was built it probably would have gone a long time before it reached the point where it wasn't worth renovating."

For Nemitz, bringing the 102-year old building up to code was a major challenge, as was designing it to bring

The award-winning Tannery Row

charm that would attract tenants to downtown living. Tannery Row was one of the first warehouse properties to be renovated for housing. This beautifully created building now serves as a model for future downtown development and is toured by developers from around the country.

Cummings, a graduate of Calvin College, opened his firm in 1989. He is involved in charity and promoting Grand Rapids at every turn. From the Grand Rapids Foundation to the Grand Rapids Art Museum, his tastes include anything cultural for the city that he is dedicated to preserving.

"My wife and I spend a lot of our free time looking at other cities. We are always taking notes and trying to apply some of the knowledge to Grand Rapids," he says. "We're both architecture and design fanatics and amateur urban planning aficionados. We love old buildings. We spend most of our time seeking out historic districts, and thinking about how we could apply what we learn there, here."

PIONEER GENERAL CONTRACTORS, INC.

Scattered across the landscape in West Michigan are standing tributes to the motto adopted almost 40 years ago by Pioneer General Contractors, Inc.: "We Build with Pride."

Whether it's Bridgewater Place, Foremost Insurance Co. or Grand Valley State University, these buildings reflect the quality craftsmanship of one of West Michigan's oldest construction companies.

It's a tradition that began in 1933 when the late Earl H. Beckering Sr. founded Beckering Construction Co. in Grand Rapids. Over the years, the firm has earned a reputation for quality work, meeting deadlines and the ability to complete its own concrete and steel work — all within budget. It's a tribute, Beckering family members say, to the company's competent supervisors and skilled tradesmen that have constructed countless commercial, industrial, educational and retail buildings.

Today, the award-winning company employs about 350 skilled workers, with annual sales consistently hitting $100 million, making it one of the largest construction firms in the area.

The company began simply enough as the dream of an immigrant from the Netherlands, Earl Beckering Sr. At age 19 he worked his way across the ocean as a carpenter on a ship, joining thousands of others from the Netherlands who immigrated to Grand Rapids at the turn of the century.

Though the teenager was more interested in building, his fine carpentry skills landed him a job as an expert cabinetmaker in Grand Rapids, where the city's growing economy was based on furniture.

As the economy struggled to recover from the Great Depression, Earl Sr. felt the time was right to start his own construction business. He first worked out of his home on Horton Street SE, eventually moving to an office on Kirtland Street SW along Plaster Creek.

Earl Sr.'s religious beliefs were an essential part of his business and his life with his wife, Deana, and their three sons and one daughter. Eventually all of his sons, Ralph, Jim and Earl Jr., joined the business. But it was his youngest, Earl Jr., who would ultimately take charge of the family business.

(Top to bottom) The late Earl Beckering Sr., who immigrated to America at age 19 from the Netherlands at the turn of the century, founded the business in 1933. His son, Earl Jr., began leading the company in 1954 followed by the family's third generation and current CEO, Thomas Beckering.

Earl Jr. had grown up in the construction industry, first driving a company truck during the summers as a teenager. Because technology was rapidly transforming the way buildings were erected, Earl Jr. earned a degree in architectural engineering from the University of Michigan and a degree in construction engineering from the Chicago Technical College.

After serving as an engineer in the U.S. Air Force during World War II, Earl Jr. returned home to his wife, Sereta Morten Beckering, and their young son, Jerry. He acquired management experience when the family lived in St. Johns, Michigan, where the family business was building a new plant for Federal Mogul.

When Earl Jr.'s brother, Jim, died and his father, Earl Sr., semi-retired, Earl Jr. moved his growing family back to the Grand Rapids area in 1954 to take over the family business.

Earl Jr. quickly enlarged the scope of operations. He became known for his handshake agreements, his word of honor and his community contributions.

Though the company did well, Earl Jr. was growing weary of jurisdictional disputes with union workers that sometimes halted work on the job sites. In 1963 he created a partnership with long-time friend Kenneth Harmsen and formed another company, Pioneer Construction Co. It was one of the industry's first local non-union companies and became allied with the Associated Builders and Contractors Merit Shop.

Pioneer General Contractors, Inc., one of West Michigan's oldest construction companies, built its present headquarters on Kirtland Street SW in 1998.

Despite bitter union disputes at Beckering Construction in 1964-65, both Pioneer and Beckering remained viable and separate construction companies until the early 1970s when Beckering Construction was dissolved.

Earl Jr. went on to become president of Michigan's Associated Builders and Contractors, and later served on its national board of directors. He also was president of the Builders Exchange of Grand Rapids.

Ken's son, David, and Earl Jr.'s son, Thomas, joined Pioneer in 1968 and 1971 respectively. Armed with a business administration degree from Ferris State University, Tom brought new vitality to the company by creating the development division, which generated innovative projects such as Riverview Center and Anchorage Marina. It was the beginning of another expansion period observed with pride by Tom's father. By 1980 sales soared to $30 million.

Double-digit interest rates in the early 1980s hampered new construction. Pioneer survived until the economy turned around by working on numerous school projects financed by lower-interest-bearing bonds. By 1990 sales reached $60 million.

It was Tom Beckering, now the father of four, who gradually bought out everyone's interest in the company to become its sole owner by 1996.

Today, Tom looks forward to passing the company reins to the next generation. His oldest son, Tom Jr. (Ty), and his son-in-law, Tim Schowalter, who married his daughter Barbara, are both vice presidents, and his youngest son, Christopher, is studying engineering at GVSU and may eventually join the company.

The company's headquarters remains on Kirtland SW, where Earl Beckering Sr. realized his dream. But it has grown considerably, sprawled over four buildings totaling almost 50,000 square feet.

Forklifts, cranes, electric drills and skill saws have replaced the manual methods Earl Sr. relied on at job sites. E-mail, voice-mail and computers have replaced the communication methods relied on by his son, Earl Jr.

But one thing that hasn't changed is the company motto established by Earl Beckering Jr., now 80 years old: "We Build with Pride." He once told a writer, "We will proudly live with everything we build for the rest of our lives."

One Pioneer project, The Beckering Family Carillon Tower, will undoubtedly endure not just for a lifetime, but for many generations to come. Completed in 2000, it rises magnificently into the sky just west of the Grand River near downtown Grand Rapids. It's a gift that Tom & Earl Beckering gave to Grand Valley State University when Pioneer built the college's Richard M. DeVos Center on W. Fulton Street.

Built in 2000, the magnificent Beckering Family Carillon Tower was a gift to Grand Valley State University when Pioneer built the college's Richard M. DeVos Center on W. Fulton Street in Grand Rapids.

The stately tower features a clock on each of its four sides and surrounds 42 bells. Each bell was cast in France by one of the top foundries in the world.

Every day, the carillon rings out across the beautiful downtown campus. But it's more than just a pleasant melody. It's a gentle reminder of one landmark among hundreds built with pride by Pioneer workers.

Pioneer's skilled workforce live up to the company's motto: "We Build with Pride" every day while on the job.

BUSINESS, FINANCE
& PROFESSIONAL SERVICES

Banks, insurance companies and office equipment companies provide essential services to the Grand Rapids area.

FOREMOST INSURANCE GROUP

U.S. soldiers, fresh from the battlefields of World War II, came home to face another crisis — a postwar housing shortage. Compact, efficient and easy to relocate, mobile homes helped solve the nation's housing crunch in the years following the war. But the lack of financing and insurance became a major stumbling block for new buyers. On June 12, 1952, Edward Frey, president of Union Bank, founded Foremost Insurance Company. Frey recognized that there was a need for consistent and dependable mobile home insurance to meet the specific needs of mobile home owners, lenders and dealers.

Foremost's first office was located in downtown Grand Rapids in 1952.

The Foremost Insurance Group world headquarters is set on 580 pristine acres in Caledonia, Michigan.

But Foremost management soon realized that in order to grow, they must take a lead role in developing the mobile home industry. The company helped manufacturers establish dealer organizations and encouraged lenders to enter the market.

Working as a catalyst for industry growth was a brilliant strategy. Foremost more than tripled in size from 1952 to 1957.

During the early 1960s, Foremost started to diversify and explored new ways to insure recreational vehicles. In 1961 Foremost Insurance Company introduced TravelSure®, the first insurance policy designed specifically for travel trailers.

By 1966 Foremost wrote its one millionth policy. Rapid expansion continued as mobile home sales topped $1 billion and more Americans started buying recreational vehicles.

With its rapid growth came the need for more capital to fund expansion. Thus, Foremost formed a holding company, Centennial Corporation, and became a publicly traded company in 1972. Foremost wrote more business during 1973 than in the first 15 years combined — more than $224 million in premiums.

Then, in 1974, a cloud of political and financial uncertainty settled over the nation in the form of the Watergate scandal and an OPEC oil embargo. Double-digit inflation and a huge increase in crude oil prices caused a major recession in 1974 and 1975. Out of work, with no way to pay their loans, more than 150,000 people had their mobile homes repossessed in just two years. Those years would be some of the most challenging the company would face.

By 1976 the industry picked up steam again. Foremost returned to profitability and the lessons learned from battling an industrywide recession left it leaner, smarter and better positioned for growth. By the end of the 1970s, Foremost had earned more than $1 billion in mobile home and recreational vehicle premiums during its 27-year history — writing three times more mobile home insurance than its nearest competitor.

The mobile home evolved into today's manufactured home, longer, wider and with more amenities typical of site-built homes. Foremost kept evolving during that time as well, and in 1981 Foremost introduced a group of products to meet the need of mobile home owners over age 50. Several other products, including auto insurance, were added during the early 1980s as Foremost broadened its customer base. Development of these new programs was a major factor in Foremost's continuing growth.

A large part of the company's success was due to its attention to detail. Extensive research, market studies, focus groups and interviews helped Foremost pinpoint trends and alter its products and services to fit the changing needs of its customers.

During the mid-1980s, Foremost developed new strategies to ensure the company's success. Deciding to

Starting with three employees nearly 50 years ago, Foremost now employs more than 1,400 people countrywide.

focus on the core manufactured home and recreational vehicle products, Foremost discontinued many other insurance products and formed several different companies to better compete in target markets. The new companies became part of Foremost Insurance Group.

Foremost had weathered many storms over the years, but in 1989 Hurricane Hugo hit Carolina residents — and Foremost — with the weight of a freight train. Foremost's Claim Response Team rushed into the area to help stricken customers and settled more than 8,000 claims in just 30 days.

Foremost not only weathered the storm, but also found new ways to serve customers more efficiently. Its proven experience in serving its customers helped it receive the endorsement of AARP in 1989.

The AARP program represented a milestone for Foremost. Although the company continued to sell its products through independent agents, the new program allowed Foremost to sell insurance directly to the end consumer.

Building on the success of the AARP program, Foremost established additional relationships with recreational vehicle associations, mobile home owner associations and manufactured home lenders. By 1995 Foremost once again was looking to diversify. A new auto insurance program was created and marketed to employees and members of select companies and associations.

The program took off in 1997 when Foremost secured the right to offer auto and home insurance to 1 million distributors representing the world's largest multilevel marketing company. Growth ensued and by mid-2000 Foremost was promoting the program to over 250 organizations representing 2 million households.

As the century came to a close, Foremost began a new chapter in its history. Recognizing Foremost's strengths, Los Angeles-based Farmers Insurance Group, which is managed by Zurich Financial Services, announced plans to purchase Foremost in October 1999. When the purchase was completed early in 2000, the merger added approximately 15,000 Farmers agents to those doing business with Foremost, nearly doubling Foremost's sales base. Within months manufactured home policy sales increased dramatically. At the same time Foremost began to increase the recreational products it offers.

Today, Foremost is focused on its goal — to become the largest insurer of specialty dwellings and recreational products in the country. As 2000 comes to a close and the company looks ahead, Foremost is busy with the expansion of its recreational product line to include motorcycles, off-road vehicles, snowmobiles and marine products.

With the addition of these product lines, coupled with the company's well-known and respected manufactured home, motor home and travel trailer insurance products, Foremost has grown as a Grand Rapids employer. Today, Foremost continues to look to its future as a key player in the Farmers Insurance Group of companies, while keeping with its tradition of growing with Grand Rapids since 1952.

Foremost is a leading specialty insurer of mobile homes, motor homes, travel trailers and other recreational vehicles.

OLD KENT FINANCIAL CORPORATION

Since its founding in 1853, Old Kent has emerged as the largest and oldest financial services organization based in West Michigan, with a rich history as a community leader. The cornerstone of Old Kent's tremendous success lies in its unswerving commitment to making banking easier for its customers, employees and community, along with achieving its goal of maximizing long-term shareholder value through consistent, superior financial performance.

As a landmark in downtown Grand Rapids, Old Kent continues to build on its historic success. In 1999, Old Kent was named to the prestigious S & P 500 list, a leading benchmark for the U.S. equities market. For the third consecutive year, *The Detroit News*, the state's largest newspaper, gave Old Kent an A+ rating in its 1999 Michigan Corporate Report Card, which rates companies on their commitment to shareholders. In addition, Old Kent was listed third among 16,000 publicly traded companies for consistent performance in Bill Stanton's annual publication, *America's Finest Companies* 2000. On March 31, 2000, Old Kent Financial Corporation (NYSE-OK) reported assets of $20 billion, with more than 8,000 employees.

In 1966, Old Kent stepped solidly into the wave of downtown urban renewal when it constructed its new headquarters. It was the first office structure to be built in downtown Grand Rapids in 40 years.

This stellar performer traces its roots to 1853, when Daniel Ball opened a private bank inside his business at the Daniel Ball & Company on the corner of Canal, now known as Monroe Avenue, and Pearl Street.

Ball was a merchant, steamboat builder, realtor and manufacturer who was very influential in the village of Grand Rapids. The railroad and telegraph had yet to arrive in the lumber town of less than 4,000. And there were no other banking facilities in the area primarily because of the monetary confusion and wildcat financial practices that characterized the time.

Soon, his bank was known as Daniel Ball Exchange Bank. In 1861, the bank rechartered as Martin L. Sweet & Co., reorganized in 1864 as the First National Bank and rechartered again in 1883 as the Old National Bank.

Over the next 45 years, many new local banks opened and consolidated. Old National Bank eventually merged in 1929 with Kent State Bank and the united company was named Old Kent Bank. It was Michigan's largest banking institution outside of Detroit, with three downtown banks and 11 community offices.

Six months later, the stock market crashed. More than 10,000 banks closed during the Great Depression. But by the end of 1934, Old Kent had survived to be the 155th largest bank in the nation as listed by *American Banker.*

After World War II, the bank experienced tremendous growth as the nation turned its attention and resources from the war to returning servicemen. Old Kent led the way with the changing times. The economic boom pushed bank deposits from $83 million in 1943 to more than $150 million by 1952.

When the automobile became a necessity for nearly every family during the 1950s, Old Kent took to the road, too. It opened the first drive-in bank in Grand Rapids in 1953 at its Division Avenue branch office just south of Franklin Street SE.

During the 1960s, as new regional shopping malls dotted the suburban landscape and downtown seemed stagnant, Old Kent boldly joined the commitment to downtown urban renewal. It announced plans to build a new corporate office in downtown Grand Rapids, making it the city's first business to step solidly into the wave of downtown construction that followed. The bank's 11-story structure at the corner of Ottawa Avenue and Lyon Street NW was completed in 1966, the first office structure to be built in downtown Grand Rapids in 40 years.

Old Kent Bank also continued to grow with the merger of other banks, including Michigan Trust Co., Peoples National Bank and Community State Bank.

Since 1978, the Old Kent River Bank Run has grown to become a distinguished world-class event, now attracting more than 10,000 participants each year.

In 1972, Old Kent Bank became the lead bank of the newly formed holding company, Old Kent Financial Corporation, which first traded on the NASDAQ and now on the New York Stock Exchange. At the time, Old Kent was a $340 million bank with 27 offices. Its strategy for continued growth was based on strategic acquisitions and diversification. For long-term investors, that strategy paid off handsomely as Old Kent Bank's stock soared over the years.

During the 1970s, when running became a popular fitness activity, Grand Rapids joined the race with the Old Kent River Bank Run. The first race in 1978 drew an estimated 1,250 runners who ran along a 25-kilometer course (15.5 miles) starting and finishing downtown. Immediately, the Old Kent River Bank Run became a much-celebrated community event for thousands and marked the beginning of what has become the largest 25K race in the nation. Today, the world-renowned race draws more than 10,000 participants, with runners holding world records for the 25K run, set in 1998, and the 25K wheelchair event, established in 2000.

In addition to the race, Old Kent also has been a key partner with Old Kent Park. Built in the early 1990s, the park brought minor league baseball games back to Grand Rapids, featuring the West Michigan Whitecaps. Watching baseball quickly became a family-attraction staple to Grand Rapids residents.

In the late 1980s, the bank began aggressively expanding its base of customers to areas outside the state, most notably in the Chicago area. In 2000, Old Kent's latest acquisition, Chicago's Grand Premier Financial, Inc., gave Old Kent the fifth-largest market share in metro Chicago and the state of Illinois.

Today, Old Kent operates more than 300 banking offices in Michigan, Illinois and Indiana. It has diversified tremendously to meet the sophisticated needs of its customers, evolving from a business that met basic banking needs to one offering a comprehensive array of financial services, including a national mortgage company ranked among the top 25 mortgage lenders in the nation.

In an industry that has changed rapidly over the decades, Old Kent remains committed to making banking easier through growth and operational excellence. There's little doubt that Old Kent will continue to be a leader in both Grand Rapids and the other communities where it has become a presence.

In 1999, Old Kent opened the first fully automated banking center in the Rivertown Crossings Mall.

COMMERCIAL EQUIPMENT COMPANY

The challenge currently facing the office equipment industry is keeping abreast with ever-changing, ever-advancing technology. A trio of Grand Rapids companies — The Reed Group — is answering that challenge. The Reed Group comprises the parent company, Commercial Equipment Company, and it subsidiaries, The W.S. Reed Company (est. 1981) and Reed Office Systems, Inc. (est. 1989). The Reed Group is now one of the largest independently owned office machine dealers in the Midwest.

The "Worst Copier in West Michigan" was dropped for charity.

In 1957 three sales representatives from Burroughs Corporation in Detroit — Bob Chase, Bud Locke, and Bill Reed — took a risk and founded a small company in Grand Rapids to sell and service 3M Thermofax copiers. Using onion-skin-type paper, the Thermofax virtually eliminated the need for carbon paper to make copies.

Bill Reed eventually bought out his two partners and gradually brought his three sons, Mike, Russ and Tom, into the business. In 1992 Bill Reed sold his interest in the company to Mike, Russ and Tom, the current owners.

Advances in technology and an increasing quest for ease of use have presented challenges to the office equipment industry. The MFD — multiple function device — is a single, compact, versatile office machine that performs the duties previously delegated to several machines. "Copy, fax, print and even scan can now be performed by one machine," says President Mike Reed. "All of our products are going to digital technology now, from old analog technology. The reason for that is to allow our equipment to interface and network with computers."

According to Reed, approximately 60 percent of all office machines sold in 1999 featured analog technology, with the remaining 40 percent having made the switch to digital. Reed expects a complete reversal of those figures in 2000, with 70 percent of the office machines featuring digital technology. He expects more than 90 percent of all new office machines to have switched to digital technology by 2001.

The Reed Group, on a combined basis, carries several quality brands of office equipment such as Lanier Copiers and Fax, Canon Imaging Systems, Minolta Copiers and Fax, Proxima LCD Projectors, Konica Copiers and Fax, KIP Engineering Copiers, Riso Digital Duplicators, H-P Printers, Toshiba Copiers and Fax, and Panasonic Fax.

The company provides technical service and support for the above equipment with a team of 75 factory-trained technicians strategically located throughout the state of Michigan. The company has enjoyed close to double-digit sales growth over the past 20-plus years, through a combination of quality products, 225 knowledgeable and competent associates, and a strong Michigan economy.

Giving time and money back to the community through local charitable donations and involvement with organizations such as the Rotary, Jaycees, the Chamber of Commerce and other nonprofit organizations is important to the company owners.

Commercial Equipment Company headquarters

The Reed Group has branch offices in Kalamazoo, Muskegon, Traverse City, Lansing, Alpena, Saginaw and Southfield, Michigan, as well as Toledo, Ohio. The company's goal is simple: to continue to rank No. 1 in customer service by providing the best available equipment, optimum service and support, and to be a leader in technological advancement. The Reed Group offers its customers longevity, stability and experience.

HUNTINGTON NATIONAL BANK

The story of Huntington National Bank from birth to present is one of tradition combined with innovation. On January 3, 1886, Pelatiah Webster (P.W.) Huntington partnered with his father-in-law to create P.W. Huntington & Company, a private banking house. It remained a family-owned corporation until 1958 and became Huntington National Bank in 1979.

In October 1997, Huntington, based in Columbus, Ohio, acquired more than 90 offices of First Michigan Bank Corporation in West and Upper Michigan, expanding the bank's presence shoreline to shoreline in Michigan and establishing its Northwest regional headquarters at Monroe Center at the heart of downtown Grand Rapids.

The bank became active in the trust business in 1923. During the early years of the 20th century, hard times led other banks to fail, but the Huntington family employed conservative practices to ensure that assets covered obligations. When the Depression forced the federal government to close all banks for four days in March 1933, The Huntington reopened within one week to continue serving its customers while many other financial institutions foundered. These same solid business principles continue today, a reflection of the company's proud family roots.

The decades of the 1950s, 60s, 70s and 80s brought continual regulatory changes in the banking industry. Huntington started its own holding company, Huntington Bancshares Incorporated, in 1966. The Huntington Mortgage Company was founded in 1976 and Huntington Leasing Company in 1977. The business principles and practices of P.W. Huntington have enabled the bank to survive and prosper during economic downturns and to help others capitalize on opportunities.

But it was the 1990s that positioned Huntington as a pacesetter in a new era of banking when innovation means being not only where the customer is, but also where the customer wants to be. Huntington brought Direct Bank to its customers in 1992, giving 24-hour, 7-day-a-week access to Personal Bankers by phone for most banking needs. Four years later Huntington continued to make banking more convenient with the introduction of Web Bank, consistently ranked in the top nationwide for ease of use. Huntington Bank now holds a number of technology patents and proudly celebrated its 100,000th Internet customer in 1999.

Bill Kleven, president of Huntington's Northwest Region, says, "West Michigan is an outstanding place to do business and raise a family. In retaining P.W. Huntington's spirit, the bank has remained sensitive to the needs of family businesses as well as public corporations and individuals." Huntington National Bank has a positive local impact on the Grand Rapids and Michigan economies. In 1999 the bank committed significant resources to various charitable causes and educational institutions. Its scope is broad and diverse. For example, in 2000 Huntington began a three-year sponsorship of the Great Lakes Intercollegiate Athletic Conference Championship in Grand Rapids. The bank also participated in "Walk for Warmth," a fundraiser to avert utility shut-off for people during the cold winter months, and has supported, through staff volunteerism and financial partnerships, numerous community initiatives in the arts, education and affordable housing.

The elegant lobby of Huntington National Bank from eras past

As Huntington National Bank approaches the future, it remains committed to excellence, innovation and community, a modern counterpart of the family legacy it honors.

MANUFACTURING & DISTRIBUTION

In addition to producing and delivering exceptional goods to individuals and industry, Grand Rapids manufacturing and distribution companies provide employment for area residents.

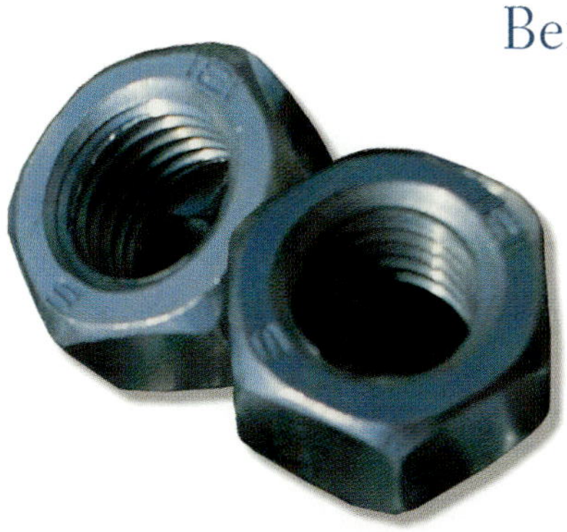

CARAUSTAR CUSTOM PACKAGING GROUP

"One name says it all" is the slogan for Caraustar, Inc. in Atlanta, Georgia. That's why in June 1999, employees at Tenneco's Packaging Corporation of America were excited to learn that Caraustar had purchased their plant on Beverly Avenue SW.

The Wyoming, Michigan, facility would now be known as Caraustar Custom Packaging Group and be part of one of the top 10 folding carton companies in the country.

Since 1992 Caraustar has more than tripled in size, mostly through strategic acquisitions, in an industry that has rapidly undergone consolidation. Today, as a $1 billion operation, it is North America's largest producer of recycled paperboard and a leading folding carton company. The newly acquired Wyoming plant is just one of 23 in Caraustar's Custom Packing Group.

"It's very exciting to us because Caraustar is one of the few paperboard and converting companies in the country that's growing," says Paul Curtis, general manger of the Wyoming plant. "The history of Caraustar marries well with the stability our company has had in Wyoming. Through an aggressive acquisitions strategy, Caraustar is changing the face of the industry."

Situated on almost 14 acres, the 180,000-square-foot plant in Wyoming employed 200 and enjoyed sales exceeding $35 million in 1999. It serves such high-profile brand-name customers as Keebler, Gerber and Nestlé.

TODAY, AS A $1 BILLION OPERATION, IT IS NORTH AMERICA'S LARGEST PRODUCER OF RECYCLED PAPERBOARD AND A LEADING FOLDING CARTON COMPANY.

When the Spees family founded the business in 1923, it was known as the Wolverine Carton Company.

The Caraustar Custom Packaging Group in Wyoming, Michigan, is one of 23 folding carton facilities operated by Caraustar, Inc., an industry leader.

By employing the latest technologies, Caraustar maintains its competitiveness.

Employees worked in a small but new manufacturing plant erected in 1919 to build cars. The short-lived Lorraine Motors Corp. assembled four-cylinder, medium-priced cars until shutting down in 1921.

As Wolverine Carton Company grew, so did its facilities. After building the business for 35 years, the Spees family sold the company in 1958 to American Boxboard Company of Grand Rapids.

A year later, the firm merged with a company in Rittman, Ohio, and one in Quincy, Illinois. The united businesses called themselves Packaging Corporation of America. In 1965, Tenneco, a large oil conglomerate, purchased the plant but retained the PCA name for many years.

As an industry leader, Caraustar is capable of handling almost any folding carton request because it keeps pace with technology, encourages innovation and employs talented workers dedicated to producing quality work. In 1974 the plant was the first carton company in the United States to make its own cutting dies with a laser. From 1989 to 1997 the plant was re-capitalized with more efficient printing, die cutting and gluing equipment, making the plant state-of-the-art.

In 1999, as an ISO 9001 certified supplier, it became North America's second carton plant to become QS 9000 certified. Over the years, it also has won numerous safety and design awards from industry trade associations.

Equally important is the dedication of its employees. "In my five years here, I'm still impressed by the West Michigan work ethic," Paul says. "It has greatly contributed to our success. We look forward to maintaining our tradition of providing outstanding service and quality to our customers while earning an acceptable financial return to our shareholders."

FUTURE TOOL & DIE, INC.

Colleagues during the day — and bowling partners at night — Dennis Bosch, Dave Hurley and Bill Roon were already primed to take charge of their collective destiny when the Grand Rapids company they were working for was sold in 1978. Realizing it was a "now or never" proposition, the men quit their jobs and founded Future Tool & Die, Inc. Hurley was 34 years old, Bosch was 35 and Roon was 38.

The trio owned one machine, still in the crate, and went a year and a half without paychecks. At the time, interest was at 22 percent and everyone told them their business would fail. Instead, the fledgling company — originally located in Grand Rapids, off 28th street on Viaduct — thrived. Four years later, the business was relocated to Grandville Industrial Park.

The park, a former gravel excavation site, had several available lots. Unbeknownst to Bosch, Hurley and Roon, they had staked out the area where sludge had been dumped; a fact revealed to them by soil sample tests completed an hour before they were supposed to close on the property. Had the tests not revealed this fact, the sheer weight of the massive tool and die machines would have when they sunk into the ground upon production.

The trio's real estate agent suggested the following options: set the building on pilings, dig all the sludge out or move to another lot. They opted for the latter.

Future Tool & Die, Inc., located in Grandville

The original 6,400-square-foot building was constructed in 1984. Three years later, Bosch and his partners added a second bay, followed by another in 1992. A two-story addition, consisting primarily of offices, was built in 1995. A small grinding room was added in 1997 and a new front entry and additional offices were completed in January 1999, giving the company a total of 30,000 square feet of space.

As in most businesses, technology has had a dramatic impact on the tool and die industry. The majority of the work at Future Tool & Die was done by hand 20 years ago. Today the company has eight computer-controlled mills and wire cutters on the shop floor. Everything is designed and programmed by computer; there are approximately 40 computers located throughout the shop.

Founders of Future Tool & Die, Inc.: Dennis Bosch, Dave Hurley and Bill Roon *Photo by Todd Zawistowski*

Future Tool & Die works with Tier-I suppliers, with each of its dies meeting the specifications of the contracting company. Approximately 95 percent of the dies manufactured by the Grand Rapids company are related to the auto industry — from ashtrays to door panels.

Dies are required to last the life of the production run. For example, a part for the original Ford Taurus ran for 10 years. Most of the company's dies are made of a

Computerized technology is exemplified with this wire burn machine.

special alloyed steel that can be heat-treated and hardened. A machine loaded with copper wire, held by tension, burns a precision cut — with electricity — through the material. This allows employees to cut closer than one-tenth of 1,000 of an inch, even with blocks as thick as 15 inches.

Hydropower is also used to cut steel. A water-jet cutter is capable of taking a 40 thousandths of an inch cut of steel. Employees can cut to within five thousandths of an inch. While most of the steel is approximately an inch and a half thick, material up to 10 inches thick can be cut with high-pressured water. A garnet stone is siphoned into the water and forced through a nozzle at 55,000 pounds per square inch. The particles of garnet are actually what cut the metal.

Dies are thoroughly tested before they leave the plant under the watchful eye of the production manager and customer. Test parts are re-run through the various automakers' systems. After thorough inspection, they are used primarily in destruction experiments.

On-site testing is just part of the post-production step. For added quality assurance, a die maker accompanies each shipment; often with one of the owners.

Mixing friendship with business can be an explosive combination. But for Bosch, Hurley and Roon, it has proven to be a winning combination. Each owner has his area of expertise and responsibility. Hurley is in charge of purchasing and personnel; Bosch is in charge of engineering and bid preparation; and Roon oversees accounting and quality.

The men credit hard work, diligence and the support of family and friends with their survival during their company's early days and — again — 12 years later, when their bank unexpectedly called in the company's loan. Suffering a substantial loss when another tool and die company went out of business, the bank responded by calling in the loans of some other tool and die shops. Future Tool & Die had 90 days to find a solution. Unable to call in their accounts receivable fast enough, the businessmen gratefully accepted a $100,000 loan from a friend.

To increase production and speed the recovery process, the three owners went back to work on the manufacturing floor where they remained throughout the summer. Today the company's employees continue to perpetuate that legacy of dedication and commitment.

For the owners of Future Tool & Die, teamwork is the cornerstone upon which they have built a thriving international business. Teamwork helped them weather the storms associated with starting up a new business, inflation and financial challenges. Teamwork, among its employees, has made the company an industry leader. And, it is teamwork that will see employers and employees through the future, as they continue to grow and expand their collective dream.

This 400-ton press is just one of Future Tool & Die's impressive pieces of machinery.

GENERAL DIE & ENGINEERING, INC.

As the new millennium dawns, General Die & Engineering, Inc. (GDE) is emerging stronger than ever in the fast-paced and challenging automotive industry.

In the fall of 2000, construction began to consolidate its two businesses and expand into one 62,500-square-foot facility on Clay Avenue SW in Grand Rapids. Located strategically at the intersection of U.S. 131 and M-6 (South Beltline), the company has easy access to its many customers throughout North America.

The expansion is a testament to the success the company has enjoyed in the design and manufacture of die-cast dies, thermoset and plastic injection molds. Approximately 95 percent of its customers purchase these molds to produce die-cast and plastic parts used in the automotive industry.

Following the year 2000 expansion — estimated at $2 million — the combined work force would exceed 100 employees.

GDE's success is by no means an easy accomplishment in the automotive industry, which demands excellence. Over the last few years the industry has changed by placing greater demands for quality from first- and second-tier suppliers while facing increasing global competition.

Founded in 1971, GDE began building molds in a small "garage shop" on Porter Street SW in Wyoming, a suburb on the south end of Grand Rapids. A few years later the business moved into a larger facility on Boston Street in Grand Rapids.

In 1979 Impact Industries, a die cast company located in Sandwich, Illinois, purchased GDE. In 1981 it moved GDE to a new 15,000-square-foot facility on 47th Street in Grand Rapids. GDE has continued doing business at this location for almost 20 years.

During the ups and downs of the tool and die industry throughout the 1980s and early 1990s, many companies ceased doing business. GDE found opportunities from larger companies that have provided steady and stable business.

Following the death of Impact Industries' owner, GDE was spun off from Impact and purchased by four business partners in 1994. Like many mold shops, GDE has succeeded by growing internally and through acquisitions. In 1996 these four partners purchased Arbor Mold &

General Die & Engineering's previous facility on 47th St. SW in Grand Rapids

Arbor Mold & Engineering's facility was purchased in 1996 by General Die & Engineering business partners.

only the finest-quality molds. It has built die-cast dies that have produced instrument panels for vehicles such as the Chrysler Neon and the General Motors Opel. In addition, it has built thermoset molds that have supplied headlamp assemblies for General Motors, Ford, Chrysler, Mitsubishi and Honda. In fact, the mold used to produce headlamps for the Lincoln Mark VIII — the largest headlamp assembly in North America — was built by GDE.

Moreover, GDE has built numerous plastic injection molds that have produced armrests, grab handles and map pockets for Ford Motor Company.

With such an impressive track record and a strong economy, it's no wonder company officials are optimistic about the future. The consolidation allows the company to take advantage of economies of scale while at the same time increasing its capacity for more business. Poised for growth, GDE is stronger than ever to compete in the challenging automotive industry in the new century.

Engineering, Inc., a 25,000-square-foot tool and die shop on Clay Avenue SW in Grand Rapids, which provided a different niche with its ability to manufacture larger molds up to 100,000 pounds.

By the year 2000, with both facilities nearing capacity, plans were made to expand the Clay Avenue facility and merge both operations into one. Ultimately the consolidation will streamline operations and allow the company to be more competitive.

GDE prides itself on servicing every customer by striving for 100 percent on-time delivery and providing the best quality at competitive prices. The company was registered to the ISO9002 standard in early 1999. Over the last several years, a booming economy has brought steady and stable growth.

A key factor in GDE's success has been the teamwork of its highly skilled work force. To attract and retain the best in a highly competitive labor market, GDE offers virtually the same benefits as much larger corporations offer, including vacation time, health care, 401K retirement plans and tuition reimbursement.

GDE is committed to meeting rigorous delivery schedules, tight tolerances and producing

General Die & Engineering's new 62,500-square-foot facility on Clay S.W. in Grand Rapids

GORDON FOOD SERVICE

Gordon Food Service, a successful, family-owned company headquartered in Grand Rapids, is hardly a mom-and-pop business. Founded more than 100 years ago by Dutch immigrants, GFS has exploded into a technology-driven, $2 billion company operating in only a handful of states.

During the past decade, GFS has experienced double-digit growth, making it the largest independent food distributor in the nation. In the past few years, GFS has been listed in *Forbes* magazine as one of the top 100 privately owned businesses in the United States.

One of the first VanWestenbrugge & Erb delivery trucks

The business was started simply enough in 1897 by Isaac and Cornelia VanWestenbrugge. Isaac, then 23 years old, borrowed $300 from his older brother, Martin, to begin delivering butter and eggs to Grand Rapids grocery stores. The goods were delivered in a wagon pulled by Isaac's sturdy horse, Dobbin.

The first distribution center was the barn behind the couple's home on Travis Street NE. The neighborhood was known as "Little Netherlands" because of its high concentration of Dutch immigrants. Cornelia ladled butter from 50-pound tubs into 1-pound earthen crocks and used candles to check each egg for freshness.

Grocery stores depended on their products, and by the early 1900s, their business began to grow. Isaac took on William Erb as a partner in 1905. They renamed their business VanWestenbrugge and Erb and moved to downtown Grand Rapids on Ottawa Street NW.

Dobbin was retired as the company started using a motorized truck for deliveries, the city's first delivery truck. It was an example of many pioneering moves as the company embraced new technology while expanding its product line to include potatoes, bananas, lard and renovated butter.

Isaac and William built a successful partnership, but by 1913 it was time for Isaac to regain sole proprietorship, forming the I. VanWestenbrugge company. Isaac hired Ben Gordon, a high school senior who impressed him, to help out in 1916. Ben also eventually impressed Isaac's daughter, Ruth, whom he later married.

Like all businesses, the company struggled during the Great Depression. Ben eventually became a partner, and in 1933 the firm was renamed the Gordon-Van Cheese Company. Ben's brother, Frank, began developing business in Traverse City. As Isaac shifted his focus to ministry, Ben and Frank reorganized the corporation and in 1942 named it Gordon Food Service.

During World War II, as shortages abounded, the company scrambled to build its fleet of nine used trucks. At the time, the foodservice industry, as people know it today, did not exist. Homemade meals were the standard fare, but after the war things began to change.

As the economy grew, Ben's son, Paul, joined the company. Restaurants opened throughout Michigan and people began to dine out more often. Because GFS had an efficient distribution system in place, it was able to step in and fill a need to supply restaurants. GFS opened branches in Kalamazoo and Lansing.

By the 50s GFS was at the forefront of the emerging foodservice industry. John Gordon Sr. joined the company, marking the beginning of the company's leap to super-distributor status.

In 1962 the majority of Gordon Food Service's clients were hotels and restaurants. Soon to come were hospitals, schools and other institutions.

The GFS team was committed to "red carpet" service for each customer.

That same year, with annual sales of about $6 million, GFS moved to its present headquarters on 50th Street SW in Grand Rapids. Company sales were climbing at a rate of $1 million each year. In 1970 the family was compelled to invest in a huge 50,000-square-foot addition.

The company's first food show in 1972, known as Food-A-Rama in Grand Rapids, launched an important company and industry tradition. It's now recognized as the largest distributor show in the nation.

To provide a convenient source of goods for truck delivery customers, the company opened its first customer service store in 1979. Today, the cash-and-carry stores, called GFS Marketplace, are growing in popularity with the public. They offer more than 22,000 food items and supplies for special events and parties, including groceries, meats, poultry, dairy, frozen foods, seafood, produce, beverage systems and tabletop supplies.

Throughout its history, Gordon Food Service has maintained a reputation as the most innovative food distributor in the industry. It continues to meet its mission, serving customers with the highest-quality foodservice products and services through innovative systems and the spirit and integrity of its employees.

In 1980 the company became the first foodservice distributor in the country to mechanize its sorting and selection operation. Its distribution centers have long been recognized as the most technically advanced in the industry.

The introduction of GFS's innovative two-trailer hookup system helped multiply business in the 1980s. Tractors and drivers waited at relay points to pick up the second half of the tandem and move it to distant markets.

In 1983 GFS pioneered the development of a turnkey software package to help its customers with more efficient purchasing, budgeting, tracking and sales analysis.

Gordon Food Service has twice earned the status of "Great Distributor Organization" from *Institutional Distribution* magazine, the only distributor to receive this honor twice. The magazine hailed the company's Brighton, Michigan, distribution center, built in 1986, as a "preview of 21st century foodservice distribution."

GFS Marketplace stores welcome the public and are springing up across the Midwest.

Today, the company has three distribution centers — two in Michigan and one in Ohio. Its sales offices and Marketplace stores are in Michigan, Indiana, Illinois, Ohio, Kentucky, West Virginia and Pennsylvania.

In 1995 GFS moved into Canada, where today it is the second-largest foodservice distributor in that country. GFS has two distribution centers in Ontario and five in Quebec.

John and Paul Gordon are still very active in the business as their sons Dan, Jim and John Jr. represent the fourth generation to head the firm. There is no doubt that through the years, the key component to GFS has been and continues to be its people. GFS serves a multitude of great customers in the foodservice industry. But this is only half of the winning combination. The employees of GFS take pride in their work and in being part of a company that does so much for them and their families. Because of great customers and faithful employees, GFS will continue to grow and prosper through a second century of service.

GFS' tandem trailers are a key to its successful distribution system.

GR SPRING & STAMPING, INC.

The story of GR Spring & Stamping, Inc. is an extraordinary one of rebirth that's won national acclaim. Its journey began in 1960 when the manufacturer began producing one product — a cable to manually operate exterior car mirrors. The company, then known as Grand Rapids Spring & Wire Products Inc., operated in a small, aging plant known as the Tanglefoot building on the city's southwest side.

Over the years co-founders Ed Manciewicz and Dick Muncy guided the business into a small but thriving $5 million spring operation employing 50 workers and supplying 650 area manufacturers. It eventually moved into more-modern facilities on Waldorf Street NW, just outside Grand Rapids.

But by 1985 the world of manufacturing had begun changing dramatically. Like many automotive suppliers, the company struggled with an increasingly competitive global market. It had no computers, no tracking systems, no quality manuals, no numerically controlled machines, no training programs and no engineers. To survive, GRS&W had to change quickly. Even more troubling was that the original automotive cable that once brought life to the business and represented 50 percent of its sales was becoming obsolete with the introduction of electric mirrors for cars.

Despite the apparent difficulties that lay ahead, Jim Zawacki and Ted Hohman saw opportunities. Zawacki was looking to run his own business after working in the industrial engineering department at Bissell Inc. and the next 18 years at Evans Products Inc., the last 10 of which as divisional president. While working in the factory at Bissell, he had earned his B.S. degree from Aquinas College and eventually became a manufacturing engineer. But he was tired of the corporate politics found in larger companies like Evans and jumped at the chance to buy a company. Hohman, who already owned several die casting companies, became his financial partner.

As the company's new president, one of the first things Zawacki did was to help develop the technical skills of his work force and create a family-like atmosphere and culture. He was convinced that people are a company's biggest asset and an essential ingredient for producing quality products. "Quality people make quality parts," he once told a reporter. He brought in experts to conduct seminars, selected one of his millwright electricians to become a full-time sensor technician and put into place a lab so that the company could move forward with its automation process and smart tools. In 1987, Don Klein, a professor from Grand Valley State University, became a consultant, exposing employees to "soft issues" such as the importance of teamwork and a positive culture.

Because the company considers associates as its greatest asset, it encourages a family-like atmosphere.

The company also began reducing the number of its customers to simplify its business. And in 1990 the owners began an assembly operation called the Grand Rapids Products Company, now known as Optimum Manufacturing, Inc., which is a minority-owned company today.

Company achievements are marked with meetings and lunches for all associates.

As GRS&W associates traveled the world from Japan to Taiwan, to Germany to Eastern Europe, and to Singapore and China in search of better ways to do things, they realized that continuous improvement is a never-ending journey. The company began basing its performance on five Key Performance Indicators: Quality, Cost, Delivery, Safety and Morale (QCDSM). Driving the business were the company's core values of Trust, Relationships, Integrity and Communications (TRIC). Six mini-companies composed of cross-functional, self-directed work teams of 25 to 35 employees oversaw quality, manufacturing and technical issues. This concept was learned from Kio Suzaki, author and consultant.

In 1995 the company changed its name to more accurately reflect the importance of stampings: GR Spring & Stamping, Inc. Associates were empowered to initiate ideas that improve their respective operations. GRS&S began hosting plant tours for many companies. In the summer of 1996, when many companies were just beginning to get serious about improving product quality, GRS&S joined a select group of manufacturers who were among the first in the nation to become ISO 9002 registered and QS-9000 compliant.

In 1996, as business bloomed, GRS&S moved into a renovated 117,000-square-foot plant on Bond Avenue NW. When the facility opened, Zawacki assured the city that the company would bring 100 new jobs to the downtown area.

Today, GRS&S is an award-winning, $35 million-plus business reflecting how pleasant a manufacturing operation can be for its internal and external customers. It employs more than 200 associates at three locations and ships products across North America to just 30 customers, mostly automotive suppliers.

In 1998 Zawacki told The *Grand Rapids Business Journal*, "We could be much bigger." But growth has been impeded by a shortage of skilled workers. "Anybody can buy machinery," he said. "It's finding good qualified people to run them" that's difficult. As a result, GRS&S continues to train its own employees with in-house seminars and training alliances with local colleges.

The company has earned local and national awards for excellence in safety, training, process control, product development and as a supplier. Among them is a national award for the invention of its "Smart Tool." This patented tool automatically measures parts as they run through the stamping presses to make sure the parts remain within strict tolerances, and automatically makes adjustments as it runs. The company also received industry media attention for its invention of an in-die welding progressive tool that produces and welds 70 parts per minute.

In 1999 Zawacki and Don Klein shared the company's success story in a book they co-authored called *It's Not Magic, the Rebirth of a Small Manufacturing Company,* with a foreword written by Lester Thurow, author, lecturer and professor at MIT. They also created *The Magic Workbook,* offering others "the tools you need to transform your company."

Nursing a struggling company back to health isn't easy. But the success represents another testimony to the dedication of associates working together towards a common goal and to strong leadership.

In 1999 GRS&S became one of 25 small manufacturers in America to win the *Industry Week* "Growing Companies Award." Companies were selected because they "epitomize both the struggles and strengths of U.S. entrepreneurship and are models for the U.S. wealth-creating sector." Zawacki will be the first to say, though, that the journey to continuous improvement never ends. It's a race without a finish line.

In-house training is regularly provided to associates because at GRS&S, improvement is a never-ending journey.

GWI ENGINEERING, INC.

Designing machines for the factories of the future is not easy. It requires innovative engineers and highly skilled tradesmen to pursue a complex journey involving computers, lasers, robots and other technology. It can take months — sometimes years — to design and build an automated system.

However, with patience, skill and quality engineering, GWI Engineering, Inc. has risen to the challenge. Since 1955 its skilled professionals have been solving complex manufacturing problems for many durable-goods manufacturers within the automotive, appliance and furniture industries. Solving and servicing those high-tech needs contributes to the success of Grand Rapids' healthy economy, where manufacturing is an essential component. Companies like GWI Engineering keep pace with technology and play an important role in helping to shape the city's future.

Peter A. Cordes is president and CEO.

Today, with nearly $15 million in annual sales, GWI Engineering employs a skilled work force of more than 50 engineers, electricians, welders, fabricators, computer designers, pipefitters, computer numerically controlled (CNC) operators, machinists, assemblers and other skilled tradesmen.

LaVerne R. Scherer and Earl F. Goodrich, co-founders of GWI Engineering

The company is vastly different from what it was in 1955, when a World War II veteran and his wife, while on vacation, dreamed of owning their own business. LaVerne "Vern" R. Scherer had learned metal fabricating skills while serving in the U.S. Navy. He subsequently worked as a fabricator for a machine tool company in Grand Rapids. That company was VanDyke Machine & Tool on Michigan Street NE, the current site of GWI Engineering.

With his wife Ruth's encouragement, Vern approached both his father-in-law, Earl F. Goodrich, and his good friend, Lyman Stevens, a fellow machinist, with an invitation to join him in his new venture.

Although Goodrich owned and operated his own company, Goodrich Manufacturing, located in Reed City, Michigan, he saw promise in the welding industry. Deciding to support his son-in-law's new venture, he sold his interests in Goodrich Manufacturing. Consequently, the small firm then known as Scherer & Stevens, Inc. was founded on West River Drive in Comstock Park, immediately north of Grand Rapids.

Scherer and Stevens were designing and manufacturing automobile welding equipment at the very time that America was enjoying postwar prosperity and its fabled love affair with the automobile. They prospered accordingly.

In 1958 Ron Scherer, Vern's son, joined the company as an apprentice, ultimately becoming its president during his 32-year career there. In 1960, another family member, Roy Goodrich, uncle to Ron, bought Lyman Stevens' interests, and the company was renamed General Welders of Michigan, Inc. Eventually, the new company's growth necessitated a move, which brought it to its current location — the old VanDyke Machine & Tool building. During the 1970s and the 1980s, the building was expanded three times.

Then, in 1978 Vern and Roy retired, selling the business to their respective children, Ron Scherer and his sister, Connie Scherer Vawter; and John and Earl

(Far left)
Axle welder built for Dana Corporation

Transmission sub-arc welder produced for GM Powertrain

Goodrich. Under Ron Scherer's leadership, computer-aided design equipment was implemented in advance of many other companies, and robots were introduced in the early 1980s. These innovations enabled General Welders to integrate both robotics and computers into the machines they built. Eventually, lasers were added to their technology. During this period of technological innovation, the business grew and was renamed GWI Engineering, Inc. to reflect the company's expanded capabilities.

Unfortunately, Ron Scherer died in 1990, leaving his sister, Connie Vawter, at the helm when the economy was facing a downturn. The effects of the Persian Gulf War and economic recession left the company vulnerable to cash-flow problems. During this time, faced with greater stringency in the banking industry and delayed payments from customers, Connie Vawter was forced to sell the company to Peter Cordes, a highly respected mechanical engineer, and two silent investors. Eventually, Cordes became the company's sole owner.

The company's respected reputation and its skilled work force lured Peter Cordes, a former co-founder and co-owner of Grand Rapids Machine Repair, Inc. He set out to attract additional employees within the industry while nurturing those already in place as he concurrently reinvested company profits.

Today, GWI Engineering boasts a formidable list of diversified customers in the metal-forming industry, including Mayflower Vehicle Systems, General Motors, Whirlpool, Ford, GE Appliances, Frigidaire, Daimler-Chrysler and Aetna Industries. Designing and building automated welding systems remains its specialty. However, GWI Engineering also builds automated assembly equipment, robotic work cells, specialized testing equipment, complex material-handling equipment, and hot melt and adhesive application cells.

Unlike many of its competitors, GWI Engineering builds nearly all of its machine components in-house, thereby assuring top quality. This capability derives from a full line of lathes, boring mills and CNC equipment.

Peter Cordes is rightfully proud of today's company. "It's large enough to deliver, small enough to care," he says. "People take pride in their work and like a challenge." With a skilled work force, strong leadership and its eye on the future, GWI Engineering holds the right formula for continued success.

Peter Cordes speaks to employees and spouses at the 2000 GWI holiday party.

HAVILAND ENTERPRISES, INC.

The Great Depression severely tested virtually every industry in this country and the furniture industry in Grand Rapids was no exception. Some members of the industry survived that test while many others did not. One casualty of those difficult economic times in the early 1930s was famous Grand Rapids furniture maker Berkey & Gay, which in 1929 had been the largest manufacturer of fine furniture in the world. When the company's plant on the east bank of the Grand River closed, a young chemical engineer named J.B. Haviland was out of a job.

Haviland, who created and tested wood-finishing compounds for the furniture manufacturer, convinced Berkey & Gay to preserve its laboratory. Prior to its closing the furniture company allowed Haviland to completely equip that laboratory and then, at the time of its closing, sold the laboratory to Haviland.

That laboratory and a young chemical engineer's personal effort to survive the Great Depression, has evolved into Haviland Enterprises, Inc., which is one of the largest chemical distribution companies in the United States. J.B. Haviland initially used that laboratory to test water samples for various municipalities in West Michigan. Then, in 1934, he founded a chemical supply company that now operates directly across the Grand River from Berkey & Gay's original location.

Haviland Enterprises, Inc. operated as a family business in northwest Grand Rapids for more than half of a century, with J.B. Haviland serving as chairman of the board until his death in 1982, at which time his wife, Mildred Haviland, was named to lead the company's board of directors. During this critical transition period, six of Haviland's 12 children served on the board and in 1989 made an exceptional decision to name a CEO from outside the family.

Haviland's logistical capabilities allow the company to move more than 260 million pounds of chemicals annually throughout the United States and to other parts of North America.

The Haviland family selected H. Richard Garner to lead its company and over the next decade Haviland Enterprises. Inc. doubled its business, earned International Organization for Standardization (ISO) 9002 certification, established a professional board of directors from outside of the Haviland family, purchased property upon which a new warehouse facility is being constructed and initiated an employee stock ownership program that now accounts for one-third of the company's ownership.

Haviland currently employs approximately 135 people, with another 25 employees joining the staff on a seasonal basis. "We have a group of talented, dedicated people in this company," says E. Bernard Haviland, president of the company's two divisions: Haviland Products and Haviland Consumer Products. "They are dedicated to quality and to exceptional customer service and they have played a pivotal role in helping us get where we are today. As we continue to grow and prosper, we'll work as a team to improve our business and serve our customers." Approximately 15 percent of Haviland's employees are scientists. "We test the integrity of every load of material that comes into our company as well as every load that we send out," Haviland says.

Haviland Products maintains a broad-based inventory that provides commodities and specialized chemical products and processes to industry. The company's on-site laboratory and safety departments support a vigilant quality control program that ensures the safe handling of over 2,500 chemicals and processes. Haviland Consumer Products formulates, blends, packages and distributes almost 100 different liquid- and dry-chemical products for more than 50 private-label swimming pool and retail customers.

"Making the supply chain process easier is our mission," says F. Norman Christopher, who replaced the retired Garner as Haviland's CEO in January of 2000. "Our dedication to providing expert service, a comprehensive product line and fair prices help us stand out as industry specialists with value-added services. A commitment to the world we live in also is evident in the availability of environmentally friendly products that Haviland can help successfully integrate into manufacturers' production processes." Maintaining the highest environmental quality is nothing new to Haviland. Joe Haviland, the founder's brother, was active in developing the first waste treatment equipment sold to metal finishers in Grand Rapids and was considered an expert on environmental issues.

While Haviland Enterprises, Inc. produces, packages and distributes more than 2,000 chemical products, from acetone to zinc, the company also produces specialty chemicals which meet the unique needs of a variety of industrial processes. Haviland works arm in arm with its suppliers and its customers to ensure safe chemical handling and efficient utilization and disposal of the chemicals it distributes. Haviland scientists are able to provide the technical support its customers, such as platers and anodizers, need and could not provide for themselves. These services, along with custom packaging, contract manufacturing, toll blending and a specialization in the handling and use of inorganics, heavy metals and hazardous materials are among the chemical services Haviland has and will continue to provide industry. Haviland is the link between large chemical producers and the end user. That end user could be a company as small as a one-man shop or as large as General Motors.

Whatever the size, Haviland makes all of its laboratory services technical support available to ensure safe chemical transport and handling and to help customers maximize the effectiveness of the chemical products their processes require.

Haviland Enterprises, Inc. also is viewed as an industry leader in personal and environmental safety education and training. The company's safety department is available to customers and other members of the community 24 hours a day. The company also has developed an extensive library of more than 130 video and audiotapes dealing with the safe handling of chemicals, general safety, swimming pool safety and regulatory concerns. Haviland makes these training tools readily available to customers, schools and government institutions.

With its new warehouse facility being constructed immediately west of its offices, Haviland's new CEO expects the company to continue its record growth in future years as it explores the opportunities of e-commerce and service orientation as they relate to chemical distribution.

"Business is changing very rapidly right now," Christopher says. "The studies that we have performed indicate that these changes will have a significant impact on our business and that we can be a major player in developing new business techniques."

The new warehousing and manufacturing facility begun in 2000 will be in full use in 2005.

IRWIN SEATING COMPANY

The story of The Irwin Seating Company debuts in 1907. Two Irwin brothers, Robert and Eber, established cornerstones in the prestigious Grand Rapids furniture industry with the Royal and Phoenix furniture companies, merged with two outside investors and their brother, Earle S. Irwin, to create The Irwin Seating Company. Grand Rapids, recognized as "The Furniture City" since the 19th century, embraced this business, which has since evolved into a world-class company capturing the global market in the manufacturing of public seating for movie theaters, auditoriums, performing arts and convention centers.

The youngest Irwin brother, Earle, was appointed general manager of the company, with both older brothers maintaining positions on the board of directors. As a result of perseverance and economic acumen, the Irwin family assumed majority stock in the company within a few years of its inception. The business remains a privately owned corporation.

The current Irwin Seating Company facility has evolved from historical beginnings.

In its early days, Irwin Seating Company occupied a facility on Buchanan Avenue on the southwest side of Grand Rapids and employed between 100 and 150 workers. Surviving the furniture strike of 1911, Irwin Seating continued to bask in America's Victorian-era-inspired love of furniture. The company continued under the helm of Earle S. Irwin until his son, William W. Irwin, joined the company in 1933. Father and son worked in tandem, together creating the blueprint for this unique company's success.

Upon the United States' entry into World War II, American industry's customer base shifted from citizens to the military. Irwin Seating Company joined most American businesses in supporting the war effort; it discontinued manufacturing furniture and transformed into Irwin Pederson Arms and produced M-1 carbines for the cause.

After the war Earle S. Irwin suffered from ill health, and his son, William, predominantly guided the business, although the senior Irwin remained involved in the company for the rest of his life. Profound effects from the war dictated a rebirth of the company — locating inexpensive used machinery, hiring workers and planning a new building. Ed Anderson, plant engineer at this time, played an integral role in restructuring the Irwin Seating Company throughout this era.

Continuing the legacy of family leadership, William W. Irwin gained the company's presidency in 1946. Senior Irwin brother, Robert, retired in the 1950s; however, he remained a diligent overseer and champion of the company for many years.

A decision that unequivocally shaped Irwin Seating Company's destiny occurred in the 1960s. Public school seating comprised a significant portion of the company's business through the 1950s. However, in response to the use of less-expensive plastic materials in classroom seating in the preceding decade, William W. Irwin invested in auditorium seating, recognizing that focus held stronger potential for the company's growth. This decision ushered Irwin Seating into its future.

The company did indeed flourish in response to the focus on commercial seating, and in 1967 Irwin Seating moved its manufacturing facility. Its location in the city constricted expansion possibilities, forcing the operation to move from Buchanan Avenue to its current 450,000-square-foot world headquarters on Fruit Ridge Avenue in Walker, Michigan.

In 1975 Earle S. "Win" Irwin, son of William W. Irwin and current president of Irwin Seating, joined the company. He served in a variety of capacities within the company,

The Buchanan Avenue Plant served Irwin Seating Company well until company growth dictated more space.

including vice president of manufacturing, as a prelude to his appointment as CEO and president of Irwin Seating Company in 1984 upon his father's retirement. "Win" Irwin attributes much of the company's economic progress and global growth to the tireless work of his employees, such as current Senior Vice President of International Operations Paul Winchester. Winchester, an Irwin Seating employee for over 30 years, was the primary architect in forging the company's domestic expansion and, later, international growth.

In 1973 Irwin Seating acquired Irwin Canada in Etibicoke, Ontario, a facility that manufactures and renovates auditorium seating. The next acquisition occurred in 1986 when Irwin Seating Company bought the American Seating line of classroom furniture. For the following decade, classroom seating was re-emphasized within Irwin Seating Company. This business doubled, yet at the end of the 20th century, the company discontinued its moveable classroom furniture to focus solely on auditorium seating.

Irwin Seating Company acquired Folding Bleacher Company, a business that manufactures telescopic platforms and bleachers, in 1991. Retaining its original name and location in Altamont, Illinois, Folding Bleacher remains strong in sales.

In 1996 Irwin Seating Company entered the global market with the acquisition of APM Irwin Seating Sdn. Bhd. in Malaysia. In 1999 the international market exploded for the company as it acquired facilities in China, Brazil and Spain. Domestically in 1999, Irwin purchased Country Roads, a company that manufactures and renovates auditorium seating in Greenville, Michigan. Irwin Seating Company currently holds eight facilities, employing 1,100 worldwide.

Although not a technology-driven industry, technological advances have affected Irwin Seating Company. The most significant changes rise from the burst in the late 1980s of multiplex movie theaters. Irwin Seating took advantage of this explosion, which peaked in the North American market during the late 1990s. Despite a national decline in the development of multiplex theaters, this market has experienced strong global growth, feeding the company's international presence. In the auditorium education market, new products include "e-link," the company's trade name for auditorium and lecture hall seating products featuring large writing surfaces and electrical components for power and data connectivity in the classroom setting.

Another new focus includes a line of movie theater seating called "The Signature." The Signature series can be tailored to the customer's requirements and includes the popular option of "articulation," which provides lounging movement in the chair's back.

The challenge for Irwin Seating Company's continued prosperity is for manufacturing to become leaner, connecting improved team-management skills with new ideas. Projecting a ubiquitous international presence is a company priority.

Irwin Seating Company balances industry growth with community involvement. A stronghold in the Grand Rapids area since the turn of the 20th century, the company reinvests in a vast spectrum of community activities, a reflection of the company's family-based heritage.

Versatility, ingenuity and integrity — the foundation for the future of Irwin Seating Company.

The Irwin Seating Company building on Fruit Ridge Road NW in 1968

PLASTIC MOLD TECHNOLOGY

Photos by Todd Zawistowski

It's not easy being an automotive supplier. Observers say the industry is very competitive, intense and demands a highly skilled work force. Nor is it easy to make a profit.

But over the years, Plastic Mold Technology (PMT) stands out not only as a survivor but also as a leading-edge model for success by carefully and consistently making the right choices in a challenging environment. The company makes molds that automotive manufacturers and suppliers use to produce plastic parts. Nearly all of the big automotive companies are its customers.

To stay ahead in the fast-paced automotive world, Plastic Mold continuously makes large investments in its employees, company and technology. When many suppliers were only thinking about achieving high quality standards to become ISO9001 registered, PMT earned this distinction in March 1997. Recently it also became QS-9000 compliant.

Innovation is another hallmark for the company. It recently developed and patented a new injection process that molds plastic together with leather in one cost-saving operation. The end result is an actual leather surface for the same look, color and feel of other leather-upholstered components.

Observers may attribute the company's success to its longtime owner, Gary Proos, who worked his way up in the industry starting as an apprentice. But there's no

question in Gary's mind that the credit belongs to his 120 employees. Many have been with the company for more than 20 years. "I've always said that my most important function in this company is to put together a team of people who can make us successful," he once told a writer. "And that's certainly the case here. Our employees are highly skilled and talented people. I believe the continued success of this company is the direct result of their efforts."

A goal for Gary is to create a Christian, family atmosphere that provides good wages and benefits, as well as the ability to support missions and ministries that proclaim the Gospel.

Originally the company was known as Woldring and Associates. Founded in 1958 by Adrian Woldring, the company initially specialized in selling electrical discharge machining (EDM) equipment from a small, leased building on South Division Avenue in Grand Rapids.

While giving demonstrations to customers, Woldring frequently obtained EDM work instead of machinery sales. As a result, the company gradually shifted from machinery sales to a die-cast, die-making company. By the late 1960s the company had evolved into building plastic injection molds primarily for the automotive industry.

Gary joined the firm in 1963 as an apprentice shortly after graduating from Grand Rapids Creston High School. For years he attended evening college classes while working full time. The company was just beginning to build plastic injection molds. Intrigued with the industry, Gary later became a project manager at Leon Plastics in Grand Rapids, where Woldring was a customer.

At age 31, when Gary decided to start his own mold shop in 1974, Adrian Woldring offered to sell his to Gary and Gary's partner, William DeJong. At that time, the company employed about 20. As the economy sputtered along with high gas prices, a slumping automotive industry and recession during the 1970s, the company diversified with work from appliance manufacturers and the office machine industry.

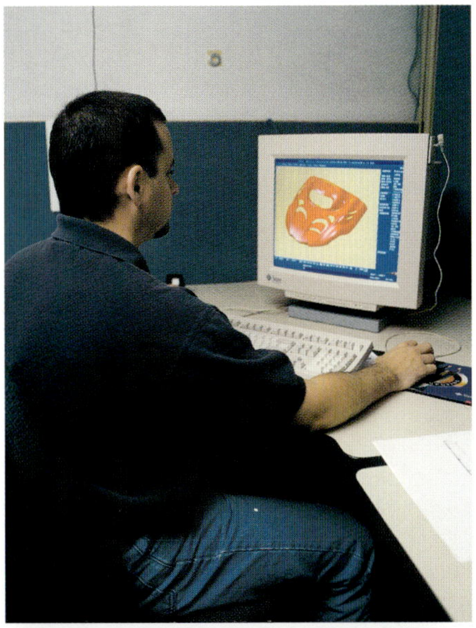

Photos by Todd Zawistowski

But when the economy improved, the company moved into its present headquarters on Broadmoor Avenue SE in Kentwood in 1978, installing the latest state-of-the-art equipment. Unbeknownst to Gary and William, the country would soon again struggle through a recession. Sales began dropping dramatically in the early 1980s. "I was broke," recalls Gary. "I was working so hard, I didn't know it." His days routinely ran 14 hours while his wife, Mary, cared for their three young children, Julie, Catherine and Gary S.

Gary became the sole owner when William retired in 1984 and sold him his stock. By 1985 the company's name was phased into Woldring Plastic Mold Technology and eventually just Plastic Mold Technology.

Plastic Mold became known for doing whatever it took to service the customer. Gary says he never intended for the company to get as large as it is today. He would have been happy with a 40-person shop. But customers began pushing the company to do more work. So from 1985 to 1987, Plastic Mold Technology doubled its number of employees, machines and factory space. Once the molds were made, Plastic Mold Technology invited customers to the plant for "mold tryouts." The molds ran on Plastic Mold's machines, which were identical to those used by the customer, saving the client time and money.

Today, Plastic Mold is a big business for its industry. Each machine in its plant cost at least $1 million; the molds themselves cost at least $100,000. Mold tryouts are conducted on 12 injection molding presses at the company's second facility on Model Court SE, directly west and adjacent to the firm's headquarters. Gary's son manages the plant while his daughter, Catherine Herron, manages Plastic Mold's marketing. Julie Buckmaster, the oldest child, lives in Lansing and is in real estate.

Because more than half of the company's employees are highly skilled tool-and-die makers, the company started its own apprenticeship program for mold making — a tool-and-die specialty. Since 1993 Harv Ribbens has taught the program, which has graduated more than 30 moldmakers.

As president, Gary no longer runs the company's day-to-day operations. He leaves that to managers, including general manager Don Boehlke, controller Dave Snellink and plant manager Ted Sarver. When the company remodeled in the mid-1990s, his managers got larger corner offices with a view. Gary took one that's closer to the size of big closet. It used to store files.

"I don't need to impress anyone with a big office," he later told a reporter from *The Grand Rapids Press*. "Those guys have customers coming in to see them all of the time."

After all, as Gary knows, it's those loyal customers who recognize quality and value that will help keep Plastic Mold Technology successful in the future.

RoMan MANUFACTURING INC.

A rich heritage brimming with tradition, family and friendship serves as the basis upon which a world leader in resistance welding power sources, RoMan Manufacturing Inc., builds today.

The history of RoMan Manufacturing Inc. begins years before its official founding in 1980 by Dietrich Roth and Robert Hofman. Both Roth and Hofman worked for a large manufacturing corporation as division general manager and division sales manager, respectively. As the 1970s drew to a close, Roth and Hofman found themselves at career crossroads. Faced with a decision to move if career advancement was desired, these friends sought a more creative solution to their dilemma and bought the transformer product line of Harlo Products, an offshoot of the company for which they had worked for many years. Thus in 1980 RoMan Manufacturing Inc., a merging of both their last names, was born in Grand Rapids, Michigan.

Robert Hofman and Dietrich Roth equally shared the workload in their new venture. Hofman continued in his area of expertise with sales and marketing while Roth served as president and engineer. Through their conservative business dealings, RoMan Manufacturing Inc., steadfastly expanded while maintaining its core focus on resistance welding transformers and DC power supplies. In 1984 RoMan Manufacturing Inc. bought the transformer division of Dollar Electric, boosting its already-flourishing business with the addition. Another major business coup occurred in December of 1991 with the acquisition of TransPower, an affiliate that supplies welding transformers and portable welding stations for the Ford Motor Company. In 1998 RoMan Manufacturing continued its growth with the purchase of Kirkhof/Goodrich, extending its line of resistance welding transformers and DC power supplies into the global marketplace.

The RoMan Manufacturing Inc. management team: (left to right) Donald Decorte, Mark Siehling, Kurt Hofman, Robert S. Hofman and Robert Roth

As the years progressed and the business grew, both Hofman and Roth faced another major decision: should they prepare RoMan Manufacturing Inc. for sale or would a second generation of Roths and Hofmans acquire the business reins? They approached their children regarding ownership and the transition from the first generation to the second transpired as Robert S. Hofman, Kurt Hofman and Bob Roth assumed leadership roles in RoMan Manufacturing Inc. Robert S. Hofman joined the company in 1980, learning the business from the ground up. In 1987 Bob Roth and Kurt Hofman joined the team, offering accounting and engineering backgrounds to the manufacturing fold. Although the elder Hofman and Roth turned over management in 1997, their impact continues as they contribute their skills as counselors and ambassadors for the company they created.

Currently eight people own RoMan Manufacturing, Inc.: a combination of 3 Roth and 3 Hofman siblings as well as Don DeCorte, director of sales and marketing, and Mark Siehling, vice president of engineering. While Bob Roth serves as president, Kurt Hofman is executive vice president of application engineering and Robert S. Hofman holds the office of manufacturing manager, the entire management team collaborates on operational decisions. Other siblings serve the company through their work on the board of directors. This unique formula of families working together in a productive, gracious manner challenges common conceptions of ill-fated family-owned businesses.

Due to frugal business dealings, RoMan Manufacturing has capably financed its expansion internally. In the year 2000 RoMan Manufacturing, through its diligence and perseverance, supplies 95 percent of the small but crucial resistance welding transformer market in North America.

The business of transformers is a cyclical one, with approximately 75 percent of its growth driven by the automobile industry, making RoMan Manufacturing's proximity to the automobile capital of the world, Detroit, significant. RoMan Manufacturing's Grand Rapids 47th Street location houses 125 employees on three sites: a 45,000-square-foot headquarters hosting 85 employees, an 18,000-square-foot TransPower Division employing 25 workers and a Service/Repair Division with the remaining 15 employees. Loyalty and pride are staples for RoMan Manufacturing Inc. employees. This company boasts such a dedicated workforce that retirement is a primary reason for workers vacating their positions. RoMan Manufacturing ownership attributes their reputation for quality workmanship and outstanding customer-service to employee stability and the Western Michigan community that produces this unparalleled resource.

Although the resistance welding business rarely must react to immediate changes in its trade, contemporary events have impacted RoMan Manufacturing. The area of robotic welding has influenced resistance welding in the last decade of the 20th century and promises to affect the industry's future as it alters the style of transformers from a fixture-style to a transgun-style transformer. New product areas for RoMan Manufacturing include large, three-phase DC power systems used in the welding of aluminum, and heavy fabrications such as wheels and brake shoes, which are shipped worldwide, and inverter DC welding. Another strong concentration in years to come will be miniaturization of transformers, the creation of smaller yet fully functional packaging of transformers. The use of plastics in automobiles is another area that requires proactive monitoring, as the use of this material instead of metal would negatively affect the contribution of resistance welding to this industry.

"Return, Reuse, Recycle" is the environmental philosophy by which RoMan Manufacturing lives and works. It reuses every salvageable part, recycling materials such as copper, aluminum and steel, and remanufactures old transformers that might otherwise clutter a scrap yard.

RoMan Manufacturing demonstrates commitment to the Western Michigan community in ways beyond environmental responsibility. Founder Dietrich Roth contributes his time to Habitat for Humanity activities, Bob Roth serves as an executive board member of the Grand Rapids Area Chamber of Commerce and Kurt Hofman sits on the Ferris State University School of Technology faculty advisory board.

Continuous improvement of current products and ceaseless dedication to providing impeccable customer service stand as the premier goals of RoMan Manufacturing Inc. The unique talents and perspectives of the family leadership — the technical and the marketing — complement each other. As RoMan Manufacturing Inc. encounters the challenges of the ever-evolving future of technology, it will continue to celebrate its family-rooted legacy and the stability it provides to its surrounding Western Michigan community.

RoMan Manufacturing Inc.'s primary coil-winding department is vital to making the company a world-class operation.

SUSPA INCORPORATED

When Suspa Incorporated hired its first employees in Grand Rapids during the winter of 1974-75, the country was beginning to emerge from a recession.

Suspa's parent company in Germany, then known as Suspa Federungstechnik GmbH, was a leading supplier of gas springs. It was convinced that a manufacturing and sales operation in the United States could capture part of the growing market from American automotive manufacturers.

Established in 1950 in Altdorf, Germany, Suspa chose Grand Rapids for its U.S. manufacturing and sales operation because of its close proximity to Detroit, where the major American auto manufacturers were based. Suspa Inc. established itself as a Michigan business in November 1974 a time when gas prices rose along with the price of automobiles.

The small, energy-efficient hatchback was becoming a popular car among Americans car buyers. And Suspa's parent company, now known as Suspa Holding GmbH, produced the gas cylinder that was used to raise and hold open the hatchback lids of cars. The name Suspa, in fact, is derived from the word "suspension."

As a handful of employees waited anxiously for orders in the company's leased building on Roger B. Chaffee Drive SE, they were hoping their new employer would join America's economic recovery.

Soon enough, production of gas springs for the U.S. market began for Suspa's first customer, American Motors, in January 1976. Everyone found themselves busy doing a little of whatever came along, including vacuuming on Saturdays. They were happy to be making about 80 to 100 cylinders a week. Servicing the customer was — and remains — a high priority.

Suspa's sales and manufacturing facility on Roger B. Chaffee Drive now boasts 135,000 square feet.

In September 1978 sales reached $1.5 million, forcing the company to add a second shift. The payroll now exceeded 70 workers.

Soon Suspa was experiencing phenomenal growth. And Erina Hanka, who was hired in April 1975 as its corporate secretary and human resources manager, began experiencing quick promotions.

By 1980, when sales rose to more than $5 million, the German-born Hanka rose to become the company president. She stepped down from day-to-day activites in June 2000 and is now chairman of the board of directors. And instead of producing 100 cylinders a week, the Grand Rapids facility now manufactures about 170,000 a week, employs more than 250 and hit sales of almost $58 million in 1999.

Suspa's impressive success story makes it a stellar member of a small but important group of thriving Grand Rapids manufacturers with parent companies outside the United States. Its prosperity has led management to persuade other foreign companies to set up their businesses in West Michigan.

Because Suspa made only the gas cylinders for the hatchback car, its first years in Grand Rapids were difficult. When its automotive customers worked overtime, Suspa employees worked overtime. When the customers laid off employees, Suspa cut back on its workforce.

To help level the volume of sales, the company began to diversify in the late 1970s with a vast number of additional applications for its popular gas cylinder. Under the careful direction of innovative and highly imaginative engineers and designers, Suspa developed thousands of applications for its gas cylinder. It was the start of a whirlwind ride that sent sales soaring.

Many are patented cylinders used in jukeboxes, airplanes, beds, doors, windows, treadmills and more. There are millions of gas cylinders in chairs all over the world because Suspa is a dominant cylinder supplier to the American office seating market.

Employees with more than 20 years of service are honored at Suspa's 25th anniversary in late 1999.

When the country began sliding into its worse recession since the Depression, Suspa had outgrown its original building. It moved to a new 54,000-square-foot facility on Roger B. Chaffee Drive SE, a few blocks north of its first building.

Even as sales temporarily dipped in 1982 to $6.7 million during the recession, *Inc.* magazine listed Suspa in 1983 as number 177 among its 500 "fastest growing, privately held businesses in the United States."

As the economy improved, sales soared to $23.6 million in 1987. The facility Suspa had erected only five years earlier was bursting with activity, forcing a 15,000-square-foot addition.

One of the most significant changes in the company occurred in the early 1990s when the company was reorganized into four business groups: Automotive and Suspension Components, Chair Components, Diversified Components and Lift Systems Components. Before this, all products were centralized under sales and marketing. The reorganization allowed each unit to focus on specific needs of its unique customer base.

Today, Suspa is a world leader in the design and manufacture of lift, support, damping and adjustment devices, including locking and non-locking gas spring cylinders, dampers, impact absorbers, spring struts and lift systems. Its gas cylinder remains its most popular product. Sales to the automotive market represent only a tiny fraction of its business.

In addition to its Grand Rapids manufacturing and sales facility, Suspa Holding GmbH has four manufacturing facilities in Germany, one in India and sales offices in 24 countries throughout the world. It employs more than 1,500 worldwide, with sales of almost $155 million.

To accommodate such customers as Whirlpool and Maytag, Suspa broke ground in 1999 for a 20,000-square-foot addition in Grand Rapids. It's used to produce suspension systems for home washing machines. That same year, the company also became ISO 9001 registered.

One of Suspa's newer products is a fluid drive lift system called MOVOTEC®, which is used in a variety of work settings that require variable height adjustments, including telephone operator stations, hospital surgical tables, industrial workbenches, conveyor platforms and more.

Over the years, the company has earned a reputation for taking care of its employees and helping the community. Those who have worked with the firm for years can attest to management's "open-door policy" and its unswerving dedication to keeping employees informed about anything in the company. Strong communication has resulted in good working relationships between management and workers.

Employees and independent Suspa sales representatives gather outside the Grand Rapids office during a get-together in the mid-1980s.

Hanka attributes the company's remarkable success to teamwork and the dedication of its employees. Many have stayed with Suspa for more than two decades, a tribute to the company's caring attitude and success in retaining employees.

That close-knit atmosphere is one of many reasons why the company is confident about future success. "Whether it's the staff or the janitor, it doesn't make any difference," Hanka says, "because we need them all to be successful. I'm so proud of them."

BENTELER AUTOMOTIVE CORPORATION

An automobile drives down a straight road, when suddenly another car coming from a different direction crashes into its side door. The passengers of both vehicles live. Before 1983 this happy ending was much less likely, and there were many more deaths resulting from side-door crashes.

For the past several decades, manufacturers and suppliers have searched for ways to make safer automobiles. As a result of its own efforts, Benteler Automotive produced a simple but innovative product that has been responsible for decreasing the death toll from side-impact accidents — the first state-of-the-art door beam.

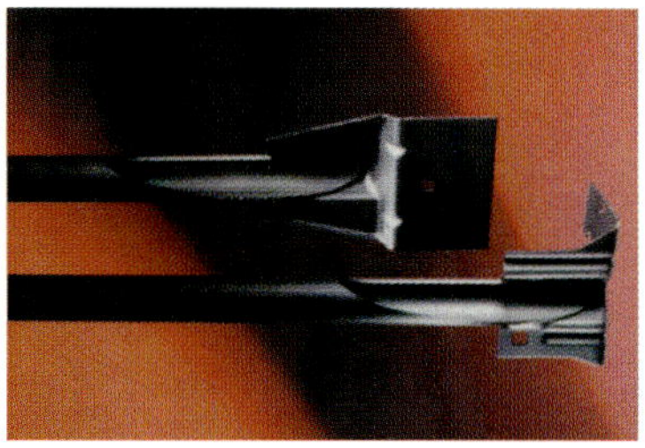
Side-impact door beam

Benteler AG was founded in Germany in 1876 by Carl Benteler, a young 23-year-old entrepreneur. Benteler was gifted with foresight and an interest in iron and the products it could create. He acquired an iron fabricator, Klopping's Bielefeld, which was a domestic hardware store that provided the foundation for the new company, Benteler Automotive.

Carl Benteler, founder

In the early days, Benteler pioneered products such as a window bar of iron tubing, welded pipes, motorcycle and bicycle parts and some of the first components for the automotive industry, including the first exhaust pipes for the Ford Eifel. Today, Benteler is a leader in the design and manufacturing of fabricated metal components, with over 16,000 associates worldwide.

In 1978 Benteler AG established Benteler Industries in the United States and based its corporate office in Grand Rapids, Michigan. It has become one of the largest employers in the local community. Later expansion of plants in the surrounding area included three in Grand Rapids, one in Kalamazoo, Michigan, and two in Fort Wayne and Goshen, Indiana.

Benteler is a leader in the automotive supply industry with its superb design and manufacturing of chassis structural components, fabricated exhaust systems and side-impact management systems. The company is one of the world's largest users of laser cutting technology, demonstrating its commitment to innovation and to using the most modern, cost-effective methods available to deliver consistently superior products.

Now renamed Benteler Automotive Corp., the company was recognized by the industry when it received the prestigious PACE Award. Benteler first received the award in 1998 for innovation and excellence in its development of the dual-wall, air-gap manifolds and tubes. But it didn't stop there. The company won the PACE Award again in 1999 — two years in a row — for innovations inherent in Ford's WIN88 axle.

Benteler supplies nearly all Original Equipment Manufacturers (OEMs), including General Motors, Ford Motor Company, Daimler-Chrysler, Honda, Toyota, Subaru and others. The company has developed this customer base by its consistent production of high-quality fabricated components designed to protect passenger safety and exceed Environmental Protection Agency (EPA) standards.

History has shown how brilliant and creative engineers can be. Benteler's engineers have proven to be among the most innovative and talented in the automotive industry, in turn, affecting the quality and safety of the cars people drive. What ingenious new technologies will Benteler design in the future? It's certain that they will be products that both protect the environment and enhance the safety of motorists everywhere.

GILL INDUSTRIES, INC.

While many people dream about starting their own business, John Gill did so in a way most would not have the courage to attempt. Gill, a Grand Rapids resident, had a successful position as a journeyman tool and die maker at the local General Motors Fisher Body plant. And in the 1960s, holding a secure, well-paid position in the automotive industry was a luxury. But Gill had a vision that would allow him to harvest even greater success than he imagined.

Gill's dream of starting his own tool and die company grew out of his conviction that he could improve production methods for progressive dies in the metal industry. He was certain that he could produce parts with less material at a lower cost while maintaining higher quality than was then available in the industry.

With a large family then consisting of his wife and their 10 children, Gill's decision to let go of the secure paycheck was both admirable and risky. But Gill was confident in himself and his dream. With a small savings and the solid support of his wife, Rita Williams, Gill and his brother-in-law, Gerald, formed Gill & Williams Tooling in a rented 1,500-square-foot building on Division Avenue.

In two short years the building was bulging at the seams, requiring a move to a larger facility. In 1966 the company moved into a new 4,200-square-foot home in Byron Center, conveniently located across from Douglas Walker Park. In these early days, Rita and her now 12 children would often come to the park for lunch. The family had grown, and so would the company. In 1985 John Gill bought out Gerald Williams' share of the company when he retired and Gill & Williams became Gill Industries.

Today, John Gill's vision has grown into a major supplier to the global automotive industry and a respected corporate citizen. Its more than 750 employees produce mechanical interior automotive parts such as adjustable headrests and latches that move seats. Gill Industries, Inc. comprises Gill Tool and Die in Wyoming and three manufacturing facilities, two in the Grand Rapids area and one in Trenton, Georgia.

"We are a people-oriented company that seeks to provide a safe and pleasant working environment with good pay and benefits," says CEO and board chair Rita Williams, who makes it a point to personally visit each new employee. "We are committed to quality and excellence in all that we do." This commitment resulted in the company being awarded the prestigious "Supplier of the Year" award from General Motors in 1994.

Gill Industries is also committed to giving back to the community. Hope Network, a local nonprofit organization dedicated to helping the disabled and disadvantaged gain productive employment, honored Gill Industries with its "Good Corporate Citizen" award in 1996. The company has also been instrumental in the construction of a Habitat for Humanity home in the Grand Rapids area.

John Gill's dream of having both a large family and a successful business has been fulfilled, and his story remains a motivational one for others. When asked the secret to success, Gill made it clear what was most important: "To make your people — family, employees and customers — your No. 1 priority."

Rita Williams is shown here receiving the Automotive News 100 Leading Women Award, 2000, with her husband, John, and their family.

GRAND RAPIDS CONTROLS, INC.

It all started in a barn.

In the early 1960s Ed Mancewicz was a working man striving to support his family. By day he worked for Wolverine Coil Spring; by night and on weekends he created a company in his barn. Today, this same cable-manufacturing company, Grand Rapids Controls, Inc., boasts $40 million dollars in annual revenue. A street sign bearing the name of Ed Mancewicz leads into the headquarters of the company he started many years ago.

In 1968, after dabbling in the growing plastics industry, Ed Mancewicz formed Grand Rapids Controls, Inc., housed with Grand Rapids Spring and Wire on Waldorf NW in Walker. In 1972, embracing his mission for company growth, Ed Mancewicz bought a 6,000-square-foot-facility on Monroe Street. Grand Rapids Controls moved in with 10 employees who produced plastic hood-release handles/cables and vent controls for Buick Motor Division. The business grew slowly, with 99 percent of its focus on supplying the automotive industry.

When a 35-acre property on Northland Drive in Rockford, the company's current location, became available through bankruptcy in 1977, Ed Mancewicz noted the opportunity and purchased it. Housing 30 employees and producing $2 million in annual business, this manufacturer of control-cable assemblies and components remained primarily committed to automotive clientele. The mid-1980s recession created peaks and valleys within the automobile industry, forcing Grand Rapids Controls to re-evaluate its business plan. Survival dictated diversity within its customer base. Targeting the strong Western Michigan furniture industry, Grand Rapids Controls formed a rewarding partnership with Steelcase, and in 1991 it began producing and shipping for the furniture maker. Business flourished.

The early 1990s witnessed dramatic growth in the automotive and furniture industries, and Grand Rapids Controls continued to thrive, growing from 80 to 300 employees and increasing annual sales from $7 million to $18 million. But that was not the only significant transformation to positively impact this company during this decade.

"I grew with the business," claims Linda Southwick, eldest child of Ed Mancewicz and owner of Grand Rapids Controls, Inc. since her father's retirement in 1996. Assuming progressive levels of management since the 1980s, Southwick took over the reins well versed in the workings of this cable-manufacturing business and dedicated to preserving the tradition of family atmosphere that pervades the company. She maintains that the destiny of Grand Rapids Controls is steered by its 460 employees who, true to her father's progressive management style, Southwick greets on the manufacturing floor with a cheery "good morning" at least once weekly. Annual employee golf outings and an employee picnic every July exemplify this company's sense of family. This commitment extends into the community as well. Southwick sits on the board of directors of the Rockford Area Chamber of Commerce, and the company sponsors internships for Western Michigan-area college students and fireworks for Rockford's annual "Start of Summer" celebration.

It started in a barn; humble beginnings for a humble man with a strong work ethic and love of family. It continues into the 21st century and beyond.

Grand Rapids Controls, Inc. boasts a street sign named after its founder, Ed Mancewicz.

THE RIGHT PLACE PROGRAM

As Michigan struggled with double-digit inflation in the early 1980s, Grand Rapids business leaders decided a single economic entity must be developed to serve as a resource for marketing the Grand Rapids area. In 1985 The Right Place Program, a unique, private/public, nonprofit economic development organization, was founded as a response to that need.

Led by Birgit M. Klohs since 1987, the primary emphasis of The Right Place Program has been retaining and expanding area manufacturers and attracting new manufacturing employers to the region. Serving as the organization's first executive director, Milt Rohwer worked hard to garner private-sector support with an initial goal of 70-percent private and 30-percent public funding. Today, The Right Place is 75-percent private and 25-percent publicly funded.

The Right Place Program has continued to leverage that community support. The organization's retention, expansion and recruitment efforts have helped businesses in the region create and retain more than 12,000 jobs. With assistance from The Right Place Program, Western Michigan companies have invested more than $1 billion in capital improvements.

In addition to providing direct assistance to area companies, The Right Place Program is aligned with the Grand Rapids Area Chamber of Commerce. Sharing space in downtown Grand Rapids, the two organizations collaborate to continuously improve the West Michigan business climate while partnering with other area economic-development entities on regional-improvement issues.

In 1995 The Right Place Program worked in partnership with area manufacturers to open a learning facility in a renovated manufacturing plant. The former Sackner Products building houses a place where manufacturers come to learn from each other and improve their collective competitiveness. Industry councils, continuous-improvement user groups and workshops all take place within its walls.

To support these and other manufacturing assistance services, The Right Place Program became the West Michigan regional office of the Michigan Manufacturing Technology Center in 1996. As such, The Right Place Program connects area manufacturers to a state and national network of manufacturing support resources. That same year The Right Place Program merged with the Research & Technology Institute of West Michigan, adding R&D and technology-transfer assistance to its complement of manufacturing assistance programs.

Later that year The Right Place Program entered a contractual arrangement with the city of Grand Rapids to provide concentrated economic assistance in the city's urban core. Rick Chapla joined The Right Place staff in 1996 as its Urban Redevelopment Specialist and worked to develop an Urban Redevelopment

Council composed of business and community leaders. With the opening of the Van Andel Institute in May 2000, The Right Place Program is working in tandem with the community to promote the growth of a new biomedical industry cluster.

The Right Place Program remains dedicated to regional economic growth through high-quality job creation and retention. To that end, its staff continues to support the development of area manufacturers and encourage new business. It proudly serves as a steward for the retention, expansion and recruitment of industry in West Michigan.

MARKETPLACE

Grand Rapids retail establishments and service industries offer an impressive variety of choices for Grand Rapids residents and visitors.

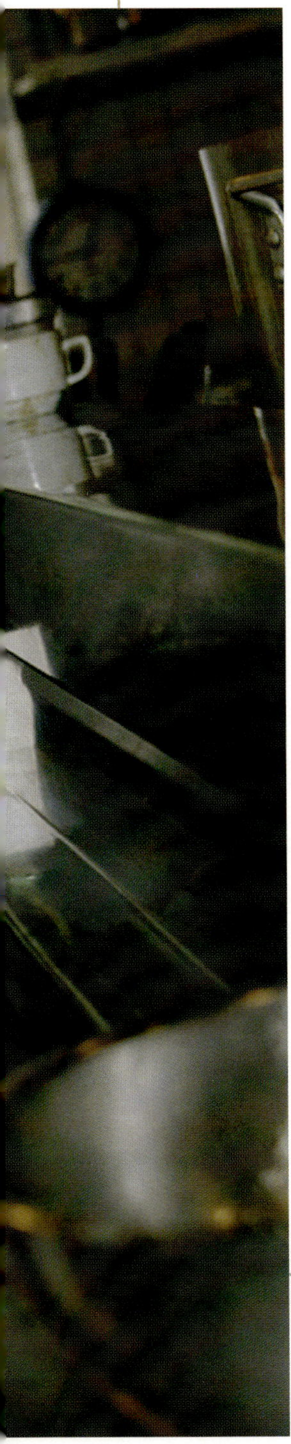

D&W FOOD CENTERS, INC.

Roy Woodrick never belonged to a formal fraternity. He did, however, have a group of young friends and acquaintances with whom he met regularly to discuss what they had learned and what they might do with that knowledge in the future. Woodrick met with his "fraternity brothers" almost every day, whenever he went to work. In the 1930s Woodrick worked for A & P, a popular West Michigan grocer, and he and his co-workers were learning every detail of the retail food industry.

Roy Woodrick founded D&W in 1943 with $2,000 of his own money and a $500 loan from a friend.

D&W first operated under the IGA banner in Grandville, Michigan.

Having spent more than 18 years learning the business, in 1943, with $2,000 of his own money and a $500 loan from a friend, Woodrick opened his own store in Grandville under the IGA logo. The store featured only two checkout lanes, but it quickly became known for its friendly service and superior meat, since it was one of the first area stores to sell exclusively USDA Choice Beef.

Three years after opening his store, within months of the end of World War II, Woodrick formed a partnership with Sid DeVries, who was one of his former A & P colleagues and who had returned to West Michigan after a stint in the Navy. As a result of that partnership formed by DeVries and Woodrick in 1943, D&W Food Centers now serves West Michigan with 26 store locations. Of the 26 stores currently operated by D&W, 16 are located within the boundaries of metropolitan Grand Rapids.

A second-generation Woodrick, Bob Woodrick, currently serves as the chairman of the board of D&W Food Centers. "My dad and Sid both worked at A & P and so many independent retailers in this part of the state got their training at A & P," Bob Woodrick says. "It was like a fraternity. A & P was their college and that was their fraternity."

Because the Grandville IGA flourished throughout the early 1950s, Woodrick and DeVries decided to open a second store in 1957. Bob Woodrick, who had been working with his father at the Grandville store, moved his family to Cascade to manage the new addition. Four years later, Woodrick and DeVries decided to become members of Spartan Stores, a cooperative distribution facility located southwest of Grand Rapids, and with that decision, D&W Food Centers was born and the company's trademark heart logo was adopted.

"When we opened that second store, we did $15,000 in business the first week and I thought that was a lot," Bob Woodrick says. "Now we have stores that do more than that in an hour. I don't think my dad ever dreamed that we would be this size. When he died (in 1974) we only had eight stores and only three of those were actually ours; five of them were controlled by Spartan."

Roy Woodrick died the year after his son began to assemble a strong management team that undertook the task of developing a company philosophy. D&W's management team wanted to establish a working philosophy, one that every member of the organization could understand, relate to and, most importantly, practice. The D&W Philosophy was developed and today remains the cornerstone of the company, and its 1973 establishment remains a significant event in the history of the company. With Bob Woodrick as chairman of the board, Jeff Gietzen serves as the company's vice-chairman and CEO. Other members of the D&W executive committee include Doug Blease, who is the president and COO; Jerry Matthews, who is a senior vice president and CFO; Wayne Boatwright, who is the senior vice president of operations and human resources; and Scott Rzesa, who is the senior vice president of sales and merchandising.

The D&W Philosophy, first presented by the management team, reads in part: "At D&W we realize that the success of our company will ultimately rest upon our ability to satisfy the needs and desires of our customers, D&W associates and the community of which we are a part. Aware of these challenges, we will always strive to promote the welfare and growth of our fellow associates and to provide the finest in services and products to our customers."

A continuing effort to practice that philosophy helped D&W Food Centers build a reputation of service, quality and innovation as the company expanded throughout the 1970s and 80s. "We have always been the service leader in West Michigan, and where we will position ourselves in the future will be in an even greater expansion of that service," says Ron Cox, D&W's vice president of marketing.

D&W's stores numbered 10 when the Walker location opened early in 1980. This facility brought more diversification to the company as it featured an in-store pharmacy and a floral shop. These departments, as well as well-stocked delis and bakeries, are now common in D&W stores. Also in the early 1980s, D&W changed the physical appearance of its stores, landscaping the exteriors and projecting a low, sharp facade. The interior of the stores now featured wallpaper rather than paint; floral and greeting card sections were carpeted, and poster art was added to the decor. Variations in lighting were experimented with and a particular emphasis was placed on the presentation of all perishables, such as meat, produce, and deli and bakery products.

D&W innovation has included numerous products and services, as well as the presentation of those products and services. "We have clean stores with wide aisles and in this market, we blazed the trail as an upscale food

Current chairman, Bob Woodrick, followed in his father's footsteps in managing a D&W Food Center early in his career.

retailer," Woodrick says. "Our stores were the first to offer delis, the first to offer pharmacies and the first to offer floral shops. If you wouldn't serve it in your home, we wouldn't put it on our shelves."

Offering delicatessens and floral shops to its customers was not enough, however, for Woodrick and the D&W management team. The company built Central Kitchen, a centralized commissary facility, to better serve the deli departments. Central Floral, a centrally located distribution center, was also constructed to serve the growing number of floral shops within D&W stores. "With Central Kitchen and the floral facilities, the deli recipes are our own and the floral products are ours and everything is fresh," notes Woodrick. D&W also has developed one of West Michigan's widest varieties of specialty foods, as well as an extensive selection of wines.

With the January 2000 opening of stores in Rockford and Portage bringing the number of D&W Food Centers to 26, the company plans to continue to develop its reputation as a quality store with quality people and quality service. "Where we are headed in the food retail world, as with all changing businesses, is to consolidation," Cox says. "The future in West Michigan, as in other markets, will see a few major players, with other smaller retailers filling in the gaps."

With its 26 stores and 4,500 employees, Cox sees D&W as one of those smaller retailers. "Those major players will have the purchasing power that they can

D&W was a leader in bringing new concepts to West Michigan supermarket shopping, including full-service delis, floral and expanded wine departments featuring imported and domestic products.

leverage, which we cannot," Cox says. "In the future we will look to serve those customers who are more focused on quality and value. Our mission is to provide the finest food shopping experience and create the best overall value for our customers."

What made D&W different and successful when Roy Woodrick and Sid DeVries first formed a partnership in 1946 is exactly what will make D&W Food Centers different and successful in the future. "We are going to have to be the food experts with different products — better products," Cox says. "We are going to have to be the people with better service and quality."

Market research within the retail food industry indicates that American shoppers now shop more often and spend less at each visit than in previous years. "D&W will be focused on convenience and quality, offering people superior products but getting them in and out of our stores faster," says Cox, who also noted that D&W could buck an industry trend in an effort to better serve its customers. "Because of that focus on convenience and quality, you might see us building smaller stores instead of larger ones, which is the norm in the industry right now."

"Instead of trying to be all things to all people," Woodrick says, "we are going to be the best for those people who choose to shop with us."

D&W Food Centers has a strong heritage of providing support to the communities of west Michigan. D&W supports many organizations through the donation of both financial and human resources. As stated in the D&W philosophy, the success of the organization is partially dependent upon their ability to help sustain a strong community. D&W believes very strongly in providing adequate assistance in meeting the social needs of the communities it serves. D&W management members serve on the boards of numerous nonprofit organizations and the company contributes to hundreds of local agencies and groups each year. D&W associates are one of the largest groups of contributors to local United Way fund drives and they have a high level of personal involvement in a multitude of organizations within their communities.

D&W's innovation has not been restricted to the products in its stores nor the quality with which its products are presented. D&W also has been progressive in its thinking, in its commitment to integrity and the elimination of racism. The company has been internationally recognized for celebrating diversity and healing racism.

"It is time in American society to embrace our founding ideas of equality, opportunity and justice for all," Woodrick remarks. "D&W Food Centers is actively working toward healing racism and celebrating diversity. These initiatives are expressions of our integrity and ongoing pursuit of excellence."

D&W has led the way among Grand Rapids-area businesses in its practice of hiring workers of all ages, from all walks of life and with wide varieties of physical challenges. In fact, D&W Food Centers boasts a relatively high percentage of older workers. "We welcome older workers," Woodrick says. "Older workers are some of our best workers because they want to be there." The company also has hired countless disabled and physically challenged workers, including hearing-impaired associates.

"Commitment to diversity goes beyond a statement at D&W," according to Woodrick. "Our associates are committed to healing racism in our company and our community. Our relationships are built on caring, fairness, honesty, service to others and inclusiveness. Our associates are recruited from the full spectrum of the work force, educated to value diversity and trained to serve all customers with dignity and respect. D&W seeks to partner with those who support our diversity commitment."

D&W has instituted a three-pronged program in which every one of its associates learns to welcome diversity and eliminate racism. The initial step in the program is entitled Living with Diversity and features a one-day workshop that each entry-level employee attends. The final step in that program is the Institute for the Healing of Racism. D&W's leadership in this area has prompted the local chamber of commerce to institute the Employers' Coalition for the Healing of Racism and prompted Grand Rapids to host the second International Conference for the Healing of Racism. D&W also has joined Aquinas College in creating the Woodrick Institute for the Study of Diversity and Racism.

"We came to the conclusion that you have to address racism and cannot ignore diversity," Woodrick says. "At D&W we have made a distinction between healing racism and valuing diversity. Healing racism is becoming aware of and correcting the effects of racial prejudice and discrimination in our personal lives and in our community."

According to Woodrick, valuing diversity means learning what and how differences among associates, suppliers and customers are relevant and valuable to the retail food industry. "We do this not just because it's good business, but because it is the right thing to do."

D&W places high emphasis on design and decor in the shopping experience, as indicated here in one of its latest stores, featuring Frank Lloyd Wright's prairie-style architecture.

(Left to right) D&W Vice Chairman and CEO Jeff Gietzen, President and COO Doug Blease and Chairman Bob Woodrick

ALTICOR INC.

The front-page headline in the October 24, 2000 *Grand Rapids Press* announced big news: "Amway gets a parent — Alticor."

Beneath the bold type, the story told how Amway Corp., a West Michigan success story for 41 years, decided to make itself an even stronger competitor for the 21st century by adding three siblings to its corporate family — along with a new parent company, Alticor Inc.

The announcement marked the latest in a long string of bold moves that had helped the company grow from two friends working out of their basements into a global direct-selling giant that employs approximately 10,000 people worldwide. Founded in 1959 by lifelong friends Jay Van Andel and Rich DeVos, Amway is a pioneer and perennial leader in the direct selling industry. From a small sales force selling a single product, an all-purpose cleaner called L.O.C., Amway has evolved into much more. Today, Alticor companies research, create, manufacture, market and distribute more than 450 company products and operate in more than 80 countries and territories. The Alticor management team is now led by Chairman Steve Van Andel and President Dick DeVos — each the son of an Amway co-founder — and other members of the second generation are also involved in guiding the company's future.

The Alticor family of companies is based in Ada, Michigan, with other operations in West Michigan and around the world. It has a vision of helping people live better lives — a goal made apparent through its products and services. Its business opportunities empower people to reach for personal goals and give them the support to achieve them. Diverse products and services meet customer needs in nutrition, wellness, beauty and home care. And Alticor is also known as a great place to work.

Alticor's subsidiaries, Amway, Quixtar Inc., Access Business Group Inc. and Pyxis Innovations Inc. carry on the founders' values while adding unique strengths and talents for competing in the modern marketplace.

(Left to right) Rich DeVos and Jay Van Andel, co-founders of Amway Corp.

AMWAY CORP.

One of the world's largest direct selling companies, Amway offers a low-cost business opportunity and top-of-the-line products, including Artistry® skin care and cosmetics and Nutrilite® vitamins and supplements, backed by a customer satisfaction guarantee. By helping millions worldwide earn extra income, Amway helps people live better lives. Today, operating in more than 80 countries and territories, Amway expanded outside the United States to Canada in 1962, Australia in 1971, Europe in 1973, the Pacific Rim in 1974, Central America in 1985, South America in 1993 and Africa in 1997.

QUIXTAR INC.

In 1999 Web-based business Quixtar launched and quickly rocketed to a leadership position in the competitive e-commerce market. Quixtar-affiliated Independent Business Owners (IBOs) generated more than $518 million in sales at Quixtar's Web site and its Partner Stores in its first year alone, making Quixtar one of the most successful e-commerce companies. Quixtar-affiliated IBOs in the United States, Canada, Puerto Rico, U.S. Vergin Islands, Guam and the Pacific Islands refer customers to the site and earn bonuses and incentives based on the business volume generated by sales made to clients, members and other IBOs. Quixtar offers dozens of top-quality products in the beauty, health and home categories plus a variety of name-brand products and services.

ACCESS BUSINESS GROUP INC.

Access works with the business-to-business market, offering other companies its services in the areas of product development and formulation, manufacturing, private labeling, logistics services, packaging design, freight and warehousing. Together with its affiliates, Access operates manufacturing facilities in the United States and the People's Republic of China. It also operates farms in the United States, Mexico and Brazil. Access provides services supporting clients such as Amway, Quixtar and a range of other name-brand and private-label manufacturers. Additionally, Access operates distribution centers across North America. Access draws on more than 40 years of experience shipping raw materials as well as storing and distributing finished goods. It also has a significant transportation, warehousing and distribution infrastructure. Access also operates Access Print & Design, which produces packaging and marketing materials.

(Far left)
Alticor Inc. Chairman Steve Van Andel

Alticor Inc. President Dick DeVos

PYXIS INNOVATIONS INC.

Pyxis is the corporate development arm of the Alticor family of companies. The company contributes to the growth of Alticor and its subsidiaries through the creation of new products, services and business opportunities and through mergers and acquisitions. It does a lot of work in the areas of nutrition, wellness and beauty, combined with the marketing power of e-commerce. An important part of Pyxis' business is staying ahead of new technology, trends and consumer needs.

THE COMMUNITY

Improving the quality of life in the communities where Alticor does business is also very important to the company and its subsidiaries. It does this by sharing its time, money and other resources. In West Michigan, where the companies are headquartered, it participates in numerous projects. Since 1980 it has helped sponsor local events such as Celebration on the Grand and August in Ada. Since 1981 the company has sponsored the West Michigan kick-off party for the Toys for Tots campaign, which in one night results in the donation of hundreds of toys to give to needy children for Christmas. Since 1989 it has partnered with Sigsbee Park Elementary School in Grand Rapids to help students academically and through programs that boost their self-esteem. Since 1990 it has been a sponsor of Children's Miracle Network of West Michigan, which provides health care programs and services for children. Alticor also continues to support the arts and other programs in West Michigan and throughout the world.

Today, Grand Rapids and West Michigan also have benefited from the tremendous community involvement of the Van Andel and DeVos families. The families have been major sponsors of the Women and Children's Center in Spectrum Health, Van Andel Arena, the Van Andel Institute of Education and Medical Research, the downtown business campus of Grand Valley State University and several cutting-edge medical research foundations.

Helping people live better lives is a commitment that the people of Alticor, Amway, Quixtar, Access and Pyxis dedicate themselves to every day. Not only is West Michigan benefiting a great deal from this great family of companies, so is the world.

Alticor's world headquarters complex in Ada, Michigan, is the center of an international business that encompasses more than 80 countries and territories. Most of the products offered by its subsidiaries are manufactured at this site, nestled at the juncture of the Thornapple and Grand rivers.

SUPERIOR SEAFOODS & MEATS

One day when the lake was calm, a young man watched from the shore. The view of the water offered one of the most beautiful scenes on earth. With no land in sight, it was easy to forget that this was not an ocean, but the most expansive freshwater mass in the world. Filled with hundreds of shipwrecks, coastal shoals and a vast array of fishes, these powerful, pristine waters have a force that can inspire. Lake Michigan, one of the five Great Lakes, called out that day nearly 50 years ago to the young man, Paul Osterhaven.

Osterhaven decided to create a business that would sell only the freshest fish to the Grand Rapids area, which was in need of a top-notch fish supplier. He and his 15-year-old son, Bruce, founded a small fish supplier in 1954. Back then, there were no supermarkets. The fishery sold to corner grocery stores in neighborhoods, restaurants, hospitals and country clubs.

It was a small enterprise in the beginning that sold only Great Lakes freshwater fish — but it didn't take long before increased demand made expansion a necessity. Feedback from customers provided Bruce Osterhaven with the confidence to form a larger company with an expanded product line and the name, "Superior Fisheries." As the business prospered Superior outgrew many locations as more employees were added.

Two sons, Paul and Keith, began working in the business, and in 1976 the youngest, Jim, also joined the company. Later, Keith went on to start his own smoked fish operation. As the years went by, Paul and Jim, who both grew up in the seafood supply industry, took over many of the management responsibilities of the business so that their father could retire. In the late 1990s, they purchased the business from their father and have continued to run the business with a flawless record of quality.

Today, with Jim Osterhaven serving as president and Paul Osterhaven serving as vice president, this family business and its employees place the needs of customers at top priority. This means that only the freshest, finest-quality food — with the highest standards — can be delivered. Superior has been approved by the United States Department of Agriculture (USDA) and by the United States Department of Commerce (USDC) since these inspection endorsements began. Additionally, Superior is now certified as a Hazard Analysis of Critical Control Points (HACCP) plant. This plan identifies the hazards involved in handling seafood or any food product. By becoming HACCP Certified, Superior has demonstrated the highest standards of both sanitation and safe manufacturing procedures. Commitment to quality does not end with government inspections, however. Superior provides rigorous training to its employees in sanitation and sound manufacturing procedures. Superior will maintain its commitment to product safety by meeting or exceeding federal standards and investing in new technology as it becomes available.

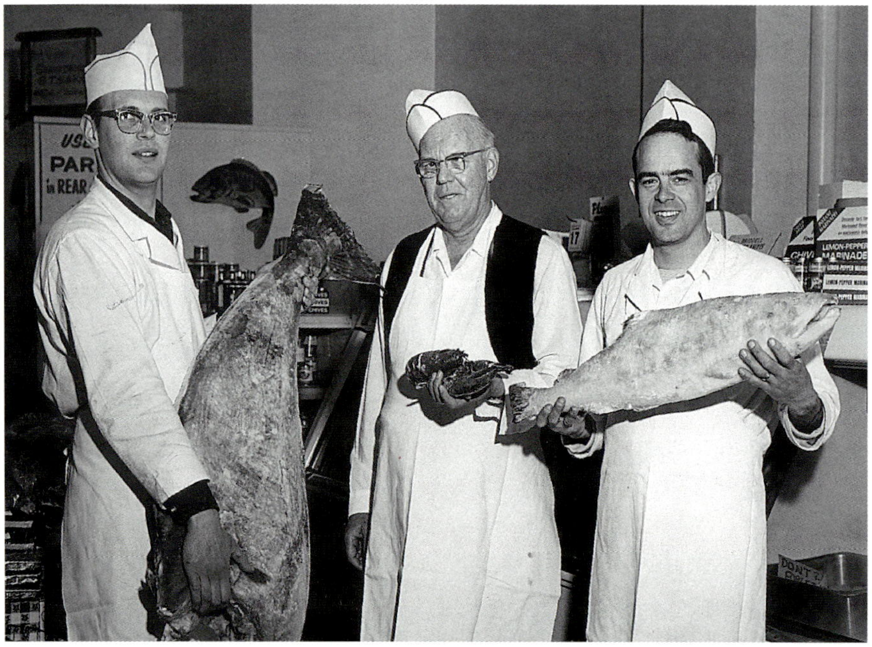

Paul Osterhaven with his son, Bruce, and his son-in-law, Harry Start.

"We are the only seafood facility in the Midwest to achieve this level of inspection," Jim Osterhaven says with pride. These standards have assured the growth of the company over the years. Today, seafood generates 75 percent of company sales. Meat, game and poultry are new lines that have been added in response to the full-service demands of the local marketplace. Other added products include side dishes and desserts. With these new products added to the mix, it was natural for the company to be renamed "Superior Seafoods & Meats."

One of the quality trucks in the extensive fleet

Superior Seafoods & Meats is devoted to a mission statement that guides all of its employees every day. The mission — "Our success can only be measured by the success of our customers — exceptional service and quality products on every order for every customer" — is Superior's guiding principle. Superior service means working one-on-one with customers to develop the products they want. The company remains flexible and allows special orders, custom-cut seafood and steaks, packaging and labeling to customer specifications, marketing and promotional assistance, and complete institutional service programs. Superior Seafoods & Meats is proud to have earned the right to serve over 800 restaurants and 1,200 retail stores throughout the Midwest. Still located in Grand Rapids, the company has over 100 loyal employees and a truck fleet of 25 vehicles delivering only the freshest and finest seafood and meat. Superior also has its own dock space at Northwest Airlines' terminal at the Gerald R. Ford International Airport in Grand Rapids.

"When my dad was alive we dreamed of building a business with sales of half a million," says Bruce Osterhaven. "Today, Superior enjoys almost $1 million per week. It's amazing how my father started it, not knowing a great deal about the seafood business. The entire family sure has gone through a tremendous learning process."

Great are the lakes in Michigan, and one could call them many things — prosperous, oceanlike and rich. But today, the oceans have added products Osterhaven only dreamed of in the early days, including seafood from Australia, Hawaii, Chile, Alaska, Ecuador, Iceland, Norway, Africa and many points in between. Freshwater lakes and saltwater seas have provided the Osterhaven family with the ability to bring the finest, freshest and most superior seafood to communities throughout the Midwest. And with Superior's commitment to quality and safety, there is no doubt that it will maintain its leadership position far into the future.

Superior Seafoods & Meats manufacturing facility

YAMAHA CORPORATION OF AMERICA

These days, it is uncommon to go to any type of musical performance and not see the name "Yamaha" appearing on the bell of a tuba or the face of a bass drum.

Yamaha Corporation of America's manufacturing facility in Grand Rapids is the center of manufacturing, distributing and marketing of Yamaha instruments in America.

With a complete line of musical instruments, professional audio products and other merchandise for both the amateur and professional musician, Yamaha is highly regarded by professionals, consumers, institutions and business people within the related industries. With a name that is synonymous with superior quality in the acoustics, design, technology and craftsmanship of its musical instruments and other consumer goods, Yamaha has endeavored to produce products and services that satisfy the diverse needs and desires of people worldwide.

Yamaha has endeavored to produce products and services that satisfy the diverse needs and desires of people worldwide.

With 44 subsidiaries throughout the world, it may seem unusual that such an international corporation would give and owe so much to West Michigan. Yet the presence of the Yamaha Corporation of America in Grand Rapids contributes to both the company and the enrichment of the lives of people in the area and around the world.

Since the Grand Rapids facility opened in 1973, Yamaha has relied on the skills of local artisans to produce the finest-quality instruments. In return, Yamaha has done much in organizing and sponsoring local musicians and the organizations to which they belong. Yamaha believes that manufacturing musical instruments is not an anonymous industry, but an intimate partnership between the company and community to work for artistic quality and human enrichment in all areas of music.

Although the company was founded in Japan in 1887, the partnership between Yamaha and Grand Rapids did not begin until 1972. While Yamaha was known throughout the world for its quality instruments, in the United States the company was one of many musical-instrument manufacturers on the market. At that time Yamaha had one facility in Los Angeles that established a sales-and-marketing network for the company's products, which were made in Japan. In order to create a stronger presence in the American market, corporate officials knew they would have to have a manufacturing facility in the United States.

With the U.S. band-instrument industry traditionally centered in the Midwest, officials at Yamaha focused their attention on that region and scouted cities in the areas for a prime place to build their new facility. At that time the Michigan Chamber of Commerce had an office located in Tokyo. Representatives from the chamber met with Yamaha officials and spent a considerable amount of time discussing which cities in the state would be favorable to the instrument manufacturer's needs.

After looking at several cities, it was evident that Grand Rapids was the ideal choice for many reasons. Aside from the location, the city was already an established center of national commerce. Grand Rapids also had a work force with a large number of highly skilled craftspeople from the furniture and automobile industries. This work force had the skills to create and adjust clarinets, flutes and saxophones as easily as it had created world-acclaimed cabinets, desks and cars. Almost a year after its search began,

Yamaha started moving into its new West Michigan manufacturing facility.

Today, Yamaha's 155,000-square-foot facility in Grand Rapids is the center of manufacturing, distributing and marketing of Yamaha instruments in America. Over 275 employees manufacture woodwind, brasswind and tuned percussion instruments. In addition to making more than 75 percent of the Yamaha wind instruments sold in the United States, the facility exports woodwind and brass instruments to the Canadian market as well.

To Yamaha, all of the instruments it produces symbolize the mutual respect that exists between those who make music and those who make musical instruments.

With a name synonymous with quality, Yamaha takes great pride in its Yamaha instruments. Many musicians such as clarinetist Buddy DeFranco, trumpeter Bobby Shew, flutist Jim Walker, saxophonist Eugene Rousseau and members of the Canadian Brass use Yamaha products because of the company's dedication to detailed craftsmanship. Others enjoy Yamaha instruments, such as orchestral and percussion instruments, for their musical precision and grace.

To Yamaha, all of the instruments it produces symbolize the mutual respect that exists between those who make music and those who make musical instruments. By manufacturing these instruments, many employees at Yamaha see themselves as contributors to the cultural life of the community and the country.

But Yamaha's contributions to the community go far beyond the construction of superb musical instruments. Yamaha's goal continues to be to succeed not only as a musical instrument manufacturer, but also as a corporate organizer and sponsor for activities that center on the enrichment of music in the community. For years, Yamaha has donated instruments to musical organizations and held clinics for professional musicians. Yamaha also sponsors concerts, symphonies and special events held by the Grand Rapids Symphony, the St. Cecilia Music Society and other musical societies in West Michigan and around the country.

In recent years Yamaha's focus has grown beyond helping established musicians to cultivating a new set of young performers through music popularization programs like the Yamaha Music School and the Junior Original Concert. Yamaha also hopes to interest many young minds with music and supports their exploration of music through concerts, after-school programs and scholarships.

Yamaha also strives to understand the needs of music professors and other educators. The company has established endowments to support musical programs and individual musicians at public schools, colleges and universities throughout the United States. In addition to donating funding, each summer Yamaha invites band directors and music educators from around the country to come to the Grand Rapids facility to see how its instruments are made. Here the directors and instructors can offer their input through the "Yamaha Listens" program.

Yamaha's name is synonymous with superior quality.

Yamaha's very basic corporate objective is reflected in its credo, "Play the Very Best You Can." For Yamaha the search for excellence is not only in what the company does, but also in how it does it. As the corporation looks to the future, Yamaha resolves to make further strides in fostering social and cultural development through its musical products. Indeed, everything that Yamaha manufactures contributes to the enrichment of the quality of lives for people of Grand Rapids and around the world.

AMWAY GRAND PLAZA HOTEL

It was only fitting that in 1913 the world's furniture capital, Grand Rapids, would be home to the beautifully designed and furnished Pantlind Hotel on the city's riverfront — a lavish testament to elegant craftsmanship. While the foundation of the hotel was being laid, the country had its own milestones that year: Grand Rapids-native President Gerald Ford was born, women first publicly wore silk stockings and the federal income tax was instituted.

Fashioned after English Adams Architecture by its designers, Warren & Westmore of New York City, who also designed that city's lavish Grand Central Station, it was termed "One of the Ten Finest Hotels in America" by 1925.

That tradition of beauty, craftsmanship and award-winning acclaim continues today. However, what was once the quaint Pantlind Hotel is now a towering monument of elegance: the Amway Grand Plaza Hotel.

Still sitting on the original property in the heart of the business and entertainment district, the Amway Grand was purchased in 1978 by Amway Corporation. which not only restored its original elegance by keeping the structure of the historical Pantlind, but added a 29-floor glass tower addition, complete with glass-walled express elevators and modern-day amenities.

Former President Ronald Reagan and Former British Prime Minister Margaret Thatcher are only two of the many world's dignitaries who have graced the 4-Star hotel, which is known for fabulous restaurants, stellar service and elegant decor.

The Pantlind Lobby is a tribute to splendor and drama: three Austrian crystal chandeliers, the country's largest domed ceiling of hand-applied gold leaf and a mammoth "sunburst," a golden artwork that hung for 150 years in the ballroom of the Palazzo Moroscini in Venice. The hotel's three-tiered copper fountain complements the Queen Ann and English Adams furniture.

Guests of the hotel browse the shops or relax in spacious rooms with romantic decor. All rooms retain Old World elegance while keeping up with modern amenities. The super-luxurious Grand Suites provide separate living and sleeping quarters, two baths and dazzling views.

Thirty meeting rooms and elegant ballrooms draw conventions and special events to this delightful hotel. After business is over, guests unwind in the indoor swimming pool, fitness center or lighted rooftop tennis courts. A private lounge and concierge services are available. There is easy access to the Grand Center, Plaza Towers and Van Andel Arena through the hotel's skywalk.

Among the main attractions of the hotel are the nine dining facilities. The 1913 Room is a lavish, oak-trimmed facility that recaptures the elegance of the era. The Cygnus, named for the swan constellation visible through its glass ceiling, offers gourmet cuisine and dancing under the stars. Bountiful fresh buffets showcase creative aspects of culinary art.

Condé Nast Traveler magazine ranked the Amway Grand Plaza as the 12th-best city hotel in North America and in the top 100 hotels in the world.

Standing on the banks of the Grand River and the site of the region's first trading post, the Amway Grand Plaza Hotel carries on a rich heritage of hospitality and symbolizes the spirit of timeless elegance.

BISSELL INC.

Necessity truly is the mother of invention. In 1876, as America celebrated its centennial, Anna Bissell cleaned the sawdust off the carpet of the crockery shop that she and her husband, Melville, owned in Grand Rapids. After watching his wife repeatedly struggle with the time-consuming nuisance, Melville Bissell designed and constructed a carpet sweeper that permanently ended her struggles. A patent was issued to Bissell in 1876 and soon thereafter he realized that his invention was more than a practical solution to a common household problem.

In 1883 the Bissells acquired a carpet sweeper company in an effort to amass the resources necessary to build a new manufacturing facility. By the time Melville Bissell died in 1889, making Anna Bissell the first female corporate CEO in America, the company the Bissells had founded was well on its way to establishing itself as the world's pre-eminent manufacturer of carpet sweepers, a position that BISSELL Inc. maintains today.

Where it all began: The Bissell crockery shop, c. 1876

BISSELL Inc. currently employs more than 600 production and office workers in the Grand Rapids area. The company, specializing in home cleaning products, including deep-cleaning machines, vacuums, sweepers, electrical appliances and cleaning formulas, operates sales and production facilities in the United States, Canada, Mexico, the United Kingdom, Ireland, United Arab Emirates and Australia. BISSELL also has been granted 225 trademark registrations in 75 countries.

In August 1996 BISSELL Inc. was awarded the President's "E" Award for Excellence in Exporting, an honor representative of four years of significant growth in exports from its Homecare Division.

"BISSELL has been a family-owned business enterprise for more than 123 years and the values demonstrated by our founders are the same qualities that we demand of ourselves today," says President Mark Bissell, who is the fourth generation of the Bissell family to lead the company. "This company will continue to strive to be the best there is by building upon the fundamental strength and integrity that have come to be associated with the name BISSELL."

The company's fundamental strength for more than a century has been the manufacture of home cleaning products, and it is that endeavor upon which the company plans to concentrate its future focus. The manufacturer of the first heated-solution, residential upright deep cleaner — the ProHeat™ PowerSteamer® — BISSELL recently introduced its built-in heating system to the company's popular Little Green® portable deep cleaner. The Little Green® ProHeat™ is the only small-area deep cleaner on the market equipped with a built-in heating element, which is a natural extension of the company's line of small-area deep-cleaning products.

"Our first responsibility is to the consumers who use our products, and if we are to meet their needs, everything we do must be the best there is," Mark Bissell says. "Our goal is to continue to produce the best home-cleaning products available."

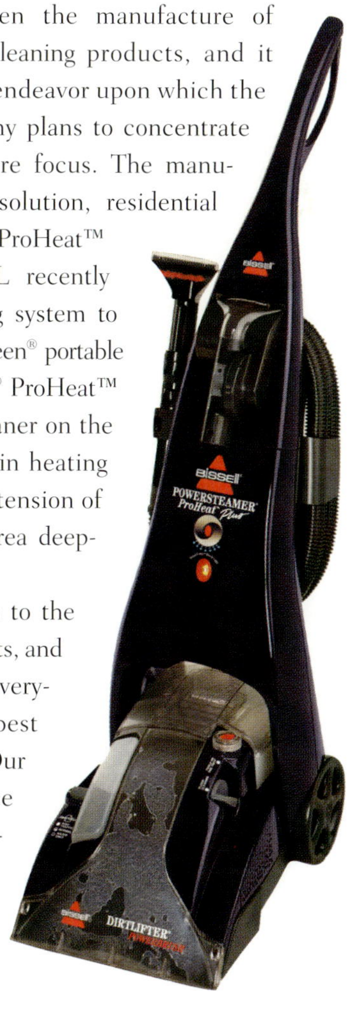

ProHeat™ is the first upright deep cleaner with a built-in heater.

CRYSTAL FLASH

For over 65 years Crystal Flash has been an innovator in the petroleum marketing and distribution industry. Offering convenience goods and services at its stations as well, CF's commitment to preserving the environment and supporting activities in the local community has established this family-operated business as a good neighbor in Grand Rapids.

Crystal Flash began in 1936 when Frank Fehsenfeld was sent to Grand Rapids to investigate a relative's faltering oil company. Impressed with his analysis of the company, Frank's father, John, founder of Crystal Flash Petroleum Group in Indiana, put his son in charge of the company.

In addition to wholesaling oil as his relative had, Frank opened a retail gas station. The outlet was successful, having excellent sales and profits in spite of competition. From 1936 to 1939, CF opened more stations throughout Grand Rapids. One station on Alpine Avenue became the company's headquarters.

A Crystal Flash station in the 1950s

Although CF flourished during the Depression, it struggled in the 1940s. During World War II, CF faced gas rationing and lost employees to the draft. In 1940 CF successfully expanded into the home heating service but struggled with this industry during the United Mine Workers strike in 1946. But the 1940s were also a period of development. On the suggestion of a CF station owner, Carl Henry, the company painted stations and fixtures white, gave their employees white uniforms, and began serving customers 24 hours a day. The innovation went over well and Henry was promoted to station supervisor of the company.

CF flourished until the Middle East crisis erupted in the 1970s. The company's previous oil contracts supplied local demand, but the uncertainty of the crisis halted station expansion. Instead, CF concentrated on other ways to expand business. Merging with smaller companies across the state, CF became the largest fuel oil marketer in West Michigan. In 1975 the company opened the first self-service station in Michigan. The same year, Tom Fehsenfeld, Frank's son, joined the company.

Like his father, Tom looked for new services to offer CF customers. On a test station, he remodeled the service bay into a grocery store. By 1980 most CF stations contained a convenience store. Franchise restaurants, bakeries and laundromats were later incorporated in some CF stations. In the late 1980s Tom expanded CF's home heating industry to offer propane service to customers.

Today, CF continues to be an innovator in the petroleum marketing industry. Committed to the environment, CF operates a profitable oil- and product-recycling program throughout Michigan. Believing that the company depends on the strength of the community, CF sponsors many nonprofit organizations and encourages employees to volunteer in these groups on company time.

An ability to look ahead and help develop innovative approaches to meet the ever-changing needs of its customers has kept Crystal Flash on the cutting edge. As the company looks to the future, Crystal Flash continues to be a leader, providing innovative products and services at its local stations and making further strides to be a good neighbor in the Grand Rapids community.

Crystal Flash today

GILMORE PARTNERSHIPS

John F. Gilmore and his son, Gregory, enjoy a passion for providing tremendous dining experiences in a variety of establishments throughout West Michigan. Couple this with an appreciation for historically significant buildings and locations and you have a legacy of landmarks. They currently operate over a dozen completely unique and outstanding restaurants while preserving some interesting architectural history. Their keen sense of value has helped them to collect excellent real estate as well as popularity.

Their largest establishment, excluding Redstone Inn in Colorado, is in downtown Grand Rapids. Located across from the Arena, the 70,000-square-foot, four-story, red brick building was constructed in 1903 as Judson's grocery warehouse. It stood vacant for decades before Gilmore Partnerships began its transformation, saving it from demolition. Its casual appeal, large size and age inspired the name The B.O.B. — an acronym for Big Old Building. The B.O.B. offers every individual a different experience, depending on the time of visit and the path taken once inside.

The B.O.B. houses several restaurants, an arcade, a cigar lounge, a microbrewery, banquet rooms, a comedy club, a dance club, a billiards hall, The B.O.B.ware shop, live jazz and a wine cellar. Changes and additions are planned. The restaurants include Gill's Fish House, Judson's Steakhouse, Sweet Wallace's Smokin' Blues BBQ and Bobarino's. The microbrewery — B.O.B.'s House of Brews — regularly wins awards around the country. It supplies all Gilmore Partnerships' Michigan locations with draft beer and just began bottling its beer. The B.O.B. hosts several weekly activities like Mug Club, Wine School, Jazz night and free swing dance lessons, not to mention performances by nationally touring comedians, concerts and theatre productions.

Another Gilmore property, Rose's on Reeds Lake in East Grand Rapids is a busy, cozy, bistro. It once was a boating and bathing club, which is depicted by vintage photos. Summer finds the lakeside deck packed with patrons enjoying wood-fired pizzas and daily fresh seafood creations. Rose's Express, opened in 2000, offers Rose's menu items to go from a charming storefront in Gaslight Village. Their oldest area restaurant, Thornapple the Bistro hosts weddings on its rolling lawn alongside the Thornapple River and parties in its rustic wine cellar. Its innovative simplicity and seasonal freshness attract those seeking unpretentious comfort in its fireside, garden or casual Taproom. Located in the charming village of Ada, it boasts a well-crafted menu and wine list. The lakeshore areas near Grand Rapids are home to other Gilmore projects such as the recently opened steakhouse, The Grill Room, and The Kirby, a social institution, both in Grand Haven, and Pinheads on White Lake with its bowling alley.

The Gilmore Partnerships maintain deep appreciation for their community and local history. Succeeding in the challenging, competitive hospitality industry and saving important buildings along the way, they continue to grow. They treasure their talented, dedicated team and enjoy the arduous work and requisite attention to detail and style. Perhaps most satisfying for them is the creative aspect of providing environments for people to enjoy dining and socializing. The Gilmore Partnerships are worth watching, as their creative endeavors multiply.

Photo by Todd Zawistowksi

HILTON GRAND RAPIDS AIRPORT

"They're back!" declares a hotel staff member as she receives the unusual but preferred couple that returns every year to the Hilton Grand Rapids Airport for the comfortable courtyard view and kind-hearted hospitality. They and their newborns have received first-class attention during every stay for nearly a decade. But these are no ordinary guests.

The Hilton's annual guests

This returning couple is the same pair of feathery parents that have given birth each year to new, fuzzy ducklings under a bush in the Hilton's courtyard. They are well cared for by staff employees all season long until they are able to fly the coop. But the babies cannot fly high enough to make it over the hotel from the closed-in courtyard, so the sympathetic staff escorts the family of ducks inside the hotel. They waddle down a hallway and out a side door where they are free to fly, and are given the warmest good-bye a guest of this outstanding hotel could ever receive.

The Hilton's expansive lobby

While many hotels strive to deliver excellent customer service, this hotel is in a class of its own because of its humanitarianism and its pampering and excellent care of its guests. It is a common occurrence for the Hilton Grand Rapids Airport to receive repeat out-of-town and local guests — of the human kind — due to this kind of superlative treatment.

The Hilton Grand Rapids Airport is owned and operated by MeriStar Hotels and Resorts and is ranked a market leader in Greater Grand Rapids. The hotel hosts the same amenities as national or international Hiltons, including bonuses for both hotel and airline mileage programs. Meeting, banquet and event services are offered in a 7,000-square-foot catering facility with meeting rooms up to a 400-person capacity.

Not only are local businesses and out-of-town guests — human and not so human — impeccably treated by the Hilton Grand Rapids, it is common practice for the hotel to support worthy charitable causes and organizations.

Hotel management and staff believe in the importance of assisting human-interest nonprofits that help many individuals and their families in unfortunate circumstances. The Hilton contributes human involvement to these activities. For example, the hotel hosts such organizations as the March of Dimes, and the Hilton staff involves itself in the "Walk for the Cause." The hotel is also a notable sponsor of many events, such as the National Multiple Sclerosis Society's MS Walk, as well as a co-developer of campaigns with the American Cancer Society. These important contributions are just a few of the hotel's benevolent activities. The Hilton Grand Rapids Airport is recognized for creative community involvement that goes beyond that of the average hotel.

Even ducks are treated so well that they return time and time again to the Hilton Grand Rapids Airport, though they could stay anywhere they wish. Visitors return for the hospitality of a hotel that knows how to treat everyone — whether human or not — with first-class service.

NOTO'S OLD WORLD ITALIAN DINING

Once upon a time, far away in the city of Custonaci, Sicily, two young men joined forces to build a memory by designing and laying bricks in a stone mosaic circle in front of their town's church as a gift, a remembrance. These men were the Noto brothers, ancestors of Tony, Tom and Joann, who along with their mother, Mary Noto, are proprietors of Noto's Old World Italian Dining in Grand Rapids. Family, tradition and pride are the essence of this fine-dining establishment.

The Noto family traditionally held its annual family reunion on the first Sunday after New Year's. On that Sunday in 1985, family members decided it was time to expand their small, family-owned-and-operated pizza restaurant and video arcade located on Lake Michigan Drive by adding on and remodeling. When the head of the Noto family, John A. Noto, died the following day, his family made a commitment; the dream would become reality. In February 1997 another family dream was achieved when Noto's Old World Italian Dining, a pronounced transformation from the earlier humble Noto eatery, opened on 28th street.

Upon opening the heavy wooden front doors of Noto's Old World Italian Dining, focus is drawn to the many black-and-white photographs of children and weddings adorning the brick walls of the entryway, detailing family heritage. Warm, flavorful aromas of spices and pasta tempt; an immense, circular mosaic-tiled floor design — a unique reflection of their Sicilian heritage — creates a monastic ambiance; vases filled with colorful flowers grace white linen-covered dining room tables as classic opera floats through the air. The feel is of walking through time to another era, another country. Rough-cut flooring and thickly hewn walls boast photographs of Grand Rapids' Italian sister-city, Perugia. Statues of summer and spring add a mystical Mediterranean touch. Old World Italian culinary masterpieces, many consisting of family recipes, are prepared by long-time Noto's chef and family friend, Chef Frank Amodeo II. Guests delight in the likes of Bruschetta, hand-made crostini topped with marinated roma tomatoes, garlic, olive oil, basil and parmagiano, served with an Italian wine of choice, the meal graciously finished with a cappuccino and tiramisu.

An airy banquet room, capable of seating 400, hosts many celebrations during which guests dance the night away on its permanent black-granite dance floor. Classic French doors open from the banquet room to an exquisitely manicured outdoor garden maintained by Master Gardener and family member, Barb Stafford. From here Chef Amodeo harvests edible flowers, spices and herbs to complement his cuisine. During season, a local farmer delivers organically grown vegetables while his neighbor brings freshly picked fruit, both essentials of fine Italian cooking.

Heritage is important to the Notos, but the family is active in today's community events as well. Wine festivals held in the spring and fall raise money for local charities, and "Support the Arts" is an annual Noto-sponsored fund raiser for organizations such as the DeVos Children's Hospital and the Ronald McDonald House.

Once upon a time in Custonaci, Sicily, two brothers created a pattern and set it in stone — a foundation rich with heritage, family and tradition, a pattern their children and their children's children would embrace and preserve in the restaurant known as Noto's Old World Italian Dining.

TODD ZAWISTOWSKI PHOTOGRAPHY

Was it the goal of capturing the stark panoramic beauty — the scrubby yet delicate hue, the gradual contrasts and shadings — indigenous to the deserts of the Southwest that first persuaded Todd Zawistowski to pick up a castoff camera years ago? Or was it the influence of his photographer brother?

Whatever the impetus, it's a brave new world Todd Zawistowski embraces.

The exterior of Todd Zawistowski's studio at Godfrey SW, in the heart of industrial Grand Rapids, rivals the blacking factories of Dickens novels. Inside the spacious loft, an Everlast punching bag graces a corner, tempting fate. It is here that Todd Zawistowski shoots photographs of people, products and life.

Incorporated into all his work — whether gallery-bound fine art photography, product photos for a corporate client or a wedding portrait — is his editorial edge: the invisible stamp that designates the creation as that of Todd Zawistowski.

In the highly competitive world of professional photography, Todd Zawistowski combines a "shoot-from-the-hip" creativity with strong direction, as demonstrated within his various portfolios, each targeting a specific market. Concentrating on grabbing the image regardless of the subject matter, his niche leans towards black-and-white photography, yet his style also favors saturated colors and utilizing high contrast while illustrating selective focus.

People and products currently drive his business, but photography is an evolving art: technology a ubiquitous muse. Galleries and fine arts are embracing digital art and Zawistowski sees this in the offing, although he currently uses film for all formats. Stock photos catalogued on photographers' Internet Web sites, available from archives with a mouse click, beckon Zawistowski as well. He plans on having 500 images available on his Web site.

Simple or complex, black-and-white or color, product or people, moving or still — Todd Zawistowski aims true.

THE SIERRA ROOM AND CLUB 1894

When the Sierra Room and Club 1894 opened, they shook the Grand Rapids restaurant scene like nothing before. Situated in the heart of historic Old Town, both restaurants feature a one-of-a-kind dining experience unique to the city. Although they are only a few years old, The Sierra Room and Club 1894 are a medley of the past and present that will have a significant impact on the future of downtown Grand Rapids.

Since it opened in 1997, the Sierra Room has made a distinctive niche in Grand Rapids. Advertised as "casual dining, elegant atmosphere," the restaurant's interior is a tasteful, opulent mixture of gothic chandeliers, Italian tiles and antique statuary. The menu is equally elegant and eclectic. Created by Chef Richard Lowack, a Culinary Institute of America honors graduate, many of the bistro's entrees borrow from French, Asian, American and Southwestern cuisine. Voted "Restaurant of the Year" in 1998 by *Grand Rapids Magazine*, the Sierra Room also features a wine bar that serves 20 vintages by the glass and a cigar lounge.

Flushed with their success, restaurant owners Christine Gill, Kristi Jackson and Chef Lowack opened Club 1894 a block away from the Sierra Room a year later. The gothic-style entertainment complex has a dance floor, a stage, and both a wine and traditional bar at opposite ends of the main level. In the Dragonfly Room on the second level, patrons can overlook the main floor while enjoying Japanese, French and American style cuisine and a full-service Japanese sushi bar. The third level, the VIP Room, is a members-only club, with a private restaurant, bar and cigar lounge.

On most nights, both restaurants are packed to capacity. But the success of these Old Town restaurants signifies something more to Grand Rapids. At the beginning of the 20th century, Old Town was a business district of manufacturing companies, wholesalers and retailers that neighbored the Union Depot. The building that houses the Sierra Room was a furniture company; the one that houses Club 1894 was a warehouse. In the later half of the century, however, these businesses relocated to the outskirts of the city, causing the downtown to wilt.

Although there were attempts to draw business back downtown, it wasn't until 1996 when the Van Andel arena opened that people and businesses became interested in Old Town. Seeing the enormous potential of the historic area for their restaurant idea,

The Sierra Room, opened in 1997, has made a distinctive niche in Grand Rapids among restaurant goers and local preservationists.

Formerly a warehouse, Club 1894, a gothic-style entertainment complex, opened in 1998 a block away from the Sierra Room.

Gill and Jackson signed a lease for their first restaurant and began to carefully renovate the site. They were the building's first tenants in over 30 years.

The Sierra Room and Club 1894 are a blessing to local preservationists and an inspiration to downtown businesses and city planners. Events at the arena may draw crowds, but the fine dining experience of these restaurants attracts the people of Grand Rapids and keeps them coming back. The Sierra Room and Club 1894 are a vital part of downtown's renaissance, a celebration of the continuing artistry, beauty and prosperity that has defined Grand Rapids since it began.

PEACHES BED & BREAKFAST

Business travelers looking for comfortable lodging and gentle reminders of an era long gone will find it at Peaches Bed & Breakfast, a sumptuous Georgian country manor just a quick walk from downtown.

Built in 1916, this elegant three-story manor on Gay Avenue SE is located in historic Heritage Hill, where some of the city's wealthiest and most influential families once lived. The late Chester and Marion Idema built the red brick home for their family, including sons Chester Jr., James and David. By today's standards, the 8,000-square-foot manor seems large. But for a wealthy entrepreneur like Chester — son of Henry Idema, founder of Old Kent Bank — the magnificent home had to be spacious enough to also accommodate a staff of five, including two live-in maids and a full-time cook, chauffeur and laundress.

Built in 1916, this beautiful Georgian manor now houses Peaches Bed & Breakfast in Heritage Hill.

Built by local architects Williamson & Crowe, the five-bedroom home features innovations ahead of its time. Among them are a built-in warming oven in the butler's pantry, seven-foot bathtubs without claw legs and wall sconces for indirect light that are all in use today. While Chester was involved in several ventures ranging from farm products to timber and advertising, his brother, Walter, helped found a metal office furniture company now known as Steelcase Corp., the world's largest office furniture manufacturer.

Throughout the decades, the home's exquisite detail has been remarkably maintained, from the tiny Flemish tiles in the vestibule to the cathedral-glass skylights that let natural light into the second and third floors. Leaded glass panes enclose the library shelves. The lower-level ballroom with maple flooring has been transformed into a game and TV area. Details from the past, including Depression-era murals that depict the four seasons of sports in Michigan and a pool table from the 1950s, remain. Outside, a lovely wisteria more than 80 years old wraps around the front porch, and the grounds are colorfully accented with beautiful perennial gardens.

The family of Fred and Lyn Steiner bought the home in 1978 after Chester died, and maintained most of the home's original structure. Jane Lovett and her husband, Doug Wondergem, veterans of home-renovation projects, turned the stately building into a bed and breakfast after purchasing it in 1993. With five guestrooms, four baths and five fireplaces, the home "was just perfect" for a B&B, recalls Jane.

When it opened on Oct. 3, 1993 as Peaches Bed & Breakfast, it was the first B&B in Heritage Hill to cater to traveling business professionals. Its name is a tribute to Jane's late grandfather, who grew peaches in South Haven.

The rooms, which can be viewed on the Peaches Web site, are designed with the traveler in mind — simple, comfortable and froufrou-free. There are no stuffed teddy bears on these beds. Guests will, however, find a telephone, modem hook-up and desk in each room. A fax/copier and TV/VCR are available, too. Other amenities include a video library and an exercise room equipped with a weight machine, stair stepper and free weights. Of course, guests can expect peaches as well. The delicious fruit is served at each homemade breakfast.

QUALITY OF LIFE

Education, health care, and cultural and service organizations contribute to the quality of life enjoyed by Grand Rapids residents and visitors.

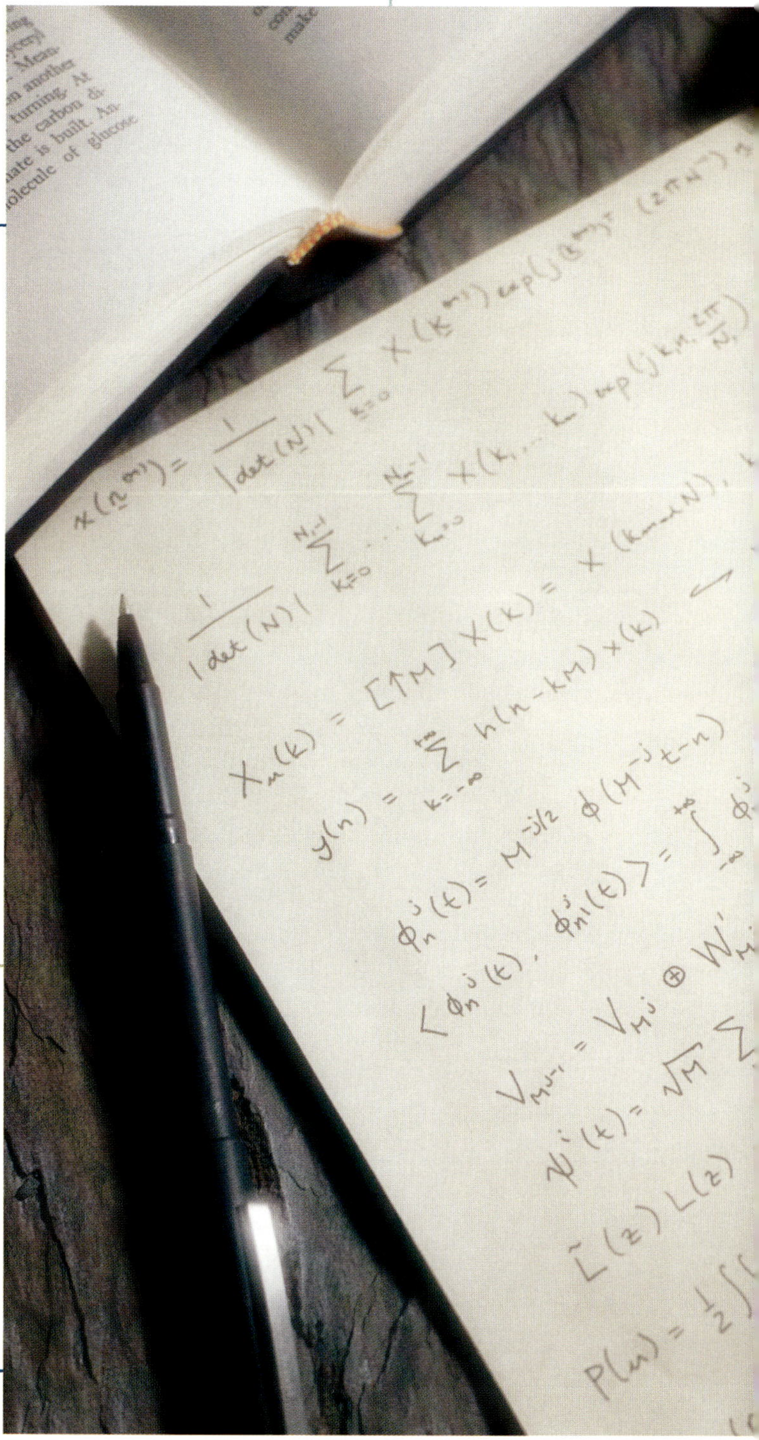

CALVIN COLLEGE

In 1876 Calvin College opened its doors in the upper room of a small building on Williams Street, near the Grand Rapids Union Station. Founded as a theological school for prospective ministers of the Christian Reformed Church (CRC), Calvin's seven students met with the school's only professor to study Dutch, Latin, Greek and Hebrew as well as history, geography, psychology, logic and rhetoric.

Calvin called a beautiful campus on Franklin Street home for almost half a century. That campus now is home to the administration of the Grand Rapids Public schools.

Since those modest beginnings, Calvin College, still affiliated with the CRC, has become one of the best Christian colleges in the country. Offering a broad liberal arts curriculum of almost 90 majors and programs, Calvin College emphasizes excellence in academics while promoting lifelong Christian service and commitment to church and community. As Calvin's Mission Statement reads:

"Calvin College is a comprehensive liberal arts college in the Reformed tradition of historic Christianity. Through our learning we seek to be agents of renewal in the academy, church and society. We pledge fidelity to Jesus Christ, offering our hearts and lives to do God's work in God's world."

Calvin's first campus was the upstairs of a modest building on Williams Street in Grand Rapids. The school began there in 1876.

The journey from a one-room schoolhouse to a top-notch undergraduate school began quickly for Calvin. Between 1876 and 1890 Calvin grew from seven students to 40 and outgrew its space on Williams Street. It then bought land at what is now the corner of Franklin and Madison and built a building that seemed palatial, with its faculty room, spacious classrooms, library and 200-seat auditorium. The building was dedicated in 1892.

In 1900 the Calvin curriculum was broadened, attracting local students who were interested in teaching or pre-professional courses with a religious basis. This expansion attracted women for the first time in the history of Calvin College, and in the 1901-1902 school year, the college had its first female enrollees. By 1906 the literary department, which provided the four years of preparatory and two years of college work, officially became the John Calvin Junior College. This junior college in time became a four-year college and the preparatory department was discontinued. In 1921 Calvin College awarded its first bachelor of arts degrees.

As the curriculum expanded, the enrollment also continued to grow. With the surge in Calvin's enrollment, administrators knew they needed to find larger facilities. Kalamazoo city officials tried to attract Calvin by offering the college the campus of the defunct Michigan Female Seminary. Muskegon also tried to convince the college to relocate to their city by offering money and land. Sentiment, however, was strong for Calvin to stay in Grand Rapids, and when the Grand Rapids Board of Trade offered to raise $10,000, the school agreed to stay. In 1909 Calvin College acquired 10 acres of land on Franklin Street, between Benjamin and Giddings. Over the next half century, this plot of land would be the school's home.

The quality of a Calvin education attracted more local and out-of-area students every year, and enrollment continued to grow. By the 1950s Calvin's enrollment made the formerly spacious Franklin campus seemed cramped. Taking such growth into consideration, the college purchased a 400-acre farm to the east of the area and began construction. Nicknamed "the Knollcrest campus," Calvin began to teach classes on this new campus in the early 1960s.

Since then, Calvin College has called Knollcrest its home and is continually adding to the campus' beauty and utility. Situated on Burton and the East Beltline, the modern campus boasts architecturally unified academic and administrative buildings, a beautiful chapel, spacious residence halls, modern dining facilities, a large field-house, the five-floor Hekman Library and much more. In the fall of 1999 Calvin completed a $20 million addition to the campus — a state-of-the-art life sciences center meant to support academic endeavors in such areas as biochemistry, biotechnology and more.

While much has changed at Calvin College, some things have stayed the same. Subjects from the original curriculum, such as classical languages, psychology, logic and rhetoric are still an important part of a Calvin education. More importantly, the relationships between Calvin professors and their students continue to be a distinction of a Calvin education. Over 4,000 students from across the continent and around the world attend Calvin. About 55 percent of its U.S. students are from out of state and 45 percent from in state. Calvin also draws substantially from Canada and from a variety of foreign countries. Calvin professors, all of whom are professing Christians, are leaders in their fields and are recognized as top-notch scholars and researchers. But they also take seriously the call to teach — to educate, encourage, mentor and shape a new generation of scholars.

With a student body of about half CRC and half other denominations, Calvin is also renowned in the Grand Rapids community for its emphasis on service. Calvin's Service Learning Center organizes a variety of efforts that connect Calvin students to the community. These efforts include academically based service learning, in which service is made part of the curriculum and carried out over the course of a semester, as well as many "one time" projects. One of these projects, Street Fest, is a massive service project in which all Calvin first-year students volunteer for community-service projects in Grand Rapids before taking a single Calvin class.

Calvin also provides its students and the entire community with numerous extracurricular opportunities on the campus. The wildly popular January Series each year brings such speakers as Francis Collins of the Human Genome Project, author and humorist Garrison Keillor, political reporter David Broder, space shuttle commander Eileen Collins and NPR's Frank Deford. In January 2000 Calvin hosted a Republican presidential debate featuring all six GOP candidates for president. The biennial Festival of Faith & Writing has brought such luminaries as Maya Angelou, John Updike and Chaim Potok to campus.

At the start of the 21st century, Calvin College has become widely acclaimed; the institution is recognized as a best college by *U.S. News & World Report,* a character-building college by the Templeton Foundation and a "best buy" by several college guides.

Seeing how the college has grown with Grand Rapids, one suspects that Calvin's founders would be pleased by its progress — and by how it has stayed true to its roots.

Calvin's state-of-the-art DeVries Hall of Science is a highlight of today's campus.

FOUNTAIN STREET CHURCH

Many people would find it hard to imagine a church in Grand Rapids, Michigan, that has maintained a national reputation for championing liberal religion and causes because of the perception that the community is highly conservative. But that's what Fountain Street Church has done for the last century.

This independent, non-denominational congregation of over 2,500 people is well-known for its commitment to freedom of the spirit and individual responsibility. Over the years, Fountain Street Church has become home to those unfulfilled by the orthodoxies and rituals of their native religions, who want to carve out their own spiritual ideologies with others who share their convictions and commitments.

The dynamic Dr. Duncan Littlefair, senior minister from 1944 to 1979, introduced more liberal beliefs and did away with many of the more traditional ceremonies.

Located in the heart of Grand Rapids, Fountain Street Church believes that its primary purpose is to provide an encouraging and supportive environment within which people can find a rich and meaningful life. Members are free to hold to their own beliefs.

The magnificent Fountain Street Church, built in 1924, featured 1,632 theatre seats.

Interestingly, despite current liberal leanings, Fountain Street Church's roots are in the traditional First Baptist Church, founded in 1842. This church grew out of earlier Baptist missions to Native Americans in the Grand Rapids area in the mid-1820s. In the 1870s members built an imposing Gothic church on Fountain Street that became known as Fountain Street Baptist Church.

As Fountain Street Baptist Church grew to become the largest congregation in Grand Rapids, two striking movements were developing in Europe that would dramatically alter the church's character. Theologians were sharing new interpretations of Christianity, upsetting many who believed in a strict, literal reading of the Bible. At the same time, the concept of a social gospel emerged, calling for community good works and the elimination of social evils. Fountain Street Baptist Church became one of the first churches in America to embrace these new ideals.

This metamorphosis became pronounced when the eloquent Rev. John Herman Randall arrived in 1896. By 1905 area Baptist churches wondered whether Fountain Street Baptist Church could legitimately be considered one of their own. Consequently, they passed a resolution that formally protested Randall's beliefs but stopped short of calling them heresy. A year later, Randall accepted another call and the feisty Rev. Alfred Wesley Wishart took over as the church's leader.

For the next 27 years, the progressive Wishart enhanced the church's position as a liberal voice in the community. One of his greatest tangible achievements was shepherding the construction of the church building that stands today. Fire had destroyed the Gothic church in 1917, forcing members to hold services in the old Powers Theatre. By 1924 the congregation had erected a magnificent Romanesque church building costing

$800,000 and boasting 1,632 theatre seats. Because Grand Rapids lacked a civic auditorium, the congregation offered its large, new sanctuary to host civic and community events.

But the cost of maintaining the large church was compounded by the financial problems caused by the Great Depression. When Wishart died in 1933, the church began to slide into difficult times.

Another modernist, the Rev. Milton M. McGorrill, was called to lead Fountain Street Church. This proved to be very difficult for McGorrill. By 1938 only 20 percent of the church members attended Sunday services. In 1943, when the church as an institution seemed perilously close to death, McGorrill resigned.

Finding a successor to rejuvenate this once-vibrant congregation was not easy. It took nearly 1.5 years to secure a new pastor. The young, intense, Dr. Duncan E. Littlefair, the pastor of a small church in a wealthy Chicago suburb, came to the Pulpit Committee's attention. Members eventually persuaded him to visit the church. Littlefair later admitted he was "disturbed" by what he saw, "particularly by the desperate condition of the congregation," wrote the Rev. Roger Bertschausen in his book, *Liberal Legacy,* a history of Fountain Street Church. But Dr. Littlefair's visit began the irreversible process of changing his mind.

The dynamic and charismatic Littlefair had an exceptionally clear direction for how he wanted the church to move — and the members followed. During his 35 years as the church's Senior Minister, Dr. Littlefair built a legacy and a devoted, loyal congregation. Within months after his arrival in 1944, Sunday attendance rose from a mere 200 to more than 1,000, making the church once again a focus of conversation in Grand Rapids.

For all of its liberalism in the 1940s, however, the church still adhered to beliefs about Jesus as the Christ. Littlefair introduced ideas that reconsidered this orthodoxy. In his booklet, *A Religious Primer*, Littlefair emphasizes Jesus as a man of history "in the line of the great Jewish prophets." He encouraged the study of other religions because religion is a "search for God." He described the Bible as "a story of the quest of the Jewish people and Western people."

Religious education at Fountain Street Church also underwent a dramatic change and growth. Instead of requiring children to memorize and recite Bible verses, "Character School" was developed in 1948. The curriculum focused on the beatitudes in the Sermon on the Mount along with eight general attitudes. By the end of the 1950s, the church had eliminated such traditional rituals as World Wide Communion and baptism. Babies were dedicated instead of baptized. These changes were so profound that the congregation eventually severed its Baptist ties in 1969 and became known simply as Fountain Street Church.

Under Dr. Littlefair's guidance, the church's doors were open to those who could not speak or meet elsewhere in Grand Rapids because they were seen as too radical. Among those were civil rights leader Stokely Carmichael and Nation of Islam leader Malcom X. Church members also took up the fight to support causes such as the civil rights movement, Planned Parenthood, the American Civil Liberties Union, and the rights of gays and lesbians. The youth group, the Fountain Club, raised money by sponsoring concerts at the church featuring many popular groups, among them Steppenwolf and The Moody Blues.

After Dr. Littlefair's retirement in 1979, the scholarly Dr. David Rankin carried on the liberal cause from 1982 to 1998. In 1999 the energetic Dr. Brent A. Smith became the present Senior Minister, continuing the Fountain Street Church legacy into the new millennium.

During the 1920s and 1930s the church hosted several community events because Grand Rapids lacked a civic auditorium.

GRAND RAPIDS COMMUNITY COLLEGE

Career and educational trends were very different in the early 20th century than they are today. In 1914 Grand Rapids Central High School principal Jesse Buttrick Davis found himself with more teachers and classrooms than the number of students justified. While Central had been the city's only four-year high school, Union High School added a 12th year in 1914 and South Junior High was scheduled to open in 1915. Davis, who had written textbooks on the subject of vocational education, proposed the idea of a junior college to school superintendent William A. Greeson.

"The idea of a junior college was in the air," Davis recalled in a speech delivered in 1939. Although Greeson feared that taxpayers would not support an additional two years of higher education, he did not discourage Davis. "That dear, good man," Davis said of Greeson in the 1939 speech. Greeson had said to him, "Davis, if you think you can get away with it, go ahead. I will not stand in your way."

The original idea for the establishment of a junior college in the Grand River valley had come more than 60 years earlier, when University of Michigan president Henry Philip Tappan foresaw a time when the first two, less-specialized years of a college education could be completed in a variety of municipal centers scattered around the state. Tappan's vision was first realized in 1882 when A.F. Lange, who had attended the University of Michigan, established the nation's first junior college in California. In 1901 that developing trend in education gained credence when University of Chicago President William Raney Harper granted the title of "associate" to those who had completed the first two years of their college education.

Despite no public demand for the school, nor any state law granting boards of education the authority to support such an institution, Grand Rapids Junior College opened its doors to 49 students on Sept. 21, 1914. After arranging for the full transfer of credits from the junior college to the University of Michigan, Davis sold his idea to the board of education as well as the community. Eight original faculty members offered Grand Rapids Junior College's first 49 students courses in rhetoric and composition, mathematics, history, biology, physics, Latin and German.

The school, founded the year that World War I was triggered by the assassination of Austrian Archduke Franz Ferdinand by Serbian nationalists, was the first junior college in Michigan and only the seventh such publicly funded institution in the nation.

In 1991 voters in the Kent Intermediate School District authorized the redistricting of Grand Rapids Junior College as a community college. For the first time in its 77-year history, the college was governed by its own board of trustees and its boundaries were extended beyond the Grand Rapids Public School District to include the 20 member districts within the Kent Intermediate School District.

Accredited continuously since 1917 by the Commission on Institutions of Higher Education of the North Central Association of Colleges and Schools, Grand Rapids Community College now enrolls almost 14,000 students in credit programs and another 10,000 students in

The college was known as "Junior on the Hill" in its earliest days.

non-credit instruction. Two-thirds of the student body at GRCC attends on a part-time basis. As the state's oldest community college, the school has developed a strong reputation as a premier transfer institution and is nationally recognized for its liberal arts and occupational programs.

Students at Grand Rapids Community College now are offered courses in 56 areas of study, and associate degrees are available in arts, science, music, nursing, applied arts and sciences, business and general studies. GRCC's School of Workforce Development features courses in Accounting/Office Administration, Applied Technology, Child Development, Computer Applications, Dental Auxiliary, Drafting and Design, General Business, Manufacturing, Nursing, Occupational Therapy Assisting, Radiological Technology, Business and Technical Training, Occupation Training and Work Based Learning. Its School of Arts & Sciences features programs in Behavioral and Biological Sciences, Criminal Justice, English, Hospitality Education, Language and Thought, Mathematics, Performing Arts, Physical and Social Sciences, Visual Arts and Wellness.

"Since our founding in 1914, we continue to serve as a strong liberal arts preparatory school. Over the past several decades, we have extended our reach beyond preparing students for a traditional degree program by adding pre-college classes, business and technical training and occupational training in the skilled trades," says Juan R. Olivarez, Ph.D., who in October 1999 became the eighth president of GRCC. "As we enter the 21st century, we continue to enhance the learning environment so students are prepared to compete in the marketplace. Occupational programs, associate degrees in technical fields and customized training for business and industry are some of the learning opportunities we extend to the community."

Grand Rapids Community College currently occupies an expansive eight-block urban campus that reflects a 20-year construction program. The most recent addition to that campus is the $30 million Calkins Science Center, named for Richard W. Calkins, who served as the school's president from 1975-98. Two decades of construction at GRCC also have brought the Applied Technology Center, which was built in an unprecedented partnership with Ferris State University, several classroom buildings, a learning center and library, a student center, a new Spectrum Theater, the Ford Fieldhouse and natatorium, a remodeled music center, two parking ramps and a pedestrian mall.

Grand Rapids Community College also expands beyond its downtown campus. The 50-acre Occupational Training Center is located in northeastern Grand Rapids, a Michigan Technical Education Center (M-TEC) opened recently in Holland and another M-TEC is scheduled for a 2001 opening in Grand Rapids' Renaissance Zone.

"Grand Rapids Community College provides the community with lifelong learning opportunities," Olivarez adds. "Our vision is focused on enriching the lives of people and a contribution to the vitality of the community."

As the "community's college," GRCC offers a wide variety of learning opportunities to the community, such as its Senior Computer Club.

The Bostwick Commons, GRCC's student pedestrian mall, opened in the fall of 1999 between Fountain and Lyon Streets, adding to the college's urban campus appeal.

GRAND RAPIDS COMMUNITY FOUNDATION

"Every dollar, whether donated by blackboot or billionaire, will do an equal amount of good work."

These words, published on the front page of the April 15, 1923 edition of the *Grand Rapids Herald*, reflect a vision that has come to fruition. The story of the Grand Rapids Community Foundation, the oldest community foundation in Michigan, is woven throughout several decades, from its inception in 1922 to greeting the 21st century as a powerhouse of financial support and community enrichment for Grand Rapids.

Grand Rapids businessman Lee Hutchins founded the Grand Rapids Community Foundation in 1922.

Lee M. Hutchins, president of Hazeltine and Perkins Drug Company in Grand Rapids, had a dream. He shared his dream of a local community foundation with the Grand Rapids Association of Commerce, an organization committed to community improvement. On May 23, 1922, he addressed the association, his eloquence resulting in the appointment of a committee to explore foundation possibilities. By September of that same year, the project had been approved, and in January 1923 Hutchins was unanimously elected chairman. The Grand Rapids Community Foundation was born.

Yet the Foundation struggled in its first years, with no money to bestow until a $25 gift, earmarked for incidental expenses, came from Association of Commerce President S. George Graves. These meager funds remained the Foundation's only asset until George and Mary Metz left the Foundation a trust of more than $100,000 in 1929, producing an annual income of $3,000. Before the ink could dry on the Metz endowment, however, the Depression of the 1930s hit the United States.

Desperation ruled throughout this trying decade, as many people relied solely on outside assistance for survival. The Foundation prioritized contributions to community welfare programs such as the Family Service Association and the Salvation Army. Most funds were distributed for necessities such as groceries, shoes and rent. This urgent need extended beyond the immediate Grand Rapids area, and an amendment to the Founding Resolution was written allowing the trustees to disperse money within Grand Rapids and "vicinity." Two new trusts from Anna Bissell and Elnora Edison increased the Foundation's assets during the 1930s.

The United States' entry into World War II created more financial strife within the Grand Rapids community. Foundation trustees distributed $35,000 to social agencies during the war years. After the war, the Foundation's coffers flourished, enhanced by a generous gift from the estate of George Ames, a former city engineer. By 1950 the Foundation's annual income had reached $30,000.

Health issues commanded Foundation funding in the mid-1940s and 1950s as the wars created a nursing shortage. A postgraduate scholarship program in the field of psychiatric nursing was expanded to include obstetrical, surgical and pediatric nursing. Foundation grants also served the Grand Rapids Public Schools by facilitating scholarships to train teachers and helping local students with postsecondary needs. The Foundation continued to stretch its dollars to serve the diverse needs of its community, often struggling to accommodate the city's many deserving causes.

The Public Museum of Grand Rapids and Grand Valley State University's Eberhard Center each benefited from Grand Rapids Community Foundation grants.

That struggle became easier in 1958, a major turning point in the Grand Rapids Community Foundation legacy. Local businessman and entrepreneur Curtis M. Wylie bequeathed $6.2 million to the Foundation with the condition that moneys must benefit "charitable and educational purposes." The Wylie bequest proved to be one of the largest gifts to a public foundation in Michigan's history and was instrumental in laying the groundwork for the foundation's future stability. Funds of this magnitude required more formalized management, so in 1959 foundation Secretary Harry B. Wagner was hired as part-time director. New challenges and successes awaited the foundation and those it served.

Throughout the 1960s, grants were bestowed upon more organizations grounded in humanities, including the Foundation's largest gift to date — $50,000 to start Grand Valley State University — followed by an additional $200,000 over the course of three years. The Foundation had come far from its initial $25 donation, which had eventually been spent on a file cabinet. Projects for Calvin College's Knollcrest Campus and the Grand Rapids Public Library were also funded. The Foundation took a proactive stance during these socially turbulent times when it awarded grants supporting a police-community relations program, a halfway house for rehabilitating prison parolees and the improvement of inner-city housing. The world was changing fast and the Foundation was keeping pace.

The Foundation's goal of establishing a permanent charitable endowment capable of generating its own philanthropic money had been accomplished. The Foundation stood as a viable charitable institution in its own right. New funding heralded exciting opportunities to broaden the scope of grant recipients. In the 1970s a $1.5 million gift established the Lucy E. Barnett Trust, restricted to use for the elderly, funded studies of health issues. In the 1980s the Foundation provided start-up funding for the AIDS Resource Center.

The 1990s comprise a kaleidoscope of accomplishments for the Grand Rapids Community Foundation: creating a consortium to address environmental issues in its community, partnering with affiliate charitable entities to help foster their success and gathering a group — Perspective 21! — to define community priorities about child welfare. At the dawn of the 21st century, just past its 75th anniversary, the Foundation holds more than $180 million in assets.

"If the Grand Rapids Community Foundation did not exist, so what?" asks Diana R. Sieger, president of the Grand Rapids Community Foundation since the 1980s, to challenge audiences of community organizations. Sieger claims that unless the Foundation can measure the impact of its grants in the community — unless the Foundation can be held accountable — it is ineffectual. She also anticipates future trends in endowments will include a concept referred to as "venture philanthropy," where the Foundation will assess community needs and present proposals targeting these needs to donors for potential funding.

Diana Sieger has been president of the Grand Rapids Community Foundation since 1987.

Foundation board members contribute wisdom and solid commitment to the community, and they follow up with grant recipients to ensure donated money is well spent. With the unflagging and dynamic dedication of its board members, the healthy status of the Foundation is ensured for many future generations.

Long ago, Lee M. Hutchins planted the seed for serving and improving his community. The Grand Rapids Community Foundation has nurtured the growth well, and today stands strong and tall, pledged to preserve its giving tradition.

Foundation staff, board members and donors observe a conductive education classroom, one of hundreds of local programs and projects funded by Foundation grants.

GRAND VALLEY STATE UNIVERSITY

Grand Rapids closed the 1950s as one of the most densely populated cities in the country that did not have an established university. A group of community leaders seeking to develop an institution of higher learning in Michigan's second-largest city petitioned Governor G. Mennen Williams for a charter to establish such a university, and with the approval of that charter in 1960, Grand Valley State University was born. Classes opened on the Allendale campus in 1963 with an enrollment of only 224 students. Six years later, Arend Lubbers became the school's second president.

Lubbers, who is the longest-serving president of any four-year university in America, led GVSU into the 21st century as the fastest-growing university in Michigan. With an enrollment that has nearly tripled since the 1980s and is now approaching 20,000, Grand Valley State University offers more than 75 degree programs, almost a third of which can be completed on an expanding downtown campus. That urban setting, which is nestled on the west bank of the Grand River in downtown Grand Rapids, is the center of Grand Valley's graduate programs, more than a dozen of which are now available.

"We are the city's local university, and we're best equipped to provide the range of programs and services the local market needs," Lubbers notes.

The Richard M. DeVos Center, dedicated in 2000, bolstered Grand Valley's presence as the city's full-service university.

Located between Grand Rapids and Lake Michigan, Grand Valley's main campus, a 900-acre spread in Allendale, reflects the school's original mission to serve the entire West Michigan community, but specifically the residents of the three counties that surround it: Kent, Ottawa and Muskegon. The school has expanded its presence in the region with the Grand Rapids campus, which opened with the nine-story Eberhard Center in 1988, as well as a campus in Holland and centers in Muskegon, Traverse City and Petoskey. It also offers a number of courses in Sault Ste. Marie in conjunction with Lake Superior State University.

While Grand Valley's rapidly increasing enrollment figures reflect the prosperity of the West Michigan region, they also reflect a concerted effort by the university's administration to keep education as affordable as possible. Grand Valley State is one of the lowest-priced universities in Michigan's Lower Peninsula and has been repeatedly acknowledged as such by *The Student Guide to America's 100 Best College Buys*, a book compiled by Institutional Research and Evaluation.

Trends in the region's population growth are reflected at the university since more than half of the students currently enrolled at the school are nontraditional students. At the Grand Rapids campus, the typical GVSU student is not one who recently graduated from high school and immediately enrolled at the university. "In the city, we cater especially to the nontraditional college student — the returning adult working on a bachelor's or graduate degree to advance in his or her profession," Lubbers says. "Grand Valley's growth has paralleled the growth of Grand Rapids. The expansion of our downtown campus addresses the need for more opportunity in higher education in the Grand Rapids market," he adds.

In response to a growing demand for graduate programs as well as an increased demand for a university presence within the city of Grand Rapids, Grand Valley State University opened its downtown campus in 1988. The focal point of that campus had long been the Eberhard Center, which features more than 40 classrooms and laboratories, conference and teleconference

Grand Valley began offering programs downtown in the late 1980s at the L.V. Eberhard Center. Courses have attracted nontraditional students, including professionals returning to college to complete or start undergraduate or graduate degrees.

facilities and the studios of WGVU-TV and Radio, the university's public broadcasting stations. Now the Richard M. DeVos Center, an ambitious expansion project estimated at $50 million, 30 percent of which came from the private sector; Secchia Hall, a new housing facility; and the Fred M. Keller Engineering Labs make the university a formidable presence downtown.

"It was a very high priority that our expanded campus blend with the existing downtown architecture, and what you see in the Richard M. DeVos Center and Secchia Hall are the newest visual assets along the city's skyline," says Lubbers. GVSU's downtown campus now features the school's highly acclaimed school of business and economics, the Seidman School of Business, The Van Andel Global Trade Center and facilities for all of the university's graduate programs.

The names such as "DeVos," "Eberhard," "Meijer," "Secchia" and "Seidman" that grace Grand Valley's downtown campus, and names such as "Padnos" and "Cook" that mark the Allendale campus are a testament to the support the university has received and continues to receive from the leaders of the West Michigan community.

While GVSU reflects the economic, social and cultural development experienced by the West Michigan region in the second half of the 20th century, it also has stayed abreast of the world's technological advancements. Grand Valley State University is ranked as one of the top-100 wired universities in the country by *Yahoo Internet Magazine*, which bases its ratings on a school's technological infrastructure as well as the number and the quality of computers available to students. Only three Michigan universities made that top-100 list; the others are the University of Michigan and Michigan State University.

Arts and athletics also are essential aspects of student life at GVSU. The Alexander Calder Art Center houses the university's visual arts programs, and the Performing Arts Center includes the Louis Armstrong Theater. GVSU students also compete in 11 sports at the NCAA Division II level and the Allendale campus is home to The Meadows, an 18-hole championship golf course recognized as one of West Michigan's best.

Every class at Grand Valley State University is taught by a faculty member — never a teaching assistant — and class sizes range from 15 to 28 students. With more than 100 companies interviewing students on campus each year, nearly all GVSU alumni find work directly related to their field of study. GVSU students graduating with degrees in broadcasting, physical therapy and hospitality/tourism have enjoyed 100 percent placement in recent years, while no fewer than 91 percent of GVSU students in any field of study have been employed in a field directly related to their major.

With almost 100 undergraduate and graduate programs available for study on rural and urban campuses, as well as a reputation for offering superior educational opportunities at a reasonable cost, Grand Valley State University is sure to continue its rapid growth and development as it approaches its 50th birthday.

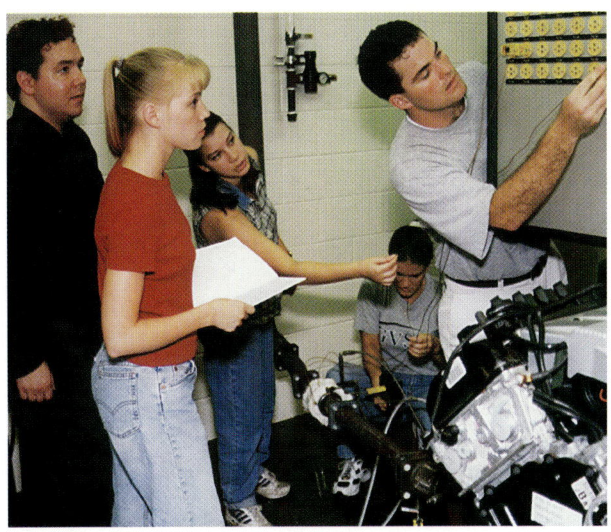

The Padnos School of Engineering, housed on the Grand Rapids Campus, provides industry in West Michigan and beyond with highly skilled engineers and leaders for the new century.

KENT INTERMEDIATE SCHOOL DISTRICT

(Opposite page, top) A Hospitality student at Kent Transition Center displays some of the skills she's learned in this popular field, which is just one of the center's programs offering job skills and placement opportunities.

(Opposite page, bottom) In the Plastics Lab, part of the Manufacturing Technology Cluster at Kent Career/Technical Center, a high school senior demonstrates one of the machines to fourth graders who were touring the center.

Kent Intermediate School District is a dynamic organization offering a wide range of services focused on learning. Dedicated to improving education throughout the region, Kent ISD serves the schools and communities of its 20 public school districts, along with non-public and charter schools. That means serving nearly 400 schools, 140,000 students and 10,000 educators and staff with programs and services that would be too resource-intensive or costly to maintain at a district level.

Created by legislation in 1962 to serve local schools and act as a liaison between them and the Michigan Department of Education, Kent is one of 57 intermediate school districts across the state and is known for its regional cooperation and the strength of its programs. Kent ISD is a shared community resource, providing an extensive network of support for schools, students and educators.

From its highly advanced, career-oriented tech center, to the hands-on outdoor nature center and adaptive vocational education center, Kent ISD is helping teach and inspire the young minds of the future throughout the Grand Rapids metropolitan area. As an educational advocate, Kent ISD helps make the needs of children and their schools known to community leaders, legislators, service agencies and the media.

With extensive professional development programs for teachers, administrators and staff, job training programs for company employees and adult education for community members, Kent ISD is a learning resource for adults, too. Hundreds of workshops, courses and professional meetings for educators are hosted or led by Kent ISD staff on the Knapp/Beltline campus each year. These programs cover topics including new curriculum, classroom ideas and techniques, technology usage, meeting student needs, administrative issues and many more. Recruiting and training substitute teachers, coordinating teacher certification requirements, communicating with area educators through the Internet and a monthly magazine are other service examples.

The entire community benefits from the millions of taxpayer dollars saved each year through extensive cooperative purchasing programs for school and building supplies. Kent ISD also serves the community by coordinating grants and state/federal monies for special education, providing professional staff and assisting special education programs in every school district. Career preparation programs and services reach into the schools, helping students envision their futures and explore career choices, exposing them to the world of work in their communities.

Another important service classroom teachers rely on is the collection of resources in the Regional Educational Media Center, serving schools in Ionia, Montcalm and Kent counties. The REMC8 offers videos, CD-ROM programs, equipment and educational services for classrooms in all three counties. Through Distance Learning, the ISD provides shared courses, video conferences, satellite broadcasts and educational experiences around the country for both students and educators.

(Far right) When toddlers from Ecuador and China were adopted by the Toering family, they needed extra help building skills for eventual school success, which was provided by the Early On program, represented here by service coordinator Sheri Meyer.

Karin McAleenan, one of the interpretive teachers at Howard Christensen Nature Center, demonstrates some of the turtle's physical features to a group of delighted kindergartners.

Student achievement is a major emphasis throughout Kent ISD programs, from school improvement efforts and research into the criteria for school success, to a teacher-led cooperative curriculum in math, science, social studies and language arts, all tied to state learning standards. Consultants from the ISD work with educator teams in local schools on these issues and others, including health, gifted and talented, truancy and at-risk, violence and substance abuse prevention, and arts and culture.

Important youth development programs led by Kent ISD include the Close Up Program, which teaches citizenship and government and includes study in the nation's capital, and the Kent Diversity Council, striving to help students better understand each other and the rich ethnic heritage in the community. In addition, ISD staff coordinate youth conferences, workshops on peer mediation and service learning projects in schools.

Three learning centers serve students from every district with a wide array of programs.

The Kent Career/Technical Center is an exciting, hands-on facility enrolling more than 2,400 high school juniors and seniors each year in more than 30 career-entry programs. These range from Certified Network Administration, Banking and Graphic Design to Plastics Technology, Aviation Mechanics and Automotive Technology. Each is guided by local industry representatives who help the experienced, vocationally certified staff ensure both instruction and equipment are state-of-the-art. They also help students make important connections with employers, including work/study, internship and apprenticeship opportunities. While many graduating students go directly into their chosen careers, more than 50 percent continue their education in a variety of post-secondary institutions.

Kent Transition Center was recently recognized as an Exemplary School for its work in providing adapted vocational training combined with work experience and eventual placement. This center offers a wide variety of entry-level skill training and a planned transition to the workplace for high school juniors and seniors who are academically challenged, at risk or who need hands-on learning. Programs range from Construction, Manufacturing and Agriscience, to Hospitality and Nurse Aid.

Both KC/TC and KTC are located on the Kent ISD campus near the corner of Knapp Street and the East Beltline.

The Howard Christensen Nature Center, located on 134 wooded acres in Kent City with lakes, ponds and a variety of natural habitats, educates 18,000 students each year with hands-on science lessons. Designed to meet local and state learning standards, the programs help classroom teachers implement their curriculum with outdoor experiential learning combined with educational displays, activities and a computer lab. Nature center staff also provide a variety of related workshops for teachers throughout the year.

The extensive range of Kent ISD services is matched by the organization's effective use of resources, as it operates with the smallest per-pupil tax levy for general education of any intermediate school district in Michigan. Kent ISD serves the community with the primary purpose of preparing all students to be successful workers, lifelong learners and contributors to a democratic society.

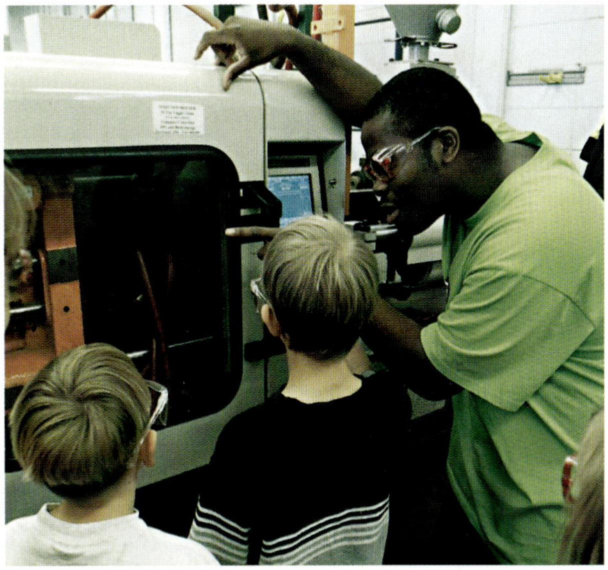

Member Districts:
Byron Center Public Schools

Caledonia Community Schools

Cedar Springs Public Schools

Comstock Park Public Schools

East Grand Rapids Public Schools

Forest Hills Public Schools

Godfrey Lee Public Schools

Godwin Heights Public Schools

Grand Rapids Public Schools

Grandville Public Schools

Kelloggsville Public Schools

Kenowa Hills Public Schools

Kent City Community Schools

Kentwood Public Schools

Lowell Area Schools

Northview Public Schools

Rockford Public Schools

Sparta Area Schools

Thornapple Kellogg Schools

Wyoming Public Schools

MARY FREE BED HOSPITAL & REHABILITATION CENTER

In the name of the "Marys."

It began with a small black purse, owner unknown, found on a snowy Grand Rapids street in 1891. Only six pennies jangled within. "Add ten pennies or more to help care for the poor," came the plea from finders of the purse. "Dedicate the donation to family or friends named Mary."

The abandoned purse passed from man to woman to child. A washerwoman placed 12 coins into the purse in remembrance of the charity her daughter Mary had once received at the Union Benevolent Hospital. Within a month 36 friends of Marys had contributed sufficient moneys to the purse to establish a "free bed" in the hospital — a place for the indigent to rest and heal. Thus commenced the first fund raiser of one of the most unique charitable not-for-profit organizations in the country — a place where today, dedicated and caring hearts remain true to the tradition of its founding — the Mary Free Bed Hospital & Rehabilitation Center.

In the late 19th century an influx of European immigrants created a population growth spurt within Grand Rapids. Demand for health care accompanied this increased number of people, most of whom were unable to pay for their medical needs. The Mary Free Bed Committee, an informal charity group initially affiliated with the Union Benevolent Hospital, was dedicated to the goal of sponsoring a free bed for an entire year. These Guild women — angels of mercy who fed, bathed and read to patients, and taught some English so they could become employed — also continued to care for patients after their release. Many an empty larder was filled with food and leg braces purchased for children with polio from the purse of a Mary as follow-up care. They were called "the Marys."

In 1911, under the leadership of Estelle Wolfe, the Mary Free Bed Guild was formed. Two years later, under the leadership of Rosamund Rouse, the All-Star Concerts, a major fund raiser in the form of a series of concerts, was developed with the goal of presenting world-class performers to raise Guild funds and enhance the limited cultural climate of Grand Rapids. Tickets to see the likes of famous Irish tenor John McCormack brought $100 each for his Powers Theatre performances. Within a year the Guild had exceeded its expected goal by providing 481 days of service to 21 patients at a cost of $850. By 1913 the ultimate goal of sponsoring a free bed for a year in the UBA Hospital had finally been achieved.

An additional feather in the Guild's cap occurred during this same period when the Hospital Day Fund transferred its moneys to the Mary Free Bed Guild, granting them the day-to-day decision-making power regarding distribution of funds for public care. In 1918, after a 27-year affiliation, the Mary Free Guild anticipated its transformation into a thriving philanthropic entity by severing ties with Blodgett Memorial Medical Center (formerly UBA Hospital). Yet within a day of this action, the Guild promised Blodgett Memorial $6,500 of its $10,300 endowment to use for needy patients, knowing the Guild's absence would create a financial hardship for the hospital.

Mary Free Bed members in 1915 pose for a group photograph. *Mary Free Bed Collection, Grand Rapids Public Library*

This humble act of giving, indicative of the Guild's mission to serve those in need, was further realized in 1920 when concern by Guild members regarding lack of quality care for children with physical handicaps, often polio-related, evolved into the Blodgett Orthopedic Clinic, under the direct supervision of Dr. John T. Hodgen. Within a year the Guild took the proactive step of hiring a full-time physical therapist and establishing a rehabilitation program to complement the orthopedic clinic. The "Marys" volunteered in the field, sometimes driving patients to the clinic in the Guild's aptly named old sedan, "Mary," or visiting children in their homes, often arriving at their own homes past dusk, weary yet rewarded.

Mary Free Bed Hospital's legend transcends history's economic and social barriers. In an effort to embrace the educational needs of physically impaired children, the Guild established an orthopedic wing inside the new two-story Stocking School in 1923, allowing children, some who had never been able to attend school because of their physical limitations, to gain an education in a welcoming environment. Despite fund-raising difficulties resulting from the great stock market crash of 1929, the Guild created the Children's Convalescent Home, which opened in 1930. Stringent cost-saving measures included staff cuts followed by economizing on patient meals. Yet the "Marys" ceaselessly volunteered their time and purses, transporting patients, sewing clothes for them, hosting birthday parties and even rolling cloth bandages for the home. In 1937 the Convalescent Home became Mary Free Bed Guild Convalescent Home and Orthopedic Center.

World War II produced hardships for the home as it lost key personnel to the military. In addition, the state curtailed its funding to orthopedic children. Nationwide economic inflation resulted in a decrease of staff, and federal authorities instituted wage-control guidelines for the convalescent home. Yet the Guild remained a powerhouse of accomplishment, managing to open a dental clinic at the home in 1942.

The 1950s through 1970s were decades riddled with change for the home. The introduction of the Salk vaccine in 1953 meant a dramatic decrease in the number of polio patients, precipitating the broadening of Mary Free Bed services to include rehabilitation of adults. In 1954 the Guild established a formal alliance with the University of Michigan School of Medicine with an agreement for the school's physical-therapy students to receive their clinical training at Mary Free Bed. The 1960s brought the distinction of accreditation to the hospital followed by expansion in the 1970s, with groundbreaking for its new facility occurring on June 28, 1974.

Mary Free Bed Hospital and Rehabilitation Center continues to evolve with the times. As health care facilities face consolidation or elimination in the late 20th century, Mary Free Bed's visionary management streamlined services to remain viable within this competitive arena. Technological advances at the hospital are many, including Parastep®, an ambulating device for spinal cord injury patients. This 80-bed, Guild-run, not-for-profit acute rehabilitation center enjoys a national reputation for excellence for the care it provides while contributing to the heart of its community through the sponsorship of advocacy activities. "Bikes for the Rest of Us" provides bicycles for special-needs children, while the "Old Kent River Bank Run," with a wheelchair division, raises awareness of rehabilitative needs. The Mary Free Bed Fund provides financial support for many other important community needs.

It began over a century ago with a few pennies; it resulted in a timeless treasure, a continuous cycle of unselfish devotion, a commitment to helping those in need.

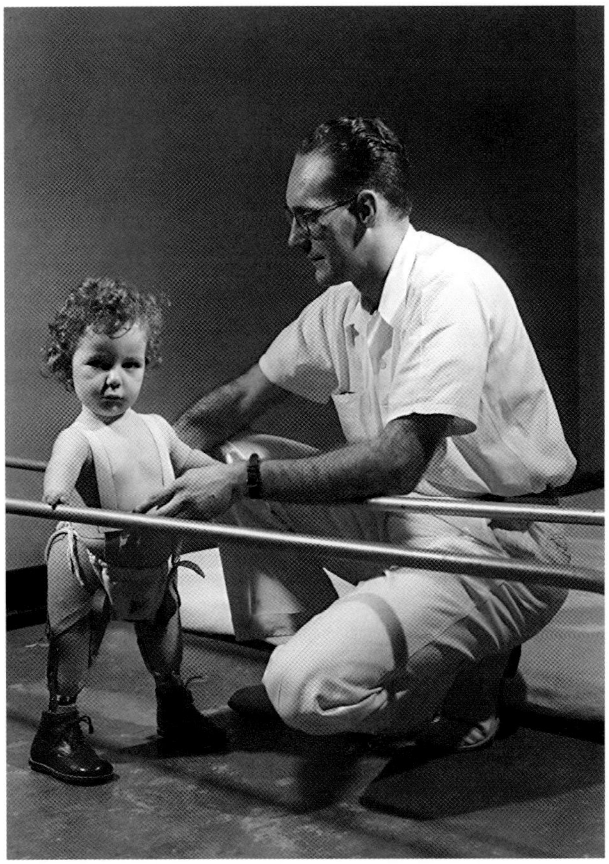

A toddler with prosthetic legs is taught to walk as part of the Juvenile Amputee Training Clinic Pilot initiated after World War II. *Mary Free Bed Collection, Grand Rapids Public Library*

SPECTRUM HEALTH

A woven cord's strength comes from the integration of its individual strands. The merger of Blodgett Memorial Medical Center and Butterworth Health System in 1997 is a perfect example of this truth. The merger resulted in the creation of Spectrum Health.

Richard E.E. Butterworth

John Wood Blodgett Sr.

The mission of Spectrum Health — to improve the health of the community by serving each individual and family with superior quality, personal care — draws on the rich history, tradition and commitment to personal care instilled by the staffs of the founding organizations.

The most recognized Spectrum Health facilities include the Downtown Campus, East Campus, DeVos Children's Hospital, Reed City Campus and Kent Community Campus. All five Spectrum Health hospitals are fully accredited, offering the community 1,231 intensive-care, acute-care and general-care beds.

The operations of Blodgett Memorial Medical Center and Butterworth Health System were merged to keep pace with a national climate demanding more coordinated services, reduced costs and improved access. The merger was also seen as a way of remaining regionally competitive and assuring the continuation of locally controlled health care organizations. The merger was not the first time the Blodgett and Butterworth names were joined together, however.

Butterworth Health System was founded in 1873 as St. Mark's Home and Hospital. It was renamed for Grand Rapids industrialist Richard E. E. Butterworth in 1890 to honor his donation of land for a new hospital previously located in a residence donated to the church in 1887.

It was his grandson, Edward Lowe, who initiated the first merger by marrying Susan R. Blodgett — uniting the families of the benefactors of Grand Rapids' two major hospitals.

Initially established in 1847 as "The Female Union Charitable Association," Blodgett Memorial Medical Center is the oldest of the two hospitals and brought to the merger an impressive track record. Along with several name changes, each expanding and/or redefining its mission, the early hospital had numerous facilities. By 1895, under the "Union Benevolent Association" name, the facility was a full-fledged hospital.

For 30 years, from 1886 to 1916, the Union Benevolent Association was located on Lyon Street. It was board member John Wood Blodgett Sr. who would take the hospital to its next incarnation by donating land and money to build a new facility, subsequently named Blodgett Memorial Hospital, in honor of his mother, Jane Wood Blodgett.

The new hospital, which was located on Plymouth Road at Wealthy Street, opened in March 1916 and underwent its first expansion in 1953.

Blodgett Memorial Hospital's history includes several stellar chapters. Its staff performed the area's first cardiac catheterization (1953); provided one of the nation's first 24-hour intensive-care nursing units (1958); developed treatment for sickle-cell anemia with Wayne State University (1970); opened the area's only Regional Poison Center (1975) and Regional Burn Center (1977); began the area's most advanced In Vitro Fertilization program (1983); installed a 3-D scanner — then offered in only a few cities nationally (1989); operated the state's first mobile cardiac catheterization lab (1992); operated the area's first flow cell cytometer for cancer diagnosis (1992); and was among the first hospitals in the state to use a special coil to repair inoperable brain aneurysms (1996).

A consummate leader in the health care industry, Butterworth brought many firsts of its own to the merger. It was the eighth U.S. hospital to obtain a deep-radiation therapy unit for cancer treatments (1936); the first hospital in West Michigan to own a defibrillator (1952); the first to introduce cobalt therapy to West Michigan (1956); and the first in the United States to offer outpatient surgery (1960). Hospital staff members also established the first neonatal unit in West Michigan, the Gerber Neonatal Intensive Care Unit (1973); treated the first patient with the city's only hyperbaric oxygen chamber (1982) and introduced the first laser center in West Michigan (1990).

Butterworth's position as an innovator in medical technology and research made it a top medical teaching hospital, as was the case for Blodgett. Educating nurses was important to both organizations. Blodgett opened the second nursing school in the state of Michigan in 1886, which operated until 1987, while more than 2,500 nurses graduated from the Butterworth Hospital School of Nursing from 1890 to 1985.

Spectrum Health Downtown Campus

Spectrum Health East Campus

Spectrum Health, in keeping with its name and the spirit of its predecessors, continues to provide a wide range of health care services through a large network of sites. At its five main campus sites, including West Michigan's only recognized children's hospital, Spectrum Health provides emergency/trauma care; highly specialized heart and vascular services; high-risk obstetrics, perinatal and infertility programs; neonatal services; comprehensive neurological care for patients with head and spine injuries; comprehensive orthopaedic programs; a regional burn center; cancer treatment and screening programs; radiology services; digestive disease services; and a regional poison center.

Other Spectrum Health services include subacute and skilled nursing facilities with 557 beds; a network of physician practices; the largest managed care organization in West Michigan (Priority Health); home care and hospice services; urgent care, occupational health and senior health services; air-medical transport services; the Blodgett Butterworth Health Care Foundation; the Cook Institute for Research & Education, now the research division of the Grand Rapids Medical Education Research Center for Health Professionals; and a network of outpatient services and facilities with more than 70 locations providing rehabilitation, laboratory, radiology and radiation oncology services. The 1997 merger of Blodgett Memorial Medical Center and Butterworth Health System also paved the way for the creation of the Community Commitment Fund to assure quality health programs for the underserved.

From 1994 to 2000, Spectrum Health, Blodgett Memorial Medical Center and Butterworth Hospital received 18 national honors given for quality, consumer choice, cost-savings and as a top-100 employer in health care. By pooling resources and eliminating duplication of services, it exemplifies the numerous advantages of collaboration. The awards also highlight the expertise of the medical staff and all staff members' commitment and contributions to excellence and quality.

The history of Blodgett Memorial Medical Center and Butterworth Health System, the foundation upon which Spectrum Health was built, will never be forgotten. Led by a community-based board of directors, it is a tapestry of vision, dedication, hard work and triumph — threads of which are now woven into the cord uniting the past with the present, a cord which truly celebrates the integration of its individual strands.

WESTERN MICHIGAN UNIVERSITY'S GRAND RAPIDS REGIONAL CENTER

Western Michigan University's Grand Rapids Regional Center has always been committed to providing high-quality academic programs and services. Primarily a center for graduate and professional education, WMU's local facility has been the first to meet the unmet needs of students in Grand Rapids. By consistently striving towards this goal for over 90 years, WMU has not only granted thousands of advanced certificates and master's level degrees to local residents, but has become an innovative, stand-alone leader in the Grand Rapids academic community.

The Grand Rapids Center is graduate intensive with 95 percent of its students enrolled in master's degree programs.

As an institution, Western Michigan University was founded in Kalamazoo in 1903. While many graduated from WMU and started careers in the Grand Rapids area, the university's alumni wanted to supplement their education with further classes. Unfortunately, no local institution offered the level of advanced study that many of Western's graduates in Grand Rapids wanted.

Six years after the university was founded, WMU started offering courses in Grand Rapids. The first class, Nature Study, taught by Dr. Leroy Harvey, began in the fall semester of 1909. Always a dedicated faculty member, Dr. Harvey taught on WMU's campus during the day and took the train to Grand Rapids to teach in the evening. Although the commute between the two cities was a moderate distance by early 1900s standards, the professor's dedication to his city students set a precedent for WMU in Grand Rapids.

As the enrollment and popularity of the university's local classes rose, Grand Rapids employers and professional groups approached WMU frequently, requesting that the university offer more specific degree programs locally. In 1964 the university brought the Master of Business Administration (MBA) degree to Grand Rapids at the request of local businesses. In 1973 WMU incorporated the undergraduate engineering program into their course offerings at Grand Rapids, providing the last two years of engineering courses to undergraduate students who had completed their prerequisites at the Grand Rapids Junior College. A few years later, several master's degrees in engineering were added to the schedule. In 1979 the Master of Social Work (MSW) program offered its first classes in Grand Rapids. Because of the success of these programs, in subsequent years WMU listened attentively to the Grand Rapids community, adding six more master's level programs, including public administration and organizational communication.

Aside from being the first to offer a wide selection of graduate programs in the area, WMU's programs were unique since they fulfilled the needs of local students like no other area institution had attempted before. In the 1960s it was unheard of to complete an MBA on a part-time basis while retaining a full-time job. Western's MBA program was innovative since it was specially designed with working business people in mind. The engineering and the MSW programs were similarly designed with evening and weekend courses and became successful among working students in the city.

The success of these pioneering programs made WMU a local leader in education. While the university had the prestige and presence in the community, it didn't have a permanent campus. In the early years, WMU taught courses in classrooms rented from high schools in the area. In 1966 the first regional office was established in what was then known as the Lear Siegler Building in downtown Grand Rapids. Subsequent offices were established on the campus of Grand Rapids Junior College and a few years later at the Fountain Place building downtown. Nonetheless, administrators knew

WMU students needed a permanent campus location in Grand Rapids.

In 1988 WMU purchased a building and property on Grand Rapids' East Beltline. As most of the regional center's classes are planned around working students' schedules, the building was completely renovated and specifically designed to be an executive-level conference center during the day and high-tech classroom facility on evenings and weekends. Opened in fall 1990, the three-story, 40,000-square-foot facility features 21 classrooms and two computer labs. With a state-of-the-art videoconference room as well as satellite-downlink connections, the WMU Regional Center offers students all the benefits of amenities generally found in modern offices, but not often in typical college classrooms.

The Grand Rapids Center is an executive-class conference center during the day and an extremely comfortable classroom facility evenings and weekends.

Today, WMU is a nationally recognized doctoral research institution with a long history of successful outreach programs in the region. In any semester the Grand Rapids branch has 2,500 active students, with 1,800 of them able to squeeze a course into their busy lives. Of these students, over 95 percent are enrolled in graduate programs.

Currently, more than 25 fields of study are offered at WMU, with a majority of these fields offered at the graduate and doctoral levels. In addition to the groundbreaking programs that defined the university in Grand Rapids, the regional center offers master's programs in fields such as industrial/organizational psychology, counselor education, counseling psychology, communications, public administration and others. As WMU has always focused on teacher education, many specialized master's and doctoral degrees are offered in areas such as education leadership, education/professional development, reading instruction, elementary and early childhood education, human resource development and many other professional education fields. WMU also grants graduate certificates in health care administration, holistic health, educational technology and human performance technology. In addition, working and transfer students can complete their undergraduate degrees in many specialized fields, including applied liberal studies, health studies and industrial management.

For most of the 20th century, WMU's Grand Rapids Regional Center has been an important part of the professional growth and development of the citizens of Grand Rapids. As the college begins the new millennium, the future of WMU in Grand Rapids remains very bright. The demand for nationally recognized, career-enhancing, professional education will continue to be incredibly high as Grand Rapids grows. Administrators are always looking for ways to offer more options and to develop the programs available at the Grand Rapids campus. Currently, WMU is negotiating for a second location downtown to accommodate the expanding array of programs available in Grand Rapids. All of this demonstrates WMU's diligence in living up to its name and following its mission — to serve the citizens throughout western Michigan. The aspiration of the past continues to be WMU's goal for the future — to be the first to meet unmet needs.

WMU has been in Grand Rapids since 1909 and offers over 25 different programs for working professionals.

AQUINAS COLLEGE

Challenging conventional wisdom may not be a practice some would typically associate with a small Catholic college. But at Aquinas College, where spirit and energy abound, critical thinking plays a vital role in every class.

The 2,400 students at this rigorous liberal arts school are encouraged to challenge untruths, question new truths and analyze old truths in new ways. Students philosophize and theorize about subjects from literature to human rights in the rich tradition of St. Thomas Aquinas, the patron saint of school.

Aquinas enjoys all the advantages of Michigan's second-largest city as well as the intimacy offered in its 107-acre forested campus. The mission of Aquinas College is to provide a career-oriented liberal arts education in a Catholic Christian context to all students capable of profiting from such an education, regardless of gender, age, religion, ethnicity, racial background or disability. But the student body is not exclusively Catholic. Students come from a rich mix of backgrounds, with more than 40 percent being non-Catholic.

Aquinas College traces its heritage to 1886, when the Grand Rapids Dominican Sisters established the Novitiate Normal School. Lit by kerosene lamps and heated by a coal furnace, the school evolved first into a women's college and in 1931 reorganized as Catholic Junior College in Grand Rapids.

Under the leadership of Monsignor Arthur F. Bukowski, the school began to operate as a four-year institution when it was renamed Aquinas College in 1941 in honor of St. Thomas Aquinas, the revered Dominican scholar regarded as one of the most brilliant minds of the 13th century.

From its earliest days, the college has been known for its quality, rigor and innovation. It was the first Catholic college in the country to introduce coeducation. The college later would establish the first continuing education program in Michigan and became one of the first institutions to offer a master of management degree.

Aquinas College moved to its present location in 1945 after the Dominican Sisters purchased the former estate of Edward and Susan Blodgett Lowe. Built in the early 1900s, Holmdene, a magnificent English Tudor manor, now houses administrative and faculty offices. The beautiful campus sits nestled among the trees yet is just minutes from downtown Grand Rapids.

Some observers might not expect this tiny college to be a pacesetter for the 21st century. But the college's new high-tech Jarecki Center for Advanced Learning is considered to be a model for classrooms of the future. Onlookers who challenge conventional wisdom — like St. Thomas Aquinas — often discover that things aren't always what they seem.

Today, *U.S. News & World Report* consistently ranks Aquinas College as one of the top liberal arts colleges in the Midwest. Students from more than 22 states and 15 foreign countries are drawn to the campus, where they can pursue more than 40 majors and a dozen degrees, including three graduate degrees. With 90 full-time and 102 part-time faculty members, Aquinas offers a student/teacher ratio of 13:1.

The former Lowe estate called Holmdene is a magnificent English Tudor manor that now houses Aquinas College's administrative and faculty offices.

GRAND RAPIDS DOMINICANS

On her deathbed in May 1877 in New York City, Mother Augustine Neuhierl, one of the original four Dominican missionaries who emigrated from Germany, had a vision. She saw "a peninsula in the West dotted white with Dominicans."

Interestingly enough, a few months later the Dominicans, with their familiar white habits, received a request to establish a school in Traverse City in the peninsular state of Michigan. The Sisters agreed to the mission, marking the course that many more Dominican Sisters would follow, taking them to nearly every corner of the state.

Marywood-gathering in prayer at the conclusion of the 1997 General Assembly

They arrived in Grand Rapids in 1889 to staff two new institutions: St. John's Home, a diocesan orphanage for children on Leonard Street NE, and its neighbor, St. Alphonsus School.

Guided by their mission, "to live the Gospel," their ministries were blessed with success. By 1977 the Dominicans were in the hallways and classrooms of more than 100 institutions, primarily in Michigan and New Mexico, including elementary schools, high schools, two academies, Aquinas College, a sanatorium, two hospitals and a mission in Peru. They were devout about their work — but not uninteresting. One Sister unwittingly became the inspiration for the role of Mother Superior in the highly successful, off-Broadway musical comedy *Nunsense*.

Perhaps their most visible achievement in Grand Rapids, however, was their role in establishing two thriving institutions: Aquinas College and Marywood — a 34-acre wooded campus established in 1922 on E. Fulton Street. Marywood is not only the Motherhouse of the Grand Rapids Dominicans but also was the home of Marywood Academy.

St. John's Home — The Golden Jubilee of Mother Aquinata, Aug. 4, 1914

For almost nine decades, as the number of Sisters climbed to over 800, Marywood's predecessor — Sacred Heart Academy, on Ransom NE (1900-1922) and Marywood Academy (1922-1989) attracted an elite student body with their rigorous academic standards.

After the sweeping changes of Vatican II in the 1960s, enrollment began to decline. Marywood graduated its last high school class in 1975. After its grade school closed in 1989 and the number of Sisters decreased, the Dominicans began some soul-searching about the future use of Marywood.

In the early 1990s, with renewed vigor, they launched a $3.5 million renovation at Marywood and turned their energies to meeting community social and spiritual needs.

Today, the primary corporate ministries of the Grand Rapids Dominicans are twofold: prayer and liturgies at Dominican Chapel/Marywood; and programs for spirituality, leadership, ministry development and holistic health at the retreat-like setting inside Dominican Center at Marywood.

Also to be found on the campus are leased sites for homeless women and children, Kent County Head Start, child care and health-care services.

Marywood is Motherhouse to more than 300 Grand Rapids Dominicans, including 36 who live in the congregation's nursing home. Another 90 reside on campus, while the rest serve in more than 20 states or in faraway places such as Peru and Honduras. In the 1990s they labored in neighborhood organizations, classrooms, law offices and former Soviet-bloc countries. The places are diverse as they reach out to serve modern needs. Indeed, with changing times, Mother Augustine's vision for the Dominicans has expanded far beyond the "peninsula in the West."

CITY OF GRAND RAPIDS

The Grand River is a source of beauty during any season.

With the cultural and entertainment choices of larger cities and the values and convictions of smaller towns, Grand Rapids is becoming an increasingly popular place in which to live and do business. Once known as the "furniture city," Grand Rapids earned a reputation as a place to nurture families by offering affordable housing, a diverse manufacturing base, low unemployment and low health care costs.

Grand Rapids, which celebrated its sesquicentennial in the spring of 2000, is becoming an increasingly popular place to live because of its nationally registered historic district of restored Victorian homes, 100 neighborhood parks, a public museum with a planetarium and nature center, a zoo with an aquarium and two art museums. Grand Rapids also is home to a presidential museum and the Gerald R. Ford International Airport.

According to Mayor John H. Logie, "Historic preservation got its start in Michigan in the City of Grand Rapids. Recognizing the intrinsic value of our historic residential district adjacent to downtown, a concerned group of citizens first lobbied to create the state law to permit historic districting in cities and then drafted and implemented the first historic preservation ordinance in Michigan. The Heritage Hill Historic District is now also on the state register as well as the national register of historic places. It has maintained itself as a viable residential community of choice while retaining a broad spectrum of income, ethnicity, and race. The Cherry Hill, Fairmont Square and Wealthy Business Historic Districts have followed. It is an essential component of the city's economic development plans."

The sun shines on the comfortable, colorful and friendly downtown.

While the nation's manufacturing job growth increased by 3.5 percent from 1986-96, it increased by 20.5 percent in Grand Rapids. Grand Rapids has actively encouraged sustained development by creating a 530-acre Renaissance Zone in which property owners are free of state and local taxes for 15 years.

Grand Rapids is composed of well-tended neighborhoods. The members of 38 neighborhood and business associations are dedicated to preserving the unique character of every one of them. Of the 100 largest metropolitan areas in the United States, Grand Rapids has been ranked fourth by the Reliastar Financial Security Index, which measures family earnings and wealth, income protection and job creation, and quality of life.

In the past few years, downtown Grand Rapids has undergone unprecedented growth. Much of this is due to the construction of the Van Andel Arena, a 12,000-seat, state-of-the-art facility that is home to teams in the International Hockey League, Continental Basketball Association and Arena Football League. The opening of the Van Andel Institute is making Grand Rapids a major medical research center. The city also is home to 13 colleges and universities.

Finally, Grand Rapids also is a popular place to do business. While the area's 10 largest employers represent eight different industries, companies employing fewer than 50 workers account for 94 percent of the area's almost 25,000 business establishments. This diversity and dedication to employees has helped put four West Michigan manufacturers on the list of "The Best 100 Companies to Work for in America."

DAVENPORT UNIVERSITY

M.E. Davenport, a former president of Davenport University, had a simple formula for graduates' success: "make a living, make a life, make a contribution." With an enrollment of more than 15,000 students throughout Michigan and Indiana, Davenport has become one of the largest and most highly regarded independent universities in the country. Established in Grand Rapids in 1866, Davenport University is also a community establishment that has provided qualified professionals to area businesses for 134 years.

M.E. Davenport, a graduate of Ferris Institute, joined the school in 1910 and built the foundation of the institution known today as Davenport University. Students studied a specialized curriculum and graduated with the background to grow into positions of responsibility. From 1910 to 1959 the college went through many changes in name and status, becoming a degree-granting institution in 1924.

Significant changes took place from 1959 to 1977 under the leadership of Robert W. Sneden, who was named president after Davenport's death. Under his leadership, the college received accreditation as a junior college of business and formed a public board of trustees. In 1968 Davenport College moved to its present campus on East Fulton. By 1976 the college had received accreditation from the North Central Association of Colleges and Schools.

Davenport College entered a period of expansion and growth during the tenure of Donald W. Maine. In addition to an expansion at the Grand Rapids campus, campuses were established throughout Western Michigan and northern Indiana. Detroit College of Business and Great Lakes College were both acquired by Davenport College.

Davenport was authorized to offer baccalaureate degrees in 1984 and an MBA degree through the Sneden Graduate School in 1998. Business, computer information systems, health care and legal studies degrees continue to be the focus throughout the system.

In 1982 the trustees established the Davenport Foundation to help students with their tuition costs. The endowment reached $10 million in 2000 and has provided thousands of students with financial assistance over the years.

To better manage the scope and size of the total system, the Davenport Educational System, Inc. was established in 1997. In 1998 Donald Maine was appointed chancellor of the system, and Dr. Barbara A. Mieras was named president of Davenport College.

In keeping with the expanding technology and the growing interest in distance learning, The Davenport University Learning Network was established in 1999 and approved by the North Central Association to offer full degrees in 2000.

As the new millennium began, Davenport College, Detroit College of Business and Great Lakes College became Davenport University, Michigan's largest independent university system. The mission remains the same — to prepare and sustain people for careers in business, allied health and legal studies. Davenport University will continue to be a dynamic partner with area businesses, setting trends in education so that individuals and communities can flourish.

Davenport has adapted its curriculum and its culture over the years to anticipate the changing times; however, the foundations laid by its predecessors have prevailed. In the words of M.E. Davenport, a person must be able to "make a living" in order to "make a life," and these two prepare a graduate to "make a contribution."

In 1968 Davenport College moved to its present campus on East Fulton.

GRAND RAPIDS AREA CHAMBER OF COMMERCE

Ever since the Grand Rapids Area Chamber of Commerce was founded, it has played a vital role in the city's economic development. Testimony to its success today is the booming local economy. The area is widely heralded for its high-performance renewal that's brought new jobs, businesses and people, making west Michigan a world-class manufacturing center. The Chamber now boasts a legion of 3,500 members, with many of the community's premier movers and shakers serving on its committees and boards.

The Chamber was founded as the Board of Trade in 1887 when the city was in economic distress over high railroad rates. Acting in concert, 147 local business leaders were able to secure a rate cut that saved the city's manufacturers thousands of dollars. Many of these businesses were in the furniture industry that once dominated the city. It marked the first of many achievements throughout the decades of which the Chamber can be justifiably proud.

The Grand Rapids Area Chamber of Commerce is located in the historic Waters Building in downtown Grand Rapids. *Photo by David R. Banta*

Time and again, the Chamber's leaders have demonstrated exceptional vision by responding to the challenges of the times. Whether it was to find meaningful jobs for the disadvantaged, help businesses plan for postwar reconversion, offer start-up and improvement loans, or campaign for industrial development, the Chamber could be counted on to lead the effort. Very often, its actions affect the entire community, such as campaigns to build key public facilities, or the recent establishment of Institutes for Healing Racism; a program designed to encourage executives to confront the insidious effects of racism.

Perhaps not well known is that several now-independent and self-operating organizations have evolved from Chamber activities. Among them are the Kent County Farm Bureau, the Merchants Service Bureau and the West Michigan Tourist Association.

In 1985 the Chamber helped spur dramatic job growth when it created The Right Place Program. This highly successful program is one of the country's first private sector economic development programs dedicated to job retention and creation. Within five years, the program helped create 25,000 new jobs, some from foreign manufacturers new in the area. As a result, Grand Rapids became the only metropolitan area in the Midwest to regain all manufacturing jobs lost in the early 1980s during a recession. It also gave further momentum to a gradual shift in economic strength from the eastern part of the state, to Michigan's "second heart" — thriving west Michigan. Today, The Right Place Program is a sister organization to the Chamber, with its own independent board and staff.

During the 1990s the Chamber recognized the community's unique business spirit and work force. Almost 80 percent of the businesses in west Michigan are family-owned, making it a mecca for such enterprises. To nurture this spirit of self-reliance and community mindedness, the Chamber formed the Family-Owned Business Council in 1994. A year later, it created the Cultural Diversity Council, recognizing the changing demographics of west Michigan and the nation.

Today, the Grand Rapids Area Chamber of Commerce promotes Grand Rapids as a "destination city" for people to live, work and play in. As it has proven time and again, the city can count on the Chamber to create opportunities for business success.

GRAND RAPIDS HISTORICAL SOCIETY

For more than a century, the Grand Rapids Historical Society has tended to its community's historical interests. The society was founded in 1894 when Mayor Ernest B. Fischer looked about his community and concluded its remarkable growth meant the time was right to form an historical society. Gathering several community leaders in his office, Fischer asked them to "organize an association whose purpose it would be to collect and preserve books, papers, pamphlets, maps and other material of historic value and interest...."

Once mustered, the newly formed historical society's members set about fulfilling the mayor's wishes. Among their undertakings was a series of lectures by local residents, many of them with close ties to the area's early history. John Ball's daughter, Lucy, told of her father's 1832 trip over the Oregon Trail, banker Harvey Hollister described the first banks in the Grand River Valley and Rebecca Richmond, whose father had been an Indian agent, talked on "The Fur Traders of the Grand River Valley." The society also published George Fitch's *Old Grand Rapids*, a pictorial history that remains popular 75 years later.

Another of the society's early activists, Library Director Samuel Ranck, believed the library had a responsibility to collect and preserve the manuscripts, photographs, maps and other documentation of its community's history. Under his direction the Library's Michigan Room became the region's best-known local and family history repository, housing the historical society's archives as well as those of numerous other organizations and families.

The Grand Rapids Historical Society enjoyed four decades of success before the Great Depression and World War II disrupted its activities. Ceasing regular meetings in 1938, the group did not return to full-time status until 1951. At that time, Judge Raymond Starr called together a group interested in local history and reorganized the society. The director of the Grand Rapids Public Library, Donald Kohlsted, who had succeeded Samuel Ranck in 1941, reiterated his predecessor's commitment to local history and played a key role in reconstituting the society.

Since 1951 the reorganized Grand Rapids Historical Society has been a leader in the effort to preserve and promote the community's history. Its publication program has reprinted three classics of Grand Rapids history: Albert Baxter's *History of the City of Grand Rapids,* George Fitch's *Old Grand Rapids,* and Franklin Everett's *Memorials of the Grand River Valley.* In addition, it has published *Grand Rapids Goes To War: The 1940s Homefront* by Dr. Richard Harms and Robert Viol. For the past 21 years it has also published an annual magazine, *Grand River Valley History*, and offered a popular six-part annual lecture series.

In recent decades, several new local history organizations have been formed, and the society now jointly sponsors programs with many of these groups. Its annual lecture series is co-sponsored with the Gerald R. Ford Museum and the Greater Grand Rapids Women's History Council, and publication of *Grand River Valley History* is shared with the Ryerson Library Foundation, the Greater Grand Rapids Women's History Council and the Grand Rapids Historical Commission. With the Grand Rapids Historical Commission and the Grand Rapids Public Schools, the society is currently providing financial support for local history curriculum materials that will be distributed to all area third grade classes, ensuring that future generations will respect and preserve their community's history.

Downtown Grand Rapids bustled with activity when this photo was taken in 1896, two years after the Grand Rapids Historical Society was formed. *Grand Rapids Public Library*

GRAND RAPIDS PUBLIC SCHOOLS

As more people from foreign lands have made Grand Rapids their home, Michigan's second-largest school district has evolved into a sophisticated educational system that's rich in diversity.

Whether students are refugees from Bosnia or adopted children from Russia, the Grand Rapids Public School district has risen to meet the challenge of its mission:

Built in 1875, Coit Elementary School on Coit Avenue NE is the oldest operating elementary school in Michigan.

The Math/Science Academy on Davis Avenue NW is one of many specialty schools offered in the Grand Rapids Public School System.

To ensure that all students are educated, self-directed and productive members of society. Today, 25 different languages are supported academically with various school programs.

Such diversity has been the heritage of education in Grand Rapids ever since the area's first school, Slater Mission, was established on the west bank of the Grand River in 1826. The class consisted of six students — of whom five were Ottawa Indian boys.

It was not until 1837 that the area's first public school opened in a private home east of the Grand River on Prospect Hill. It was a small beginning that eventually grew into a district boasting almost 1,700 students by 1860. That was only the start of the district's tremendous growth.

The district experienced dramatic expansion as immigrants, primarily from Europe, poured into the city. By 1906 enrollment reached 15,000 with 37 school buildings scattered around the city. Another expansion of high school and elementary schools occurred between 1910 and through the 1920s, many of which are still in use today. In the 1950s another building wave occurred with the arrival of the Baby Boomers.

The Grand Rapids Public Schools district has its share of famous graduates. Among them are former President Gerald Ford, a graduate of the district's now-defunct South High School, and his wife, Betty Ford. Mrs. Ford graduated from Central High School, the city's first high school, which opened in the 1860s.

Today, with an enrollment of more than 26,600 students and a staff of almost 4,000, there are few districts in West Michigan that rival the educational choices offered by the Grand Rapids Public Schools. In addition to neighborhood schools, families have a choice of several citywide schools that focus on a specific theme or learning method, such as Montessori. In fact, Grand Rapids is one of the few districts in the nation to offer families a K-12 Montessori program. Other programs are designed specifically for gifted and talented students. Others concentrate on environmental studies, creative arts or hospitality science.

Choices abound for athletes as well. The district's four mainstream high schools — Central, Creston, Ottawa Hills and Union — are part of the Grand Rapids City League, providing competition in 19 different sports.

The district's special education program is stellar and considered one of the most comprehensive in the country. Parents of children with special learning needs come to the Grand Rapids school district from other communities just because of these outstanding programs.

Today, as educational choices abound for parents, the district continues to achieve its mission. It recently adopted "Curriculum 2000" to raise expectations and standards for its diverse student body. Clearly, it is a step toward making sure students follow in the successful footsteps of the many graduates who call Grand Rapids Public Schools their alma mater.

INTERURBAN TRANSIT PARTNERSHIP

The concept of mass transit has existed in the Grand Rapids area since 1864. It all began with a horse-drawn line and eventually expanded to several lines serving the area. Over the years, horses were replaced by street railways and cable cars. Automotive buses were introduced into service in 1925 to feed the rail lines from the northern suburbs. By 1935 Grand Rapids was the first city of its size to have 100 percent of its fleet made up of automotive buses.

Over the next several years, the local transit industry changed rapidly. In the face of declining ridership and rising costs, many local bus and rail companies either consolidated or stopped running. By 1963 City Coach Lines had acquired the two remaining operating transit lines, thereby laying the foundation for one major transit system. Shortly thereafter, the Grand Rapids Transit Authority was formed to oversee local public transit. The city system leased it assets from City Coach Lines, which was also retained to manage and operate the transit system.

The Grand Rapids Area Transit Authority (GRATA) was formed in 1977, an outgrowth of the Grand Rapids city system, when planners and local officials realized that a truly effective transit system had to cross political boundaries. Until 2000, GRATA was a voluntary association of governments charged with providing transportation to the area, and local funding was the responsibility of the participating governments.

Since that horse-drawn line in 1864, public transportation has undergone many changes — not the least of which is the evolution of the vehicles themselves. With the passage of the transit millage in April 2000, public transportation again saw a major evolution. On October 1, 2000, the Interurban Transit Partnership (ITP) became the governing body of the public transportation system. The millage and the resulting formation of ITP provided more stable, efficient and effective public transportation. Using funds from the millage, ITP introduced evening and Sunday services — something the area had not seen for many years. Additional improvements included increased frequencies, a new cross-town route and the PASS suburban feeder system.

Building on the work of GRATA, ITP continues to offer service beyond fixed-route bus lines. Carpools and vanpools are coordinated through a ride-share program. GO! Bus operates to provide door-to-door service for seniors and the disabled. The DASH service provides shuttle service from area park-and-ride lots to downtown. In addition, ITP provides contracted service to area townships, Grand Rapids Public Schools and organizations that assist clients with the transition from welfare to work.

Over the years there have been many committees and working groups dedicated to assessing the present and future and needs of public transit in the metro area — most notably, Mobile Metro 2020, which was charged with developing a long-range plan for transportation needs through the year 2020. Grand Rapids is one of the largest urban areas in Michigan. Between 1980 and 1990, the city led the way in population growth — 16.4 percent — among Michigan cities. It is projected that more than 115, 000 new jobs will have been created between 1990 and 2015.

With growth come the challenges of congestion, pollution and parking availability. An efficient, user-friendly public transportation system is an effective way to meet these challenges and to ensure the long-term health and vitality of the Grand Rapids area.

Passengers at the Downtown Transit Center

BIBLIOGRAPHY

SOURCES CONSULTED

Altenbrandt, Edward, ed. *The Men Behind the Guns in the Making of Greater Grand Rapids.* Grand Rapids, 1909.

Annual Reports of the Secretary of the State Board of Agriculture... Michigan. Lansing, 1873-1875.

[Baker, Robert H.], ed. *The City of Grand Rapids Manufacturing Advantages, Commercial Importance...* Grand Rapids, 1889.

Ball, John. *Born to Wander. Autobiography of.* [Grand Rapids, 1994].

______. "Physical Geography of Kent County," *Michigan Pioneer Collections.* Vol. I (1877). p. 214.

Ball, Lucy. "Early Days in Grand Rapids," *Michigan Pioneer Collections.* Vol. 38 (1912). p. 92.

Baxter, Albert. *History of the City of Grand Rapids.* New York, 1891.

Belknap, Charles E. *History of the Michigan Organizations at Chickamauga, Chattanooga and Missionary Ridge.* 2nd Edition. Lansing, 1899.

______. *The Yesterdays of Grand Rapids.* Grand Rapids, 1922.

Bissell, Hillary. *The Effects of White and Non-White Population Changes in the Central City.* N.D., 1961.

Bissell, Irving J. *A Sow's Ear.* New York, [1937].

Blair, Walter, ed. *The Sweet Singer of Michigan.* Chicago, 1928.

Blois, John T. *Gazeteer of the State of Michigan...* Detroit, 1838.

The Book of Michigan Industry and Those Who Serve. Supplement Michigan Manufacturer and Financial Record. Detroit, 1924.

Boyle, Homer L. *History of Peace.* Grand Rapids, [1902].

Bradford, Thomas G. *A Comprehensive Atlas Geographical, Historical & Commerical.* Boston, [1835].

Bratt, James D. and Meehan, Christopher H. *Gathered at the River...* Grand Rapids, [1993].

Bremer, Richard G. *Indian Agent and Wilderness Scholar: The Life of Henry Rowe Schoolcraft.* Mount Pleasant, MI. 1987.

[Brook, J.D.] *Twenty-five Years of Public Health in Kent County 1914-1939.* N.P., N.D.

Bryan, William Jennings. *The First Battle...* Chicago, [1896].

Burr, C.B., ed. *Medical History of Michigan.* 2 Vols. Minneapolis, 1930.

Butler, John vs The Grand Rapids and Indiana Railroad, et al. State of Michigan Supreme Court Appeal. 14 May 1890.

Carron, Christian G. *Grand Rapids Furniture...* [Grand Rapids, 1998].

Cathcart, William. *The Baptist Encyclopedia.* 2 Vols. Philadelphia, 1881.

Census and Statistics of the State of Michigan. Lansing, 1854.

Centennial Book of Modern Spiritualism in America. Chicago, [1948].

Chesebro Family Correspondence 1873-1896. Manuscript Collection in Grand Rapids Public Library, Michigan Room.

City of Grand Rapids and Kent County, Michigan, Up To Date... [Logansport, Ind.], 1900.

City of Grand Rapids Under Commission Manager Government. 1924-1925 Review. N.P.

Cleland, Charles E. *Rites of Conquest: The History & Culture of Michigan's Native Americans.* Ann Arbor, [1992].

Clifton, James, Cornell, George & McClurken, James. *People of the Three Fires...* Grand Rapids, [1986].

Cramp, Arthur J. ed. *Nostrums & Quackery.* 3 Vols. Chicago, 1911, 1921, 1936.

Crotty, Daniel G. *Four Years Campaigning in the Army of the Potomac.* Grand Rapids, 1874.

Cunningham, Wilbur M. *Land of Four Flags...* Grand Rapids, [1961].

[DeHaven, George]. *Grand Rapids As It Is 1901. Grand Rapids,* [1901].

DeJong, David Cornel. *Belly Fulla Straw.* New York, [1934].

Dictionary of Grand Rapids Issued by the Old National Bank. N.P., [1910].

Dillenback, Jackson D. *The Grand Rapids Annual For 1875-76...* Grand Rapids, 1876.

______. *Grand Rapids in 1874...* Grand Rapids, 1875.

______. & Leavitt, [David S.] compilers. *History & Directory of Kent County...* Grand Rapids, 1870.

Dorr, John A. & Eshman, Donald F. *Geology of Michigan.* Ann Arbor, [1970].

Dunbar, Willis F. *All Aboard! A History of Railroads in Michigan.* Grand Rapids, [1969].

______. & May, George S. *Michigan: A History of the Wolverine State.* Revised Edition. Grand Rapids, [1980].

Englemann, Larry D. "Billy Sunday...," *Michigan History*. Vol. LV. No. 1(Spring 1973). p. 1.

Etten, William J., compiler. *A Citizens' History of Grand Rapids...* Grand Rapids, 1926.

Everett, Franklin. *Memorials of the Grand River Valley.* Chicago, 1878.

Faust, Patricia L., ed. *Historical Times Illustrated Encyclopedia of the Civil War.* New York, [1986].

Fisher, Ernest B., ed. *Grand Rapids & Kent County...* 2 Vols. Chicago, 1918.

Fitch, George E. *Old Grand Rapids,* N.P., 1925.

Fitting, James E. *The Archaelogy of Michigan.* New York, 1970.

Fleischer, Nat. *"The Michigan Assassin" The Saga of Stanley Ketchel...* [New York, 1946].

Freeman, Daniel Roy. *God and War.* Boston, [1915].

Friendly Fellows of Furniture Town. N.P., ca. 1900.

Gansser, Emil B. *History of the 126th Infantry...* Grand Rapids, [1920].

Georgeano, G.N. *The Complete Encyclopedia of Motor Cars.* New York, [1968].

Geschichte der St. Marien — Gemeide in Grand Rapids. Grand Rapids, 1907.

Gilbert, Angie Bingham. "A Tale of Two Cities." N.P. [ca 1897].

Gingrich, Arnold. *Cast Down the Laurel.* New York, 1935.

Goetzmann, William H. "Death Stalked The Grand Reconnaissance," *American Heritage.* Vol. XXIII No. 6 (October 1972). p. 44.

Goss, Dwight. *History of Grand Rapids & Its Industries.* 2 Vols. Chicago, 1906

______. "The Indians of the Grand River Valley," *Michigan Pioneer Collections.* Vol. XVII (1905). p. 172.

Gould, Alta Isadore. *The Veteran's Bride & Other Poems.* Grand Rapids, 1894.

Grand Rapids: Beautiful, Industrial, Commercial. Grand Rapids, [1910].

Grand Rapids, Michigan As It Is 1894. [Grand Rapids, 1894].

Grand Rapids, Michigan 1891. [Leipzig, Germany, 1891].

Grand Rapids Evening Leader. 3 April & 8 April 1889.

Grand River Valley Review. Vol. 1, No. 1 (Fall 1979) - Vol. XV (1998).

Greenly, A.H. "The Sweet Singer of Michigan Bibliographically Considered," *The papers of the Bibliographical Society of America.* Vol. 39. Second Quarter 1945. p. 91.

Grimsley, G.P. *The Gypsum of Michigan & the Plaster Industry. Geological Survey of Michigan.* Vol. IX, Part II. Lansing, 1904.

Harms, Richard. "Grand Times," *Grand Rapids Magazine*. April 1992-December 1997.

______. & Viol, Robert W. *Grand Rapids Goes to War.* [Grand Rapids, 1993].

Hayne, Coe. *Baptist Trail-Makers of Michigan.* Philadelphia, 1936.

Hess, Joseph F. *Out of Darkness Into Light...* Toronto, N.D.

Hibbard, Benjamin H. *A History of the Public Land Policies.* New York,1924.

History of Immanuel Evangelical Luthern Congregation of Grand Rapids Michigan. N.P., [1931].

Holland's Grand Rapids City Directory... Chicago, 1867.

Hollister, Harvey J. *Daniel Ball as a Banker.* Publications of the Historical Society of Grand Rapids. No. 4, Grand Rapids, 1909.

______. "Fifty Years Ago: Events in Grand Rapids From 1850 to 1860," *Michigan Pioneer Collections.* Vol. 35 (1907). p. 643.

Holt, Carol May. *The Story of Grand Rapids, Michigan, Revised.* Grand Rapids, 1932.

Hotchkiss, George W. *History of the Lumber & Forest Industry of the Northwest.* Chicago, 1898.

The House That "At" Built... Grand Rapids, 1924.

Illustrated Historical Atlas of the County of Kent, Michigan. Chicago, [1876].

Isham, Asa B. *An Historical Sketch of the Seventh Regiment Michigan Volunteer Cavalry.* New York, [ca. 1893].

Johnson, Allen & Malone, Dumas, eds. *Dictionary of American Biography.* 20 Vols. New York, 1928 -1936.

Kennedy, Stiles. *The Magnetic & Mineral Springs of Michigan.* Wilmington, Delaware, 1872.

Kent County Circuit Court Records 1837-1900. Western Michigan Archives & Regional History Collections.

Kunitz, Stanley & Haycraft, Howard, eds. *Twentieth Century Authors.* New York, 1942.

Kutz, M.J. *Wab-Ah-See. A Legend of the Sleeping Dew..* Chicago, 1868.

Lacy, Francis D. *Star Lake Romance...* Grand Rapids, 1883.

Lambert, Bernard J. *Shepherd of the Wilderness.* L'Anse, 1967.

Landrum, Charles, H., compiler. *Michigan in the World War.* N.P., [1924].

Lane, Kit. *Lucius Lyon: An Eminently Useful Citizen.* Douglas, [1991].

Lanman, Charles. *The Red Book of Michigan...* Detroit, 1871.

Lawson, Publius V. *Bravest of the Brave: Captain Charles De Langlade.* [Menasha, Wisconsin, 1904].

Leeson, M.A. *History of Kent County, Michigan.* Chicago, 1881.

Lewis, George Edward. *Heart Echoes.* Grand Rapids, [1899].

______. *Nick of the Woods.* Portland, Oregon, 1916.

Little, Henry. "Grand Rapids History," *Michigan Pioneer Collections.* Vol. IV (1883). p. 286.

Lydens, Z.Z., ed. *The Story of Grand Rapids.* Grand Rapids, 1966.

Mapes, Lynn G. & Travis, Anthony. *Pictorial History of Grand Rapids.* Grand Rapids, [1976].

Mason, Philip. *A Legacy to My Children Including Family History, Autobiography...* Cincinnati, 1868.

McCoy, Isaac. *History of the Baptist Indian Missions...* Washington, 1840.

McCracken, S.B. *Michigan & the Centennial...* Detroit, 1876.

McGee, John W. *The Catholic Church in the Grand River Valley.* Grand Rapids, 1950.

McKenney, Thomas L. *Memoirs Official & Personal...* N.Y., 1846.

Michigan: A Guide to the Wolverine State. New York, [1941].

Michigan Biographies. 2 Vols. Lansing, 1924.

Moore, Ellen Lenora. *Early Days in Grand River Valley.* Grand Rapids, 1924.

Moore, Joel, Mead, Harry & Johns, Lewis, eds. *The History of the Amerian Expedition Fighting the Bolsheviki.* Detroit, [1920].

Moore, Julia A. *The Sentimental Song Book.* New York, [1912].

Ninety-Five Years of Nursing Education 1890-1985. The Butterworth Hospital School of Nursing. [Wyoming, MI. 1986].

Official Souvenir Michigan Volunteers of '98. Detroit, [1898].

Olson, Gordon L. *Grand Rapids A City Renewed.* [Grand Rapids, 1996].

______. *A Grand Rapids Sampler.* [Grand Rapids, 1992].

______. *"In the Name of All Marys..." A History of the Mary Free Bed Guild...* [Grand Rapids], 1991.

______. & Holland, Reid. *Grand Rapids Past, Present & Future.* [Grand Rapids, 1981].

[Palmer, Russell J.]. *History Grand Rapids Fire Department 1850-1950.* N.P., 1950.

Paterson, D.D. *Casket of Poetical Treasures.* Grand Rapids, 1881.

Plainfield Charter Township History... [Shawnee Mission, KS., 1988].

"The Plague of Influenza," *The American Review of Reviews.* November, 1918. p.467.

Plat Book of Kent County. Grand Rapids, 1919.

Polk's Grand Rapids City Directory. Grand Rapids, 1883, 1919.

"Prohibition & Prosperity." *The Survey.* Vol. XLV. No. 6. (6 November 1920).

Quimby, George Irving. *Indian Life In the Upper Great Lakes.* Chicago, [1960].

Ransom, Frank E. *The City Built on Wood.* [Ann Arbor, 1955].

Record of Service of Michigan Volunteers in the Civil War. 46 Volumes. [Kalamazoo, 1903].

Reports of Inspection of Factories in Michigan. Lansing, 1895-1902.

Report of the Michigan State Commission of Inquiry into Wages... For Women. Lansing, 1915.

Rezek, Antoine I. *History of the Diocese of Sault Ste. Marie & Marquette.* 2 Vols. Houghton, 1906.

Rickman, Irwin. "Pauline Cushman...," *Civil War Times Illustrated.* February 1969. p. 39.

Robertson, John. *Michigan in the War.* Revised Editon. Lansing, 1882.

Sarmiento, F.L. *Life of Pauline Cushman...* Philadelphia, [1865].

[Shaw, L. Lloyd]. *The Industries of Grand Rapids.* Grand Rapids, 1887.

Shaw, Elton R. *Stories of Hell's Commerce...* Grand Rapids, [1909].

Shockey, Samuel W. *Twenty-five Years Fighting Fate...* Boston, 1892.

Slater, Leonard, "Annual Report to Superintendent of Office of Indian Affairs," 30 September, 1846. in *Message From the President of the United States to... Congress... 30th Congress. 1st Session. Executive Document No. 1.* Washington, D.C., 1847. p. 911-913.

Sligh, Charles R. *History of the Services of the First Regiment Michigan Engineers & Mechanics.* Grand Rapids, 1921.

Smallwood, Carol, ed. *Michigan Authors.* Hillsdale, 1993.

Souvenir of Flood Grand Rapids, Mich. March, 1904. [Grand Rapids, 1904].

Souvenir of Grand Rapids, Mich. [Columbus, Ohio, 1890].

Souvenir Program Labor Day, September 2, '01. [Grand Rapids], 1901.

Sprague, Eli W. *All the Spiritualism of the Christian Bible.* [Detroit, 1922].

_______. *Letters From Heaven.* Grand Rapids, 1931.

_______. *The Science of Magnetic, Mental & Spiritual Healing.* Grand Rapids, [1930].

Standard Atlas of Kent County, Michigan. Chicago, 1907.

The 32nd Division in the World War. [Milwaukee, 1920].

Tompkins, C. David. *Senator Arthur H. Vandenberg: The Evolution of a Modern Republican.* East Lansing, 1970.

Trainer, George F.. *Life & Adventures of Ben Hogan...* N.P., [1878].

Treaties Between the United States of America and the Several Indian Tribes... Washington, D.C., 1837.

Trotter, Melvin E. *Jimmy Moore of Bucktown.* New York, 1904.

_______. *These Forty Years.* Grand Rapids, [1939].

Tuttle, Chas. Richard. *History of Grand Rapids with Biographical Sketches.* Grand Rapids, 1874. (Black Letter Press reprint, 1974).

Utley, Henry M. & Cutcheon, Byron M. *Michigan as a Province, Territory and State...* 4 Vols. [New York], 1906.

Van Vulpen, James. *Grand Rapids Then and Now.* [Grand Rapids, 1988].

_______. *On the Wings of Progress...* Grand Rapids, [1989].

Verwyst, P. Chrysostomus. *Life & Labors of Rt. Rev. Frederic Baraga....* Milwaukee, 1900.

Views of Grand Rapids. Grand Rapids, [ca. 1905].

"Western Michigan's Front Rank." A Register of Industrial & Professional Leadership. Grand Rapids, 1921.

White, Arthur Scott. *Grand Rapids, A.D. 1873...* Grand Rapids, 1874.

_______. *Grand Rapids On Parade...* Grand Rapids, 1926.

_______. ed. *Historic Michigan.* Vol. 3. Devoted to Kent County. N.P., [1924].
_______. compiler. *Incidents In the Lives of Editors.* [Grand Rapids], 1920.

_______. *Old Grand Rapids.* Grand Rapids, 1925.

The White Printing Company's Street & Railway Service Directory of Grand Rapids... Grand Rapids, 1912.

White, Stewart Edward. *The Betty Book.* New York, 1937.

_______. *The Glory Hole.* Garden City, 1924.

_______. *The Riverman.* New York, 1908.

Whiting, Perry. *Autobiography of...* Los Angeles, [1930].

Widder, Keith R. "Magdelaine Laframbois, Fur Trader & Educator," in Troester, Rosalie R., ed. *Historic Women of Michigan.* Lansing, [1987].

Wilson, James Grant & Fiske, John, eds. *Appleton's Cyclopedia of American Biography.* 6 Vols. New York, 1888.

Withey, Marion Louise Hinsdill. "Personal Recollections of Early Days in Kent County," *Michigan Historical Collections.* Vol. 39 (1915). p. 345.

Woodford, Frank B. *Lewis Cass The Last Jeffersonian.* New Brunswick, N.J., 1950.

Young, Georgie. *A Magdalen's Life.* N.P., [1889].

[Youngstrand, C.O.], compiler. *Our Michigan Friends "As We See 'Em."* [Detroit, 1905].

INDEX

Please see following page for Partners Index

PARTNERS & WEB SITE INDEX